Northern England

FIFTY GREAT SEA KAYAK VOYAGES

Jim Krawiecki

Pesda Press

WWW.PESDAPRESS.COM

First published in Great Britain 2011 by Pesda Press

Galeri 22, Doc Victoria
Caernarfon, Gwynedd
LL55 1SQ
Wales

Maps by Bute Cartographic.

Dedication

This book is dedicated to the memory of my father. He brought up my brothers and me, giving us the inspiration, skills and freedom that led me to my appreciation and love for the outdoors. He taught us to respect the elements, seize the moment, and take pride in achievements, whilst not taking ourselves too seriously.

Sadly, Jurand passed away before this book could be completed.

Acknowledgements

I would like to express my thanks to those who contributed anecdotes and photographs that are credited throughout the book. During the time it took to compile information, take photographs, and write text for this guide I have had the benefit of help from others. The paddlers that accompanied me on the scenic sunshine tours, as well those as who stuck with me when it got 'grim up north', are too many to mention. However, they know who they are and my thanks and my respect goes to them all.

When it came down to the nitty-gritty of local information, the support and inspiration from local paddlers was invaluable. Keirron Tastagh and his wonderful family always make me welcome during my trips to the Isle of Man. Kate Duffus (Cumbria), Terry Hailwood (Yorkshire), Pat Murray (Tyne-Tees) and Ollie Jay (Northumberland) all took the time to help, advise and criticise at various stages of this project.

One non-paddler is pilot Bill Tiplady, whose flying helped to gain unique viewpoints along the eastern shores of northern England for research and photographs.

Most importantly, this book would not have been possible without the unending support of Kirstine Pearson, Sean Jesson and Peter Roscoe. I would like to acknowledge their efforts and extend my heartfelt thanks to them.

Finally, thanks are due to Franco Ferrero and his production team at Pesda Press. Franco's dedication to this project and his patience (when things didn't go according to plan) has been extraordinary.

Photographs

All photographs by Jim Krawiecki except where otherwise acknowledged in the captions.

Foreword

Life as a journalist with a passion for the outdoors can be both opportunity and trial. In the first instance I get offered fun jobs, like my first sea kayaking experience when Jim Krawiecki took me out for a short paddle along the Menai Straits. I felt like a new window on the world had been opened. Everything I love about being in nature, about making a journey, however small, and seeing things afresh were instantly obvious to me as I was expertly shepherded along.

I also immediately recognised that sea kayaking is just about the best way to watch wildlife without sitting still for weeks on end. I remember being grateful to Jim and his publisher Franco, who was also helping keep me upright, for their patience and the same indefinable ease they showed in their chosen environment that I've seen so often among mountain climbers. I felt immediately that I wanted to do more sea kayaking and within a few weeks was off to the Isle of Skye, where within five minutes of getting in the water I was paddling behind an otter.

The trial in outdoor journalism comes in how the media often choose to portray adventure sports as being something for adrenaline fiends who barely notice the world they live in. I'd be lying if I said I didn't enjoy the odd rush of the good stuff, even in my dotage, but it seems to me grotesquely unfair to assume that this is all that the outdoors has to offer. Five minutes with this book reveals the richness of the experience available paddling in our own backyard. And that's your own, individual, salt-flecked experience, not one absorbed with millions of others sitting on their sofas watching *Coast*.

If paddling off Lancashire isn't quite on the same scale as Odysseus sailing through the isles of Greece, it's astonishing how different the familiar can look from the radical new angle of a kayak. Having received an invitation from Jim to cross the Pennines by kayak, I foolishly went to the Himalaya instead, but looking at the journey described in this book I should have tagged along when I had the chance. Paddling up the River Lune into Lancaster with him was some compensation. It was bitterly cold, and we made the amusing discovery, after hauling our boats up a steep hill, that the Lancaster canal had been drained for maintenance and so had to float back down the river instead.

Apart from all the useful, practical information, I love the pictures chosen for the book: boats left high and dry; bizarre, abandoned structures; remote rock arches, those arches of experience that we seem inexplicably drawn to pass through. It's always a treat to see the North of England re-imagined, but I doubt many books will allow you to do so as comprehensively as this one.

Ed Douglas

Contents

Contents

Access & Environment

ENGLAND

Access to the outdoors in England is becoming increasingly encouraged and revisions to the Countryside and Rights of Way Act of 2000 has brought access to many additional areas of coastal land. While engaged in sea kayaking it is rare to encounter access problems. Most of the routes described in this book start and finish at beaches or harbours where public access to the foreshore is already established. Areas of coast between the high and low water mark are often described as 'foreshore', and most of this is owned by the Crown Estate. Neither the Crown Estate nor any other owners normally restrict access to the foreshore.

One exception to this is where it is important to protect areas from human disturbance at nature reserves like those at Spurn Head, South Walney and Lindisfarne. Another exception is where there are MoD firing ranges like those at Whitburn and Eskmeals. Details of these ranges along with contact details are given in the relevant chapters of this guide.

Access on the sea is only restricted in rare and extreme cases and information is given by HM Coastguard during regular maritime safety information broadcasts.

At busy ports like Liverpool and Tyne it is important to seek permission from the relevant authority, either by VHF radio or by mobile phone, before entering or crossing busy harbor entrances.

ISLE OF MAN

The Isle of Man is not part of the United Kingdom; it is a self-governing British crown dependency. However access to its foreshore, harbours and coastal land is much as it is in England.

RESPECT THE INTERESTS OF OTHERS

Acting with courtesy, consideration and awareness is very important. If you are exercising access rights make sure that you respect the privacy, safety and livelihoods of those living and working in the outdoors, and the needs of others enjoying the outdoors.

CARE FOR THE ENVIRONMENT

Sea kayakers can access remote and special places that others cannot. Many of these places have sensitive plant, animal and bird life. Be aware of, and respect landing restrictions around nature reserves. Look after the places you visit and enjoy and leave the land as you find it. Natural England (www.naturalengland.org.uk) has created www.natureonthemap.org.uk, a source of detailed maps that outline protected sites and habitats. The Marine Conservation Society (www.mcsuk.org) offers advice on how to act appropriately around marine wildlife.

TAKE RESPONSIBILITY FOR YOUR OWN ACTIONS

Remember that the outdoors cannot be made risk free and that you should act with care at all times for your own safety and that of others.

WILD CAMPING

This guide provides information on many 'paddler friendly' commercial campsites. However, wild camping provides a special experience and forms an integral part of sea touring. There is no right to camp on the English or Manx coasts, and areas that lend themselves to wild camping for sea kayakers are few and far between. If you do decide to add a wild camp to your journey plan, be sure to choose a remote location away from dwellings, roads and paths. Always arrive late in the day and do not pitch your tent until dusk. You should take your tent down early the following morning. "Leave nothing but footprints and take nothing but photographs."

Important Notice

As with many outdoor activities that take place in remote and potentially hostile environments, technical ability, experience and good planning are essential. The sea is one of the most committing and unforgiving environments. With this considered, it should be treated with the constant respect that it deserves. This guide is designed to provide information that will inspire the sea kayaker to venture into this amazing environment; however it cannot provide the essential ingredients of ability, experience and good planning. Before venturing out on any of the trips described in this book, ensure that your knowledge and ability are appropriate to the seriousness of the trip. The book is purely a guide to provide information about sea kayaking trips. For the additional essential knowledge of safety at sea, personal paddling skills, environmental considerations and tidal planning, the author recommends gaining the appropriate training and advice from experienced and qualified individuals.

WARNING

Sea kayaking is inherently a potentially dangerous sport. Users of this guide should take the appropriate precautions before undertaking any of the trips. The information supplied in this book has been thoroughly researched; however the author can take no responsibility if tidal times differ or if the information supplied is not sufficient for the conditions on the day. Conditions can change quickly and dramatically on the sea and there is no substitute for good judgment and personal risk assessment during the planning stages of a sea trip, or out on the water. This guide cannot replace or diminish the need for these essential skills. The decision on whether to go out sea kayaking or not, and any consequences arising from that decision, remain yours and yours alone.

How to Use the Guide

To use the guide you will need an up-to-date tide tide table for the relevant area, the appropriate Ordnance Survey maps and the knowledge to use them.

Each of the fifty trip chapters is set out into seven sections:

Tidal & Route Information - This is designed as a quick reference for all the 'must know' information on which to plan the trip.

Introduction - This is designed to give the reader a brief overview of what to expect from the trip and to whet the appetite.

Description - This provides further detail and information on the trip including the coastline, launching/landing points, the wildlife and environment, historical information and places of interest to visit.

Tide & Weather – Offering further tidal information and how best to plan the trip which takes the tides, weather and local knowledge into consideration.

Map of Route – This provides a visual outline of the route's start/finish points, landing places, points of interest and tidal information.

Additional Information – This section provides further information (including Admiralty Charts and other useful maps) that will complement the trip, or be of interest if in the local area.

Using the Tidal & Route Information

Each route begins with an overview of pertinent details beginning with the following information: grade of difficulty, trip name, route symbols, and trip number.

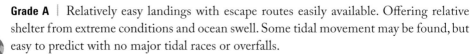 **Grade A** | Relatively easy landings with escape routes easily available. Offering relative shelter from extreme conditions and ocean swell. Some tidal movement may be found, but easy to predict with no major tidal races or overfalls.

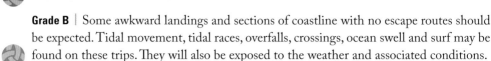 **Grade B** | Some awkward landings and sections of coastline with no escape routes should be expected. Tidal movement, tidal races, overfalls, crossings, ocean swell and surf may be found on these trips. They will also be exposed to the weather and associated conditions.

 Grade C | These trips will have difficult landings and will have no escape routes for long sections of the trip. Fast tidal movement, tidal races, overfalls, extended crossings, ocean swell and surf will be found on all these trips. They will be very exposed to the weather and sea state, therefore require detailed planning and paddlers to be competent in rough water conditions. With this considered, the journey may require good conditions for the trip to be viable.

	Distance	Total distance for the trip.

Distance — Total distance for the trip.

OS Sheet — Number of Ordnance Survey 1:50,000 Landranger map required.

Tidal Port — The port for which tide timetables will be required to work out the tidal streams.

Start — △ map symbol, name and six-figure grid reference of starting point.

Finish — ◎ map symbol, name and six-figure grid reference of finishing point.

HW/LW — The high and/or low water time difference between local ports nearest to the trip and the tidal port.

Tidal Times — Location or area of tidal stream movement, the direction to which the tidal stream flows and the time it starts flowing in relation to the tidal port high water.

Max Rate Sp — The areas in which the tidal streams are fastest and the maximum speed in knots attained on the average spring tide.

Coastguard — Name of the relevant Coastguard Station.

MAP SYMBOLS

About the Author

Jim Krawiecki

Jim started paddling in any old kayak he could muster during the school holidays. He has since paddled (and swum) many of the exciting white water rivers of England, Scotland and Wales, as well as many of those in the French Alps.

A passion for sea kayaking combined with an interest in writing and photography, brought about the first comprehensive Guidebook to the Welsh coast, for sea kayakers. *Welsh Sea Kayaking* was co-written by Andy Biggs and published in September 2006 by Pesda Press. Since then, Jim has travelled overseas to paddle along French coastlines, Greek islands and the shores of east Greenland.

Jim lives in Manchester, is a prominent member of North West Sea Kayakers, and regularly organises meets and sea trips. So a sea kayakers' guide to northern England and the Isle of Man was the obvious choice for an encore. This project has taken Jim to far-flung and remote coastal stretches as well as northern England's industrial and urban tideways.

The Isle of Man

Introduction

The Isle of Man is a beautiful, rugged and wild place at the geographical heart of the British Isles. The interior has rolling hills with heather moorland and crags. The highest peak, Snaefell, rises to 621m. This mountainous land meets the sea with jagged shores and towering rock faces that reveal dramatic and beautiful geological displays. The 160km coastline is an exploratory paddler's paradise. Golden beaches and rock gardens stretch out among huge layered cliffs with deep caves and gullies. The Isle of Man has few rivers to cloud its surrounding waters, leaving their depths unusually clear and blue.

Being an island, you can paddle round it. A typical circumnavigation will take between 3 and 5 days. John Willacy holds the current record for the fastest circumnavigation at the time of writing; he completed the 116km in 12hr 38min. If you want to save the ferry fare, you can paddle to it. There are details on a Scottish crossing in this section and information on a crossing from the Cumbrian coast in the Cumbria section of this book (Route 14). Crossings are also occasionally completed from Northern Ireland and Anglesey.

You can walk to the top of it! The 8km walk from Laxey to the summit of Snaefell takes in the famous Laxey Wheel, Laxey Glen and the beautiful surrounding moorland. It is also possible to make the ascent by the Snaefell Mountain Railway.

The wildlife is exceptionally plentiful and varied. Bird life on the island is generally similar to that of the nearby coastal regions of the UK. The coastal lowlands of the north and the Calf of Man in the south attract huge numbers of migrating birds during spring and autumn. The Calf of Man and Calf Sound are particularly good places to watch seals. From mid-summer to autumn, basking sharks move through these waters to feed on blooms of plankton. The south and west coasts are where these huge but harmless marine mammals are frequently encountered by paddlers.

Visitors to the Isle of Man experience a pleasing step back in time. Most of the island is rural with picturesque small towns and villages. The traditional rural economy of farming and fishing is turning increasingly to leisure, tourism and hospitality. There are two well-established sea kayaking centres on the island. Other adventure sports such as mountain biking, rock climbing and hill walking are also well catered for and attract an increasing number of visitors.

Tides and weather

Tidal streams in the Irish Sea are formidable and races with overfalls form around all of the significant headlands. This provides excellent sport for proficient, well-led groups, but would be better avoided by inexperienced paddlers.

The Isle of Man is generally oblong-shaped and lies along a SW–NE axis. This means that when strong winds blow from the southwest, there are few places to find shelter. When the wind blows from other directions, however, long stretches of sheltered coast can be found.

Sea mists are frequent in calm weather. Mananan is the deity who, according to folklore, takes care of the island and its inhabitants and will frequently draw down his misty cloak whenever invaders approach.

The Isle of Man lies in the middle of an area where the tides of the North Channel meet and diverge from those of the southern part of the Irish Sea. Strong winds, extremes of barometric pressure or huge spring tides can have a considerable effect. Occasionally, tidal streams have been known to change significantly earlier or later than predicted. Be aware of possible anomalies in the waters around the Calf of Man and Maughold Head.

VHF reception is generally poor beneath the cliffs of the south and west coasts. In these areas, it may be possible to make contact with Belfast under good conditions instead of Liverpool Coastguard. Mobile phone networks do not work well in these areas either, although they generally work well throughout the rest of the Isle of Man. Visitors to the island can expect roaming charges similar to mainland Europe.

Getting there

The Isle of Man has a busy airport called Ronaldsway on the southern part of the island. There are flights there from many of the regional airports in the British Isles as well as several destinations in northern Europe. Most paddlers will arrive at the island's capital, Douglas, by the ferry services run exclusively by the Isle of Man Steam Packet Company (www.steam-packet.com). Regular services run from Liverpool, Heysham, Belfast and Dublin.

Many parking areas in busy towns are regulated by the use of parking discs; these are often available at the sea terminal, tourist information offices and on car ferries. Road traffic law is broadly similar to that of the United Kingdom.

It is worth making use of regular bus services and the Manx Electric Railway. This means that if you take only one car, you can still include plenty of one-way paddles during a visit to the island (www.iombusandrail.info).

Expect frequent road closures during the TT and Grand Prix motorcycling events. Manx Tourism is able to advise on how to avoid the worst of any disruption (www.visitisleofman.com).

© Santon Burn

Douglas to Derbyhaven

Douglas to Derbyhaven

No. 1 | Grade B | 16km | OS Sheet 95

Tidal Port	Liverpool
Start	△ Douglas Harbour public slipway (SC 386 750)
Finish	○ Derbyhaven (SC 285 676)
HW/LW	Times of high and low water are similar to Liverpool.
Tidal Times	At Douglas Head, the NE-going stream starts around 6 hours after HW Liverpool and the SW-going eddy stream starts around 3 hours before HW Liverpool. At Santon Head, the NE-going stream starts around 5 hours 15 minutes after HW Liverpool and the SW-going eddy stream starts around 4 hours before HW Liverpool. The main offshore SW-going stream starts around HW Liverpool.
Max Rate Sp	Tidal streams in this section can reach 2–3 knots.
Coastguard	Liverpool, tel. 0151 931 3341, VHF weather every 3 hours from 0130

Introduction

Leaving the island's capital and main seaport, you will be immediately exposed to the wild and rugged shores of the southeast-facing Manx coastline. Towering cliffs composed of twisted rock

© Rock gardens near Port Soldrick

layers cascade down to a myriad of tiny inlets and coves. Kelp-infested rock gardens and pebbly beaches will keep you entertained along the way. The stature of the cliffs gradually decreases as you approach the shallows of Derby Haven, nestled within the northern clutches of the Langness Peninsula.

Description

Douglas is a bustling busy town, the main seaport and the island's capital. If you arrive on the Isle of Man by ferry then this is where you will land. The harbour, marina and ferry terminal are at the southern end of Douglas Bay, sheltered from south-westerly winds by the high ground of Douglas Head. On the south side of the harbour there is a public slipway beside a large wooden jetty with roadside parking nearby.

Douglas Head is marked clearly to mariners by the lighthouse. The original was built here in 1831, but following structural problems was demolished and replaced in 1892 by the lighthouse that remains in operation to this day. A foghorn was added in 1908 but its poor sighting and orientation gave rise to a barrage of complaints from the townsfolk. As a result, 'Moaning Minnie' (as the foghorn had become known) was moved to a more remote location along the coast. Higher up the headland is the recently restored Camera Obscura. This popular Victorian idea was to project images of the view outside onto the walls inside like a gigantic pinhole camera. The elevated position gives excellent views across the whole of Douglas Bay.

Douglas Harbour is often busy with ferry services, fishing boats and pleasure craft. It helps the harbour authorities if you let them know your plans before you launch and follow any advice they give you (VHF channel 12, tel. 01624 686628). Between the outside of the south breakwater and Douglas Head, there is a small sheltered cove with a shingle beach. This is a useful place to sort out any initial snags or problems. A steep path with steps leads from the beach to the lighthouse and the Camera Obscura.

Paddling south from Douglas Head, the coastline rises dramatically from the sea and there are towering exposed cliffs. On calm days it is possible to get close in beneath the cliffs, to where swell surges through small gullies and channels. The small shingle beach at Port Walberry can provide a little respite before carrying on around the craggy headland of Little Ness. The heather moorland of Little Ness is popular with walkers as it descends steeply through crags to the rocky foreshore. It is usually possible to paddle through the gully that separates the headland from a low rocky stack; the rock hopping here is excellent. Following the shore around from Little Ness, the coastline quickly rears up steeply once again but this time there are shingle beaches in sheltered coves at the foot of the cliffs. Weaving your way in and out of the coves leads you into the depths of a beautiful bay and the sadly neglected haven of Port Soderick.

Port Soderick was a fashionable destination for discerning Victorian holidaymakers in the late 1800s. There were walks through the shaded leafy woods of the glen, suspended walkways that led into smugglers caves and a funicular railway leading to a cliff-top tramway. Nowadays, Port Soderick Glen is still popular with walkers but little can be seen of the other attractions; the Anchor pub and restaurant has been closed for a number of years. There is road access and a car park at Port Soderick, but launching and landing here below half-tide would be treacherous as

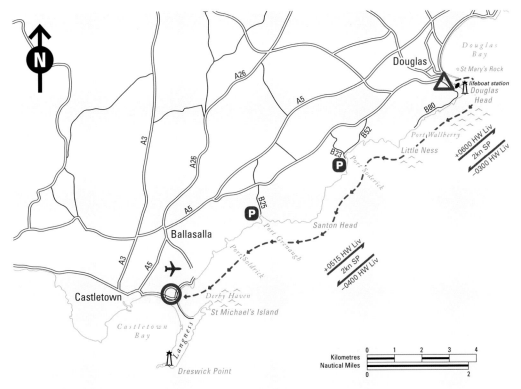

Sheltered cove outside south breakwater, Douglas

a slippery, seaweed-infested boulder field has to be crossed. If you have to land here at low water, the old sloping concrete jetty can offer a useful escape route.

The stunning scenery of the Manx east coast remains unrelenting, dramatic and intriguing. The layered rock structures form a multitude of gullies and coves around Santon Head, leading to the deep sheltered inlet of Port Grenaugh where you can find road access and a few parking spaces. The gently shelving pebbly beach offers better landings than Port Soderick and is only tricky with slippery rocks when the tide is at its lowest.

The shores between Port Grenaugh and Derby Haven have rocky cliffs that are riddled with caves and gullies. The clear shallow waters at the foot of the cliffs surge through a network of channels bound by reefs and boulders, adorned with forests of kelp. Port Soldrick is a deep semi-circular bay with a pebbly beach sheltered by the surrounding high ground. Less than a kilometre further along the coast is the deep inlet known as Santon Burn. The rocky entrance stands guard over beaches of silvery sand littered with seashells. Further in, the shallow waters narrow into a dark, steep-sided ravine where peregrine falcons spy out unwary rock doves.

Ronaldsway Airport is just over a kilometre away from the entrance of Santon Burn; the gantry which supports the approach lights juts out into the sea.

The village of Derbyhaven can be seen spread delightfully along the sandy shore of the bay that carries the same name. A few small fishing boats and pleasure craft gather for shelter behind an insular breakwater opposite the centre of the village, where there is a slipway. The shallow sandy beach dries a long way as the tide goes out, so starting or finishing here at low water is best avoided.

Tides and weather

This area of coast is exposed to any winds with a southerly or easterly component. There is good shelter from north-westerly winds for much of this coast, although the cliffs around Douglas Head, Little Ness and Santon Head are particularly prone to swirling downdraughts.

The tidal streams around Douglas Head, Little Ness and Santon Head can reach 2–3 knots and overfalls can form in wind-against-tide conditions. The tidal streams are generally much weaker for the rest of this section. Due to eddy effects along this section, the SW-going stream lasts approximately twice as long as the NE-going stream.

Additional information

Marine Drive was originally a tramway that ran along the top of the cliffs between Douglas and Port Soderick. The route was opened up as a road when the tramway fell into disuse, but has since been partly closed following several landslides. The parts that are still open are accessible by car from Douglas and Port Soderick, and offer terrific coastal views along the northern half of this section.

There are two campsites off the main A1 road between Douglas and Peel. Cronk Dhoo campsite is possibly the nicer of the two, with views to the hills across the glen (www.cronkdhoo.com). Glenlough campsite is also quite pleasant. It is closer to Douglas and only a short walk to the nearby village of Union Mills, where you can find a shop, petrol station and pub.

© *Douglas Head from the south*

Variations

This route can be paddled in the opposite direction, but there will be less in the way of tidal assistance. If you do not wish to use the public slipway in Douglas Harbour then the alternative is to use the promenade beach. The easiest access and parking can be found close to the north end of the promenade (SC 392 772). Port Soderick and Port Grenaugh can be used as alternative places to start or finish, but Port Soderick should be avoided below half tide.

 # Castletown & Langness

No. 2	**Grade C**	**16km**	**OS Sheet 95**

Tidal Port	Liverpool
Start	△ Derbyhaven (SC 285 676)
Finish	○ Port St Mary, lifeboat and public slipway (SC 212 673)
HW/LW	Times of high and low water are similar to Liverpool.
Tidal Times	In the vicinity of Dreswick Point, the NE-going stream starts around 6 hours after HW Liverpool. A significant back-eddy begins to run SW along the eastern shore of Langness, resulting in an almost continuous SW flow. The main SW-going stream starts at around HW Liverpool.
Max Rate Sp	At Dreswick Point the streams can exceed 5 knots on spring tides. The tidal streams along the shores of Castletown Bay and Bay ny Carrickey rarely exceed 1 knot.
Coastguard	Liverpool, tel. 0151 931 3341, VHF weather every 3 hours from 0130

Castletown & Langness

Introduction

The low-lying peninsula of Langness is exceptionally beautiful in a windswept, rugged sort of way. Rolling coastal moorland is bound by jagged shores with few opportunities to land. Rock

© Castletown Beach

hopping is particularly rewarding, but the spiky nature of the rocks present an added element of risk. Strong tidal streams make themselves known here, with overfalls forming at both ends of Langness. A more sheltered coastline leads from Castletown Bay to Port St Mary, with beaches and civilisation close by.

Description

The pretty village of Derbyhaven lies less than 2km to the east of Castletown on the southeast part of the Isle of Man. The main A12 road from Castletown enters the village leading directly to the beach via a slipway. Derby Haven is a natural harbour protected by the peninsula of Langness and St Michael's Island. An insular breakwater built upon a reef adds extra protection to the beach and village from strong easterly winds.

Paddling east from the beach and past the breakwater, you will be heading for the northern tip of St Michael's Island with its distinctive circular fort. There have been fortifications here since Viking times, but the circular building we see today was constructed during the reign of Henry VIII and reinforced during the English civil war.

Once you have rounded the north tip of the island, the shores of Langness will lead you southwest. Playing amongst the jagged rocky channels and lagoons of the southeast-facing shore is great fun. The northern half of the peninsula is largely occupied by the Castletown Golf Links. The southern half is open grassland with gorse and heather. The southernmost point on Langness and the Manx mainland is Dreswick Point, marked by the Langness Lighthouse. It only takes a gentle breeze to make the seas here chaotic and threatening when the tide is running. The roughest of the water cannot always be avoided by staying close to the shore and, in any case, the shore here is lined with sharp, dagger-like rocks. In calmer conditions this stretch is great for rock hopping and there are a couple of isolated shingle beaches for a quick stop. As you round Langness Point, you will enter the calmer waters of Castletown Bay.

Castletown was the island's capital and the seat of political power until 1874, when the House of Keys moved to Douglas. Castletown Bay faces the prevailing south-westerlies and the broad sandy beach to the east of the town picks the surf up nicely following a day or two of strong winds. The town and harbour are tucked away at the northwest corner of the bay. There is a public slipway in the outer harbour, which is a short walk along the quay from the Castle Arms Hotel, Castle Rushen and the original House of Keys.

Scarlett Point forms the western entrance to Castletown Bay. Following the jagged rocky shore will lead you to shallow sandy coves of Poyll Vaaish and the northern reaches of Bay ny Carrickey. The bay is around 3km across and has a succession of low rocky reefs that separate the sandy beaches, many of which have easy access to the main A5 shore road. Port St Mary and its harbour are nestled snugly in the western corner of the south-facing Bay ny Carrickey. It is possible to land inside the outer breakwater on or beside the lifeboat slipway in the shadow of the harbour office building. There is plenty of parking beside the harbour office, as well as toilets and coin-operated showers.

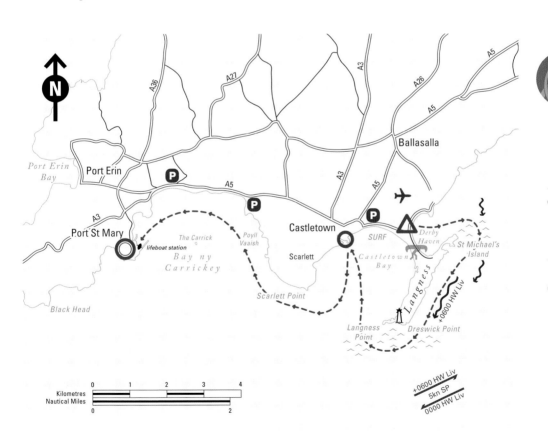

© Herring Tower, Langness

Tides and weather

The land in this area is low lying, leaving this coast exposed to winds from any direction. There is some limited shelter from northerlies along the lee shore of Langness and around Scarlett Point, but these winds tend to funnel out of Castletown Bay and Bay ny Carrickey.

A small tide race forms off the northeast tip of St Michael's Island during the SW-going ebb. For experienced paddlers, the overfalls that form during the ebb off Dreswick and Langness points can be anything from exhilarating fun, with near-shore eddies, to downright intimidating and exposed. If you wish to avoid the overfalls it is best to leave Derbyhaven a little under an hour before HW Liverpool; you should then arrive at Dreswick Point close to slack water. The tidal streams between Castletown and Port St Mary are weak and can be considered insignificant.

Additional information

King William's College offers bunkhouse accommodation (01624 820400) near Castletown. The Harbour office (01624 833205) is staffed during 09:00–16:00.

Variations

To avoid the Langness tidal streams start from Castletown Beach. There is a car park midway between Castletown and Derbyhaven along the A12 road (SC 278 677). The narrow neck of land between Derby Haven and Castletown Bay can be portaged via a public footpath that crosses the golf course at the narrowest point, leaving a straightforward portage of around 200m.

Calf Sound on a stormy day

 Calf Sound ▦▦◪▱

3

No. 3 | Grade B | 10km | OS Sheet 95

Tidal Port	Liverpool
Start	△ Port St Mary, lifeboat and public slipway (SC 212 673)
Finish	⭕ Port Erin Beach (SC 195 690)
HW/LW	Times of high and low water are similar to Liverpool.
Tidal Times	The W-going stream between Kallow Point and Spanish Head starts at around HW Liverpool. The E-going stream starts around 6 hours after HW Liverpool.
	The N-going stream in Calf Sound starts around 1 hour 45 minutes before HW Liverpool and the S-going stream starts around 3 hours 45 minutes after HW Liverpool.
Max Rates Sp	The streams in Calf Sound can exceed 6 knots on spring tides.
Coastguard	Liverpool, tel. 0151 931 3341, VHF weather every 3 hours from 0130

Introduction

The distance between Port St Mary and Port Erin by sea is relatively short but the experience is intense. The towering cliffs on the southwest corner of the Isle of Man bear the brunt of winter

© Looking north over Calf Sound

storms. There are caves, gullies and stacks surrounded by clear, luminescent blue waters. During spring and early summer, the cliff ledges, gullies and caves echo to the clamour of guillemots, razorbills and fulmars. Calf Sound itself has strong tidal streams that give rise to overfalls and standing waves. This tidal gateway provides great sport for confident paddlers with a good roll. If you pass through here close to slack water, smoother seas may tempt you to hang around and watch the many grey seals before heading off to the sheltered haven of Port Erin.

Description

Port St Mary and Port Erin are only 2km apart by road at the southwest corner of the island. The outer harbour at Port St Mary is well sheltered, facing northeast inside the western entrance of Bay ny Carrickey. The slipway between the harbour office and lifeboat station leads down a beach of shingle and seaweed-covered rocks. Kallow Point lies to the southwest of the harbour entrance and is made up of layered rock slabs that dip gently into the sea. This is the eastern entrance to Perwick Bay and from here you will be able to see the southern end of the Calf of Man. The high ground around the bay provides good shelter from all but southerly winds, making this rocky foreshore an ideal place to get warmed up with a little rock hopping and exploration of the caves and gullies. Moving on from Perwick Bay, the true might of the southern Manx coastline is gradually revealed as the layered cliffs rise sharply from the sea. The alternate hard and soft layers have eroded over time to provide perfect nesting ledges, like a series of stone bookshelves.

Tucked into a recess among the tall cliffs is a sea stack known as The Anvil. Nearby, running deep into the cliff, is a long sea cave in which the deep clear waters seem almost luminescent.

The Sugarloaf is a huge pinnacle-shaped sea stack beside the promontory that stands at the eastern end of Bay Stacka. A second cave can be paddled right through the promontory, where you emerge right beside the Sugarloaf. One Victorian description of the area states that no trip to these shores is complete without taking a boat trip into these caves. The remaining shores of Bay Stacka are boulder strewn and steep, with grass and heather slopes leading to a popular rock climbing area above known as The Chasms.

The western entrance to Bay Stacka is marked by the tall dark headland of Black Head. Close inspection of this headland reveals that parts of the layered rock shelves appear to be missing. These were removed by enterprising Victorian quarrymen, lowered into barges and taken round to Port St Mary to be used as ready-made door lintels. A short way beyond Black Head stands Spanish Head, which is the mightiest cliff of all and leads the way into Calf Sound. This narrow stretch of water separates the Calf of Man from the mainland. The depths of these fast-moving rock-infested waters are littered with shipwrecks.

Calf Sound is only 500m wide at its narrowest point. The rocky islets of Kitterland and Thousla Rock further constrict the tidal streams that can exceed 6 knots. Kitterland is home to a thriving community of grey seals. Thousla Rock is submerged at high water and is clearly marked by a white octagonal tower. These two mid-stream obstructions divide the flow into three distinct streams, with eddies in the lee of each. The deepest (and therefore smoothest) passage is through the middle, between Thousla Rock and Kitterland. The favoured spot for playing the race and surfing the standing waves is between Kitterland and the mainland. The Sound Visitor Centre

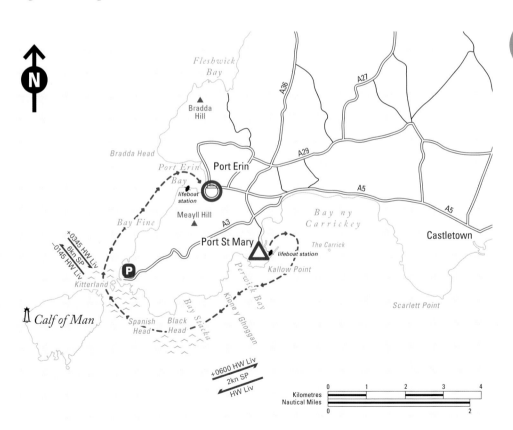

and café overlooks these waters from the lower grassy slopes on the mainland. It is possible to land on the rocky foreshore here, but only in the calmest of conditions.

The tidal turmoil and turbulent waters soon dissipate once north of Calf Sound. The last 3km of coastline that lead to Port Erin soon become hilly, with cliffs and caves. The far northern entrance to Port Erin is the mountainous Bradda Head with its distinctive Milner's Tower. The southern entrance is partially blocked by an old broken-down breakwater, which is completely submerged at high water but becomes exposed at mid tide. There is a tremendously welcoming view of the tall white houses and hotels high on the hill as you paddle into the bay. After landing on the soft sands, make time for a soothing ice cream or a hot snack at one of the nearby cafés.

Tides and weather

This section is exposed to winds from almost any direction apart from the northeast. The W-going ebb stream gains strength around Kallow Point and Kione y Ghoggan, but is even stronger around Black Head where overfalls develop from the strength of the tide.

Significant overfalls with standing waves, boils and whirlpools develop in Calf Sound, but the middle passage is deeper and wider and so tends to offer the smoothest ride.

The timings of the tidal streams that run through Calf Sound can change noticeably under the influence of the weather. Strong northerly or southerly winds or extremes of barometric pressure can alter timings by up to an hour.

The wreck of the brig *Lily*

In late December 1853, strong winter gales wreaked havoc in the Irish Sea. The wooden brig *Lily* had left Liverpool bound for West Africa, laden with general goods such as textiles, rum, firearms and 60 tons of gunpowder. Storm damage to rigging and sails left *Lily* adrift in the sea and heading for the southern shores of the Isle of Man. Despite attempts to drop anchor, the ship ran aground upon the rocks known as Kitterland in Calf Sound. The captain and four crewmen were lost, but nine of their shipmates managed to scramble to safety.

In the calm of the following days, local authorities and the survivors began to land what cargo could be salvaged. When smoke was seen coming from one of the closed holds, it was decided to make an opening so that any fire could be extinguished with water. As the hole was cut, fresh air rushed in and the cargo of gunpowder immediately ignited. The force of the explosion rocked houses as far away as Port Erin and Port St Mary, extinguished lanterns in nearby mine workings and was heard as far away as Douglas. All of those bar one attending the wreck were instantly killed. The single survivor is thought to have been protected by rocks beyond which he was answering nature's call. A white cross stands on the mainland overlooking Calf Sound and Kitterland, in memory of those who lost their lives.

© The Sugarloaf | Keirron Tastagh

Additional information

Cosy Nook Café overlooks Port Erin Beach beside the light beacon. The menu is basic but the quality excellent and, with the extensive opening hours, this café is likely to be open when many others are not. For those bad weather days, the National Folk Museum at Cregneash village and the nearby Calf Sound Visitor Centre are well worth a visit. An area of craggy moorland called The Chasms forms a popular part of *Raad ny Foillan*, the Manx coastal path. The area that overlooks Bay Stacka is also popular with rock climbers.

Variations

You may find the streams generally less significant and the waters a little smoother if you paddle this route with the E-going tide from Port Erin, round Black Head and then Kallow Point.

 # The Calf of Man & Chicken Rock

No. 4 | Grade C | 16km | OS Sheet 95

Tidal Port	Liverpool
Start	△ Port Erin Beach (SC 195 690)
Finish	○ Port Erin Beach (SC 195 690)
HW/LW	Times of high and low water are similar to Liverpool.
Tidal Times	In Calf Sound, the N-going stream starts at around 1 hour 45 minutes before HW Liverpool. The S-going stream starts at around 3 hours 45 minutes after HW Liverpool.
	At Burroo, the SW-going stream starts at around HW Liverpool and the E-going stream starts at around 6 hours after HW Liverpool.
	At Chicken Rock, the W-going stream starts at around HW Liverpool and the E-going stream starts at around 6 hours after HW Liverpool.
Max Rates Sp	The streams in Calf Sound, at Burroo and in the vicinity of Chicken Rock run at between 4–6 knots during spring tides. The E-going stream at Burroo is weaker at around 3 knots.
Coastguard	Liverpool, tel. 0151 931 3341, VHF weather every 3 hours from 0130

Passing Burroo | Keirron Tastagh

The Calf of Man & Chicken Rock

4

Introduction

Tall craggy cliffs, sea stacks, rocky islets and strong tidal streams make this a classic paddling trip. Chicken Rock and the Calf of Man are the first lines of defence when heavy seas brought by south-westerly gales come crashing upon the Manx coast. Seals, basking sharks and sea birds form an integral part of this adventure, and many rare land-based birds also come here as part of their annual migration.

Description

The closest point of departure is Port Erin, at the western end of the main A5 road that runs across the southern part of the Isle of Man. There is parking along the short promenade but this soon fills up during busy summer weekends. It is best to leave Port Erin Beach around 4hr 30min before high water at Liverpool; this way you should be paddling through Calf Sound during the last hour of the S-going stream.

As you make your way out of the bay past the lifeboat station, take care near the old breakwater. It usually becomes covered around mid-tide and leaves a row of jagged rocks just below the surface. As soon as you pass the breakwater you will be able to see the Calf of Man beyond the shores of Bay Fine. Meanwhile, there should be plenty of time to enjoy rock hopping and exploring caves along the steep rocky shores between here and Calf Sound. With good timing, the S-going stream in Calf Sound will be dying away when you arrive. This should make ferry gliding across the sound to the Calf of Man relatively straightforward.

The Calf's gentle grassy slopes overlook the sound and descend to a small northeast-facing bay. This shore is mostly made up of narrow pebbly beaches with gently shelving, seaweed-covered rock ledges below. This is the most frequently used landing for kayaks. There are two tiny harbours here: Cow Harbour and Grant's Harbour. Cow Harbour is at the northern end of the bay set in a deep, northwest-facing gully. It has an old boathouse and slipway, which can only be used in very calm conditions. Grant's Harbour lies at the south of the bay, but has high walls and no slipway.

The east-facing shores become steep as you paddle south from here, with almost 2km of tall cliffs rising vertically from the sea to over 50m. Towards the southern end of the island, the coastline relents. A narrow rocky east-facing gully leads to South Harbour, where it is possible to land among the rocks or upon the patchy pebbly beach.

It is worth taking a little time to stop here and walk across the rabbit-ridden slopes up to the rocky promontory at the southern tip of the island. A narrow channel separates this promontory from a huge sea stack known as Burroo. From the promontory, you really get the sense of being at the land's end of Manx shores. The view across to Chicken Rock lighthouse is breath-taking and you can check the sea conditions before committing yourself to the more exposed side of the island. When Burroo is viewed from the east or the west, the rock formation around the natural arch resembles a huge dragon bending down to take a drink from the sea. This gives rise to its local name of The Drinking Dragon. The south-facing bay is known as The Puddle; its shores are craggy with deep gullies and low cliffs that lead to Caigher Point at the southwest corner.

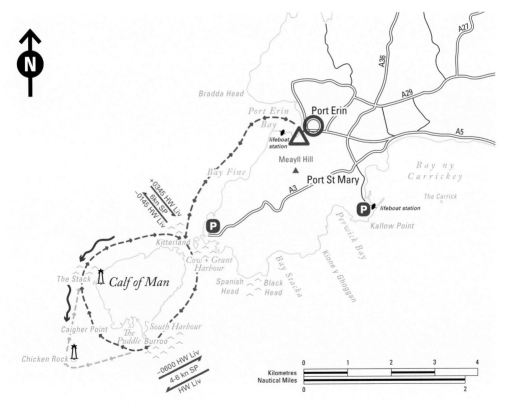

© Chiffchaff at the Calf of Man Bird Observatory

The Calf of Man & Chicken Rock

Chicken Rock lies offshore 1km to the southwest. This rocky reef is covered at high water and is the most southerly feature of the Manx coast. The lighthouse was built in 1875 after it was discovered that the high light on the Calf of Man was so often shrouded in thick hill fog that it was deemed to be almost useless. The tower is made of blocks of granite and stands 44m tall. The light can be seen as far away as 21 miles.

The gnarly western shores of the Calf rise steeply to where the old lighthouses still stand almost 100m above. A tall rocky islet simply known as The Stack stands at the most westerly point. The effects of any S-going flow are masked in the deep dark gully. The effects of the tide gradually fade as you make your way beneath the tall dark cliffs that descend from the highest part of the island. The shore is rocky and forbidding with occasional lagoons and gullies.

The cliffs at the northern side of the Calf of Man comprise steep grassy slopes interspersed with crags. High among these inaccessible crags are the nest burrows of the ghostly and elusive Manx shearwater. As you make your way round the northern tip of the island, Calf Sound and the old stone boathouse beside Cow Harbour will come into view. The tracks that wind up the hill from the harbour lead along rolling heather moorland to the bird observatory and bunkhouse near the centre of the Calf. The old farm buildings sit neatly in a sheltered hollow among a few small trees and bushes. Mist nets are stretched out here to catch migrating birds so that they can be weighed, measured and ringed. The path splits beyond the observatory with the left branch leading to the South Harbour and Burroo. The right-hand branch leads to the old lighthouses and the precipitous cliffs on the west side of the island.

The return to Port Erin is simply a case of retracing your route along the coastline. If the tide

Chicken Rock lighthouse

is running in Calf Sound, it may be necessary to ferry glide across. The tidal streams have little effect close to the shore between Calf Sound and Port Erin.

Tides and weather

Careful tidal planning is crucial to this trip being a success. Overfalls develop in Calf Sound, in the vicinity of Chicken Rock and at The Stack. Overfalls tend to develop at Burroo, mainly during the SW-going ebb. Most of this trip is exposed to winds from any direction; a gentle breeze can create difficult conditions where the wind opposes the tide.

Additional information

The Calf of Man is a nature reserve run by Manx National Heritage. The island is cared for by a couple of wardens during the summer months, and is an important site for ringing and recording numbers of migrating birds. It is well worth spending several hours exploring the island via the paths that run along the cliff tops and across the island. Camping is forbidden but cheap, basic bunkhouse accommodation is available by booking in advance with the Manx National Heritage Office (tel. 01624 648 000).

Variations

Depending on tide and weather conditions, Calf of Man trips can start or finish at Port St Mary. This will add around 6km to the trip.

© 'The Pepper Pot'. Thousla Rock. Calf Sound

4

Manx shearwater *(Puffinus puffinus)*

Having spent the winter months off the sunny shores of Brazil, these tireless ocean wanderers cross the Atlantic to the western shores of the British Isles. The female incubates a single egg in a deep burrow on a steep hillside or cliff beyond the reach of predators. The males feed at sea by day and only land at night to bring food. They are exceptionally graceful in flight but clumsy on land as they stumble along on their short and feeble legs.

Their ghostly nocturnal chunterings have struck fear into stranded mariners, superstitious crofters and even marauding Vikings. Although the breeding colony on the Calf of Man is modest in size, Manx shearwaters have a special place in local folklore. The young shearwaters normally take their first flight on a dark night when the Manx god *Mananan* brings mists over the island and watches over them as they take to the air. Once airborne, they will not reach land again until they return here to breed.

 # Port Erin to Peel

No. 5 | Grade B | 18km | OS Sheet 95

Tidal Port	Liverpool
Start	△ Port Erin Beach (SC 195 690)
Finish	○ Fenella Beach, Peel (SC 241 844)
HW/LW	Times of high and low water are similar to Liverpool.
Tidal Times	The N-going stream starts around 1 hour 30 minutes before HW Liverpool. The S-going stream starts around 4 hours 30 minutes after HW Liverpool.
Max Rate Sp	The strongest tidal streams are around Niarbyl and reach around 1 knot.
Coastguard	Liverpool, tel. 0151 931 3341, VHF weather every 3 hours from 0130

Introduction

The Manx west coast offers terrific scenery. Rolling hills and craggy coastal moorland meet the sea with pebbly beaches, rocky foreshores and towering cliffs in twisted rock layers. The proximity of these shores to civilisation makes this area a favourite for short, scenic, sunset excursions.

Description

Port Erin is a beautiful west-facing bay on the southwest part of the Isle of Man, surrounded by green hills dotted with white cottages. The beach and promenade are signposted from the main A5 road that leads into the town from the east. There is parking along the short promenade, but this soon fills up during busy summer weekends. From the promenade there is a wonderful view along the north shore of the bay towards Bradda Head, upon which stands the distinctive Milner's Tower.

The soft sandy beach and sheltered bay provide an excellent area to warm up and practise boat-handling skills before setting off. The shores along the north side of the bay quickly become steep and rocky, with plenty of rock hopping potential. The cliffs of Bradda Head and Bradda Hill rise through craggy slopes and heather moorland to almost 200m. After nearly 4km, the cliffs back away revealing Fleshwick Bay. A narrow road winds its way down to the pebbly beach, which is sheltered from all but northerly winds. The coastline to the north of Fleshwick Bay is mountainous, with the coastal peaks of Lhiattee ny Beinnee and Cronk ny Arrey Laa reaching over 300m and 400m, respectively. Streams cascade down the craggy slopes after heavy rain, sometimes making a final plunge into the sea by way of a waterfall like that at Gob yn Ushtey. From here, the pretty white thatched cottages at Niarbyl can be seen 2km to the north.

The steep rocky west-facing coastline begins to mellow to pebbly beaches at Niarbyl Bay. The name Niarbyl is derived from the Manx word for tail and refers to the rocky reef or tail of hard jagged rocks that extend seawards from the otherwise gentle shoreline. The old traditional cottages along the beach played the part of an Irish village in the late 1980s cult comedy film

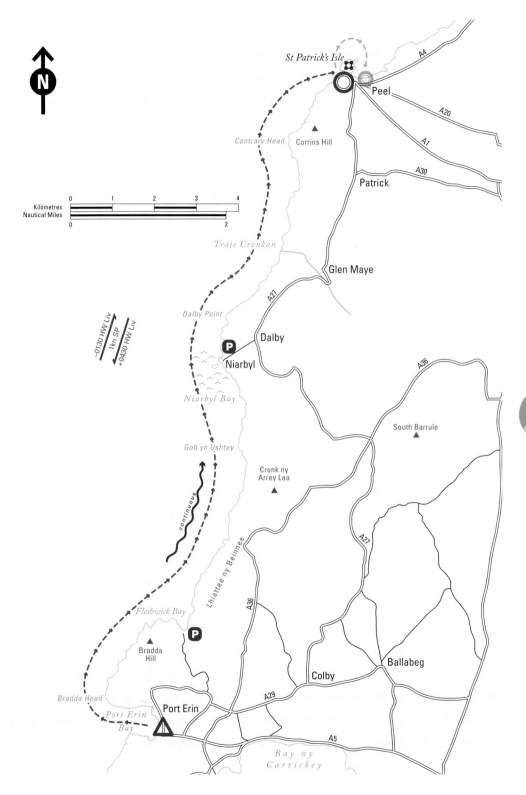

St Patrick's Isle

Peel

A4

A20

A1

Contrary Head

Corrins Hill

A30

Patrick

Kilometres
Nautical Miles

Traie Cronkan

Glen Maye

A27

Dalby Point

Dalby

Niarbyl

Niarbyl Bay

A36

−0130 HW Liv
1kn SP
+0430 HW Liv

Gob yn Ushtey

South Barrule

Cronk ny
Arrey Laa

continuous

Lhiattee ny Beinnee

A27

Fleshwick Bay

A36

Bradda
Hill

Ballabeg

Colby

Bradda Head

A29

Port Erin

Port Erin
Bay

A5

Bay ny
Carrickey

Waking Ned Devine. The Niarbyl Café and visitor centre is famed for its sunset dining and does excellent hot chocolate and fantastic snacks and evening meals. All of this should come with a gentle reminder that luxurious dining comes at a price.

On the paddle north from Niarbyl and around Dalby Point, more beaches of shingle, pebbles and boulders are passed. At Traie Cronkan the thundering waters of Glen Maye flow out across the beach. If you land here and walk less than a kilometre up the glen, you will find spectacular waterfalls in a deep wooded gorge. Looking north from Traie Cronkan, the coastline rises steeply to herald the approach to Contrary Head. As the name suggests, this is where the tidal streams of the west coast converge and divide. The huge cliffs are crazed with zigzag patterns of folded rock strata. Take your time exploring the caves, semi-submerged boulders and rock ledges in the clear waters at the foot of the cliffs.

There can be no better way to finish a paddling trip on a calm summer's evening than to follow the cliffs to Fenella Beach beneath the magnificence of Peel Castle.

Tides and weather

The tides along this section are not strong and rarely exceed 1 knot. During the strength of the S-going ebb, an eddy stream runs north close to the shore between Fleshwick Bay and Niarbyl. Fenella Beach at Peel can be awkward at high water, particularly when there is swell from the west. In these conditions, the main beach to the east of Peel harbour may be easier to land upon as it is more sheltered and gently shelving.

Additional information

To the north of Port Erin, the walk through Bradda Glen along the coastal path to Milner's Tower offers excellent views over the bay. Once you reach the tower you can see all the way along the craggy coastal moors and shores to the headland at Niarbyl.

Peel has plenty of shops for supplies and a good café on the promenade for hot and cold snacks. The Creek Inn at Peel marina serves an assortment of fine ales and has a delicious menu which includes local specialities. There is a well-run campsite at Peel with good facilities beside the leisure centre and swimming pool (tel. 01624 842341).

If you are visiting these shores for the first time, it is worth getting in touch with Adventurous Experiences (www.adventurousexperiences.com) based near Peel. They specialise in sea kayaking courses, run guided trips and can arrange basic camping facilities upon request. Adventurous Experiences also host a number of adventure sports events, including the island's annual sea kayaking symposium which is normally held in late summer.

Variations

This trip is best done in the described direction due to the N-going eddy stream that runs between Fleshwick Bay and Niarbyl. If you fancy a shorter trip, it is possible to start or finish at Niarbyl (half-way between Port Erin and Peel).

Peel to Jurby Head

No. 6 | Grade A | 16km | OS Sheet 95

Tidal Port	Liverpool
Start	△ Fenella Beach, Peel (SC 241 844)
Finish	○ Ballaugh Shore, Jurby Head (SC 336 960)
HW/LW	Times of high and low water are similar to Liverpool.
Tidal Times	The NE-going stream starts around 6 hours after HW Liverpool and the SW-going stream starts around HW Liverpool.
Max Rate Sp	The tidal streams are weak at Peel but gradually increase to around 2 knots at springs off Jurby Head.
Coastguard	Liverpool, tel. 0151 931 3341, VHF weather every 3 hours from 0130

Introduction

With its historic castle and harbour, Peel is the gateway to the Manx northwest coast. The rocky foreshores, interspersed with coves and beaches, are favoured by the local population of cormorants and shags. The rocks gradually give way to broad shingles and sands, where oystercatchers

© Looking north from Glen Wyllin

6

and other wading birds find rich pickings among the pebbles and driftwood. These shores have a wonderfully isolated feel with the convenience and reassurance of civilisation close by.

Description

Peel is a small harbour town on the mid-west coast of the Isle of Man. Following the decline in fishing, the harbour has been rejuvenated with a new marina development. There are plenty of shops, bars and other attractions for the summer tourists. Fenella Beach faces west along the short causeway that leads to St Patrick's Isle and Peel Castle. To get there, you will have to drive past the aromatic Manx Kipper smokehouse beside the marina. The taste of traditionally smoked kippers is both loved and hated the world over.

It may be best to start your journey early in the day, as the small car park that overlooks Fenella Beach can fill up quickly during summer weekends and bank holidays. As you paddle out from Fenella Beach, the castle looms over you from above the blocky cliff. As soon as you round the headland away from the beach there are several small inlets and a long, narrow, straight cave that can be paddled into as far as 20m. Legends tell of a secret cave that led from the castle dungeons straight to the sea. This may well have been the secret passage (if it existed), but if so it has been closed off for many years.

Further along, the shore levels off into a series of rocky ledges which are popular with anglers. The breakwater for Peel Harbour extends from the rocks and has a distinctive hexagonal domed light beacon at the end. Peel harbour can be busy, especially during the summer months with increased traffic to and from the marina.

Beyond the harbour entrance is Peel Bay and the broad sands of Peel Beach. When strong winds bring swell from the northwest there can be nothing better than spending the afternoon surfing in the shadow of the Castle with the cafés and bars of the promenade comfortably nearby.

Beyond the beaches of Cain's Strand and White Strand, the gently rolling hills of the northwest coast descend to steep rocky outcrops and craggy cliffs. Between the outcrops are small coves with beaches of shingle and pebbles. This is excellent rock hopping coast, which is at its best around mid tide.

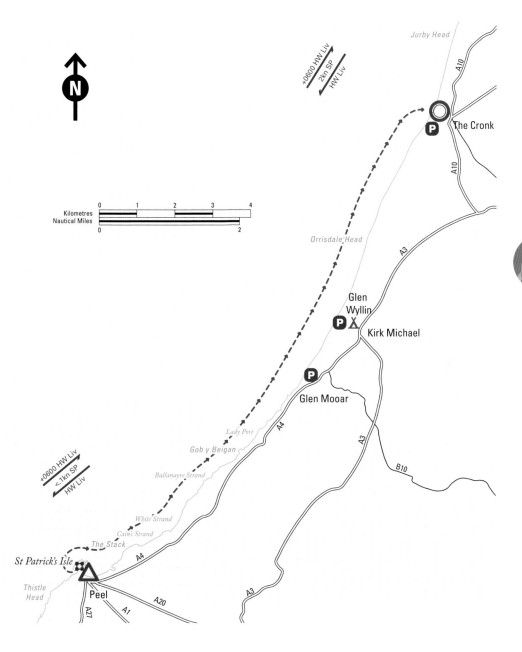

The *Raad ny Foillan* coastal path runs along a disused railway track on the cliffs above these shores. The main A4 coast road is also close by, but when you are paddling close in beneath the cliffs you would never know it. The first possible escape route is where the coastal path descends Glen Mooar and the boulder clay cliffs above the shore. There is a gravel car park (SC 302 894) with a narrow lane that leads up to the main road.

Less than 2km further along the coast is Glen Wyllin and the only public campsite on the Manx coast. It can be tricky landing here at high water when the sandy beach is covered, leaving only a steep concrete slipway (SC 309 906). A narrow lane leads from the public car park above the beach and passes through the main camping areas. The campsite is sheltered deep in the glen with plenty of trees. There is a well-stocked campsite shop with tourist information, toilets and showers. The lane then leads to the main road and the nearby town of Kirk Michael.

Paddling north from Glen Wyllin, you will pass a succession of broad beaches backed by sandy cliffs. The cliffs gradually give way to reveal lower ground that surrounds Ballaugh Shore. The trip finishes where a stream runs across the pebbly beach, above which there is a car park and picnic area. To the north, cliffs of boulder clay rise once again and a sandy beach leads to the unremarkable headland of Jurby Head.

Tides and weather

The tidal streams along this section are weak, especially close to the shore where they can be regarded as insignificant. This section is exposed to any winds from the north and west. If Fenella Beach has big surf from the west, then the rest of this coast will have tricky, choppy conditions.

Additional information

The Glen Wyllin Campsite near Kirk Michael is the only coastal campsite on the island (tel. 01624 878231). Kelvin's Tackle is a shop near Peel that sells kayaking equipment and fishing tackle. The owner has excellent local knowledge of the best beaches and kayak fishing spots.

Variations

There is a footbridge that connects the main beach in Peel with Fenella Beach beside the castle. It is possible to carry or trolley kayaks across here. There is also a small rocky slipway leading into the sheltered waters of the harbour entrance, to the north of the footbridge. This route can be done just as easily in either direction, or shortened by using the landings at Glen Mooar or Glen Wyllin that are mentioned in the route description.

Point of Ayre 🌀 ⬛🪧⬛

No. 7 | **Grade B** | **28km** | **OS Sheet 95**

Tidal Port	Liverpool
Start	△ Ballaugh Shore, Jurby Head (SC 336 960)
Finish	◯ The Mooragh Promenade Beach, Ramsey (SC 453 950)
HW/LW	Times of high and low water are similar to Liverpool.
Tidal Times	Between Jurby Head and Rue Point, the NE-going stream starts around 6 hours after HW Liverpool. The SW-going stream starts soon after HW Liverpool.
	Between Rue Point and Point of Ayre, the powerful offshore W-going stream forms a back-eddy close to the shore, resulting in an almost constant E-going flow.
	At Point of Ayre, the SE-going stream starts around 6 hours after HW Liverpool and the NW-going stream starts 30 minutes after HW Liverpool.
	Between Point of Ayre and Ramsey, the S-going stream starts around 5 hours 15 minutes after HW Liverpool. The N-going stream starts around 3 hours 45 minutes before HW Liverpool.
Max Rate Sp	In the vicinity of the Point of Ayre, streams can reach 5 knots. For most of this section, however, the tidal streams reach a maximum of 2 knots or less.
Coastguard	Liverpool, tel. 0151 931 3341, VHF weather every 3 hours from 0130

7

Point of Ayre

Introduction

The north part of the island is a relatively new feature in geological terms. It is formed of deposits from retreating ice sheets and rivers of meltwater that were here at the end of the last period of glaciation. The landscape is low lying with gently rolling hills allowing views to the hilly heart of the island, including the highest peak Snaefell. The beaches of sand and shingle, backed by sand dunes and delicate cliffs of boulder clay, are ideal for paddling trips of a less committing nature.

Description

Driving north from Kirk Michael, there is a car park and picnic site that can be reached through the north-western villages of Ballaugh and The Cronk. This is a remote and scenic beach, which makes for a beautiful beginning to a trip that starts in the shadow of the northern hills close to Jurby Head.

The extensive beaches around Jurby Head are excellent feeding grounds for redshank, turnstone and ringed plover. Beyond Blue Point, further along the coast, The Ayres Nature Reserve is home to a breeding colony of little terns. The little terns have well-camouflaged nests along the margin between the high water mark and dune vegetation. It is important to avoid landing here during spring and early summer. The level ground behind the sand dunes is known as 'dune slack'. These areas of gravelly grassland and scrub make perfect habitats for lapwing and skylark, which are preyed upon by short-eared owls and hen harriers.

The Point of Ayre is made up of extensive ridges of pebbles among which only a few hardy plants survive. The beaches are steep in places and can be tricky to land on, as the pebbles slip away from beneath your feet as you try to stand up. The tide race off the point is a happy hunting ground for cormorants, shags and gannets but you should also keep an eye out for dolphins, basking sharks and other cetaceans. On a clear day looking north, you should be able to see the Galloway Hills on the distant Scottish mainland.

At Point of Ayre the coast takes a sharp turn to the south, leading into Ramsey Bay. The sparse pebbly shoreline leads into the bay with little to attract your attention. The promenade, beaches

Scotch on the rocks

Search among the beach pebbles at the Point of Ayre and you will find granites from Scotland's craggy mountains mixed with rocks dredged from the bottom of the Irish Sea. Great glaciers once covered the whole area, grinding their way slowly southwards from the Highlands. The climate warmed and the ice melted, dumping the rocks and mud acquired on its journey. The Northern Plain of the Isle of Man was scraped flat by the passing ice and then blanketed with these erratic travellers.

By Royanne Wilding

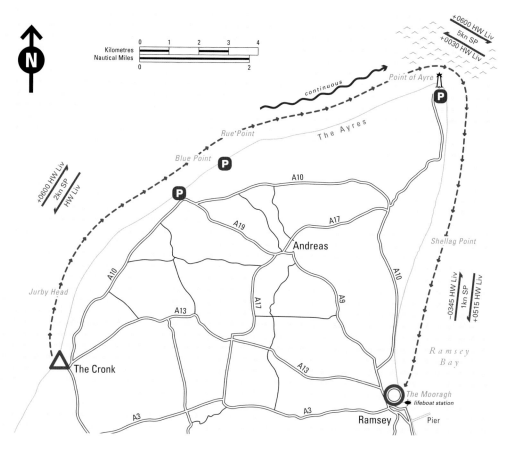

Point of Ayre

and harbour at Ramsey lie 10km to the south along this pretty (but monotonous) east-facing shore. Landing on the beach to the north of Ramsey harbour is straightforward and there is plenty of roadside parking along the Mooragh promenade.

Tides and weather

The land along this section is low-lying and offers little in the way of protection from strong winds. Tidal streams around the Point of Ayre are strong and overfalls often develop in the offshore races. In good weather conditions, it is usually possible to dodge the rough water by staying close to the shore. Due to eddy effects in Ramsey Bay, the N-going tidal stream lasts for 9 hours and the S-going stream for 3 hours.

Additional information

The Glen Wyllin Campsite at Kirk Michael is the only coastal campsite on the island. There is bunkhouse accommodation and a camping field at the Venture Centre (www.adventure-centre.co.uk) less than 1km up the lane from Port e Vullen at the southern end of Ramsey Bay (tel. 01624 814240).

Variations

For shorter excursions, there is good access by road to the shore close to The Lhen (NX 378 016), at Blue Point (NX 392 026) and at Point of Ayre (NX 468 049).

Isle of Man to Scotland

No. 8 | Grade C | 31km | OS Sheet 95

Tidal Port	Liverpool
Start	△ Point of Ayre (NX 465 051)
Finish	◎ Isle of Whithorn (NX 477 363)
HW/LW	Times of high and low water are similar to Liverpool.
Tidal Times	The E-going stream starts around 6 hours after HW Liverpool and the W-going stream starts around HW Liverpool. Across the entrance to Whithorn Bay, a strong back-eddy begins to form around 4 hours before HW Liverpool. This leads to a SW-going flow across the bay and towards Screen Rocks for all but the first 2 hours of the E-going flood.
Max Rate Sp	The tidal streams are less than 2 knots for most of the crossing, except in the vicinity of Point of Ayre and Burrow Head where streams can reach 4 knots.
Coastguard	Liverpool, tel. 0151 931 3341, VHF weather every 3 hours from 0130

Introduction

Of the four nations that are visible from the Isle of Man, Scotland is the closest. The coastline and hills of Galloway form a distinctive and tempting skyline. When the sun shines from the south,

features of the coast and hills can easily be made out. These northern waters of the Irish Sea are rich in wildlife and there is a chance you will be accompanied by shearwaters, porpoises and even basking sharks along the way. Your destination is the rugged coastline and small welcoming fishing harbour of the Isle of Whithorn.

Description

Point of Ayre is the northernmost part of the Isle of Man. The roads that lead here run through gently rolling countryside and pretty villages. The shingle and pebbles that make up the sprawling beaches largely comprise deposits left behind by Scottish glaciers during the last ice age. The shore can be steep and awkward for launching at high water, but a gentler and more user-friendly shore is revealed as the waters recede.

As you leave the beach, the initial challenge will be the tidal streams that run quickly around the point. Overfalls can develop here and confused waters with boils continue up to a kilometre offshore. The second consideration is the ferry services and other shipping which runs mainly between Liverpool and Belfast. Some vessels come quite close to the Point of Ayre while others run more offshore (but rarely more than 10 kilometres to the north). Keeping in close touch with Liverpool Coastguard will be of great benefit, as they can warn any vessels in the vicinity of your position. Once you are more than 10 kilometres away from the Point of Ayre, you are only likely to see an occasional fishing boat.

The once 'Isle' of Whithorn is now a small peninsula to the east of Burrow Head. As with any prolonged open crossing, the view towards the coast you are aiming for will seem to take ages to develop. St Ninian's Tower is a square white-painted beacon that sits on high ground southeast of the harbour entrance. Eventually, as you enter the last quarter of the crossing, the buildings around the harbour to the east of Burrow Head will become visible.

It is best to plan to arrive at Isle of Whithorn shortly before high water, as you will avoid the strongest tidal flows off Burrow Head. This will also make your landing much easier, as Whithorn harbour dries to beyond the harbour wall. There is a shingle beach beside the slipway in the eastern corner of the harbour. The slipway leads to the junction of Main Street which leads to the west and Harbour Row which leads to the south. Any thirsty seafarers that enter the harbour could not fail to notice the Steam Packet Inn, as it occupies a commanding position on Harbour Row. The post office and general store can be found along Main Street on the other side of the harbour.

Tides and weather

There is no great advantage to be gained from tidal streams because they tend to run east–west across the route. If you plan to arrive at Isle of Whithorn before high water, then you will avoid the SSW-going ebb stream that drains Wigtown Bay.

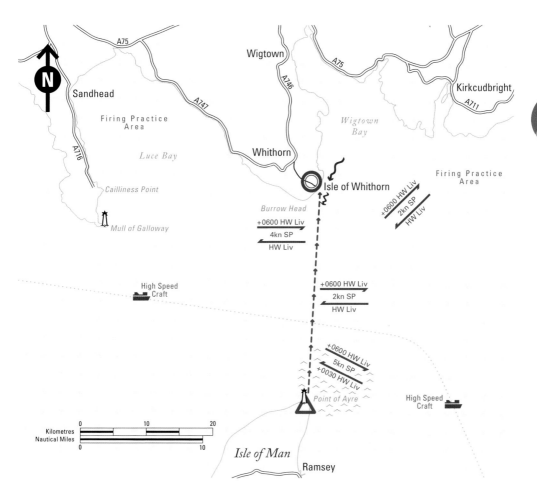

This crossing is exposed to winds from any direction. Breezes from the south can give rise to choppy conditions in the approaches to Isle of Whithorn, all the way into the harbour entrance.

Additional information

Those who wish to give thanks for a smooth crossing may wish to visit St Ninian's Chapel, which dates back to the 14th century. The ruined remains are on the ground that overlooks the harbour entrance close to St Ninian's Tower.

The harbourmaster can provide valuable local tidal information and the harbour office is adjacent to the breakwater. If the harbourmaster can't be found in his office, then his whereabouts may be determined by asking at the Steam Packet Inn. Not only does this inn serve fine ales, but there is an excellent menu and rooms are available for Bed & Breakfast (tel. 01988 500334). The local tourist and community website is also a great source of information (www.isleofwhithorn.com).

Maughold Head

 # Ramsey to Laxey

No. 9 | Grade B | 15km | OS Sheet 95

Tidal Port	Liverpool
Start	△ Port Lewaigue Beach (SC 469 930)
Finish	○ Laxey Beach (SC 442 835)
HW/LW	Times of high and low water are similar to Liverpool.
Tidal Times	Between Ramsey and Maughold Head, the NW-going stream (which runs for roughly 9 hours) starts around 3 hours 45 minutes before HW Liverpool and the SE-going stream starts around 5 hours 15 minutes after HW Liverpool.
	Between Maughold Head and Laxey, the NE-going stream starts around 5 hours after HW Liverpool. Inshore, a SW-going eddy stream starts around 4 hours before HW Liverpool. The main offshore SW-going stream starts around HW Liverpool.
Max Rate Sp	The streams are weak between Ramsey and Maughold Head and rarely reach 1 knot. Between Maughold Head and Laxey, streams can reach 2 knots.
Coastguard	Liverpool, tel. 0151 931 3341, VHF weather every 3 hours from 0130

© Port Cornaa

Introduction

The Manx east coast has everything from tall cliffs and sheltered bays to rocky foreshores and quiet secluded inlets. Port Lewaigue and Port e Vullen are at the southern end of Ramsey Bay and are excellent places to start exploring. Maughold Head is the most easterly point on the island. Seals bask lazily among the reefs below this striking headland, which towers over 100m above the sea.

Description

The pretty little inlet of Port Lewaigue is nestled among the sheltered southern shores of Ramsey Bay. The beach and car park are signposted around 2km southeast of Ramsey along the main A2 then A15 road, away from the town's busy narrow streets. Access to the shingle beach is easy via some steps and a short path down a steep grassy slope. As you paddle away from the beach to head east, you will pass the rocky headland of Gob ny rona. The headland divides Port Lewaigue from another pretty beach at Port e Vullen. There is a narrow lane to the shore here, but no parking or even a place to turn.

East of here, the coastline grows in stature. Craggy slopes and rocky buttresses descend to pebbly shores divided up by rocky reefs and small stacks. As you approach Maughold Head, steep cliffs with caves give the place a distinctly wild and exposed feel – almost like arriving at a great mountain summit. The crowning glory of Maughold Head is the lighthouse: the brilliant white tower is precariously perched half-way up the steep cliff. The residential buildings are more soberly placed on the level ground above.

Following the drama of Maughold, the coast becomes gentler with low rocky shores allowing views to the inland hills. Port Mooar is a deep inlet with rocky shores on each side of a steep pebbly beach. There is a car park from which a narrow lane leads to the main A15 road. As you paddle out of Port Mooar, the classic rock-hopping coast continues with excellent views along a series of headlands that stretch away into the distance.

Port Cornaa is a delightful cove among higher cliffs and makes an ideal lunch spot. The waters of Ballaglass Glen make their final descent to the sea through a steep wooded gorge into a still lagoon sheltered by a shingle spit. This is a popular beauty spot, with a car park from which a road leads to the main A2 road. Further along the coast, the eastern slopes of Barony Hill drop steeply to a rocky foreshore. At Dhoon Bay, water from the mountain streams crashes through the wooded glen before flowing out across the pebbly beach into the sea.

The pretty town of Laxey with its brightly painted houses lies another 3km south of the high cliffs that surround Bulgham Bay. The bay here is broad and shallow with a small harbour, a beach and a promenade at the north end.

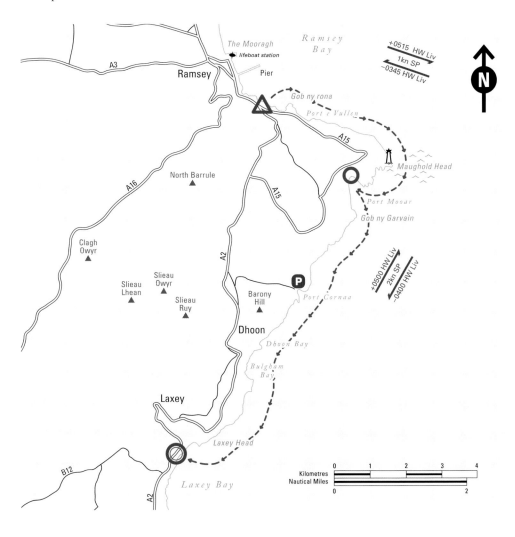

Tides and weather

This section is exposed to winds with an easterly component. However, the stretch between Port Lewaigue and Maughold Head is one of the few places on the island where it possible to paddle when there are strong winds from the southwest. Strong westerly winds cause swirling downdraughts around Maughold Head and in Bulgham Bay. Tidal streams can reach 2–3 knots around Maughold Head where overfalls can be expected. Due to eddy effects between Maughold Head and Laxey, the SW-going stream lasts approximately twice as long as the NE-going stream.

Additional information

Laxey is a popular place on the island to start a 'sea to summit' walk to the top of Snaefell. A trek up Laxey Glen will take you to 'Lady Isabella', the largest working waterwheel in the world. Walking further on up the glen you will reach the open moorland and steeper ground that leads to the highest point on the Isle of Man at 621m above sea level. A more leisurely way to the top is by way of the Snaefell Mountain Railway, which runs from Laxey to the summit.

The Manx Electric Railway (www.mers.org.im) has stops at Bellevue (near Port Lewaigue) and Minorca (near Laxey Harbour). This provides a wonderful means of returning to the car at the end of a one-way trip.

There is a small, friendly campsite with excellent facilities on Quarry Road. The site can be found by making your way up from the harbour along a narrow street called Minorca Hill, then turning left onto Quarry Road (www.laxey.org, tel. 01624 862623). The Shore Hotel in the centre of the old village serves good-quality pub grub, dispenses its own 'Bosun's Bitter' and boasts a selection of over 100 single malt whiskies (www.shorehotel.im).

Variations

This trip can be done in the opposite direction but there will be significantly less help from the tidal streams. It is also possible to do shorter trips by making use of the beaches with road access at Port e Vullen, Port Mooar and Port Cornaa.

Ramsey to Laxey

Laxey to Douglas

10

No. 10 | Grade A | 11km | OS Sheet 95

Tidal Port	Liverpool
Start	△ Laxey Beach (SC 442 835)
Finish	◯ Douglas Beach (SC 392 772)
HW/LW	Times of high and low water are similar to Liverpool.
Tidal Times	The NE-going stream starts around 5 hours after HW Liverpool. Inshore, a SW-going eddy stream starts around 4 hours before HW Liverpool and the main offshore SW-going stream starts around HW Liverpool.
Max Rate Sp	Tidal streams can reach 2–3 knots on exposed headlands.
Coastguard	Liverpool, tel. 0151 931 3341, VHF weather every 3 hours from 0130

Introduction

Laxey Bay is a wonderfully scenic and gentle stretch of coastline. Beyond the shelter of the bay lies Clay Head with its coastline of sustained steep cliffs and intriguing rocky shores. There are seals, seabirds and a restored cliff-top steam railway. Following the adventures of these stunning wild places, a grand entrance to Douglas Bay awaits you along its striking Victorian seafront.

© Garwick Bay

Description

Laxey is about half-way along the east coast of the Isle of Man. The old part of Laxey down by the harbour has the look and feel of a typical old fishing village. The main street winds down the hill among a hotchpotch of gaily painted stone cottages set between larger houses. The harbour dries out at low water, so the main beach is the best place to put in. There is plenty of parking beside the harbour and along the promenade, with public toilets at the southern end. The beach is steep with pebbles higher up, but there are gently shelving broad sands lower down.

Beyond the beach, the shores of Laxey Bay are lined with small rocky coves topped with steep slopes of gorse, bracken and heather. Paddling away from the shore, views of rolling hills that surround the bay and the mountain moorland beyond open up in front. Tucked away in the southwest corner of Laxey Bay is another bay with a character all of its own. The wooded shores of Garwick Bay lie at the foot of the shady glen that bears the same name. Fingers of rock extend into the water like natural groynes, dividing clear deep waters and patchy shingle beaches. An old tree that overhangs the beach may still have a makeshift rope swing, adding to the temptation to stop and look around.

Along the coast from here, the shore becomes more open and exposed as a line of rising cliffs leads out of the bay. The cliffs are riddled with gullies and the shoreline is adorned with rocky islets as you pass Clay Head on the way to Port Groudle. The first signs of Port Groudle will be the Sea Lion Cove station building and café, which is visible as the cliffs give way to gentler shores. While seals play among the rocks at the foot of the cliffs, you may catch sight of a steam engine on the cliff-top railway. The Groudle Glen Railway has been lovingly restored in recent years and is run entirely by enthusiastic volunteers. The shingle beach at Port Groudle is a good place to take a rest. There is also a nearby car park that is only a short drive from Onchan and Douglas.

The beach at Douglas is another 4km along another line of spectacular cliffs that lead the way to Onchan Harbour. Little remains of what used to be a busy fishing harbour. There is a beach in this deep inlet, but access to the road is steep and awkward. As you paddle round Onchan Head, the sense of wilderness will be left far behind to be replaced by views across the busy waters of Douglas Bay. The distinctive Victorian promenade arcs away to the south, where the harbour and sea terminal shelter behind Douglas Head. The nearest landing is towards the north end of the promenade. There is a broad set of steps that lead from the beach (SC 392 772) up to the promenade close to the junction of King Edward (promenade) Road and Summer Hill Road. There is roadside parking along the promenade.

Tides and weather

These shores are exposed to any winds other than those from the west or northwest; bear in mind that strong westerly winds will tend to funnel out of Douglas Bay. Due to eddy effects close to shore, the SW-going tidal stream lasts for approximately 9 hours and the NE-going stream only lasts for 3 hours.

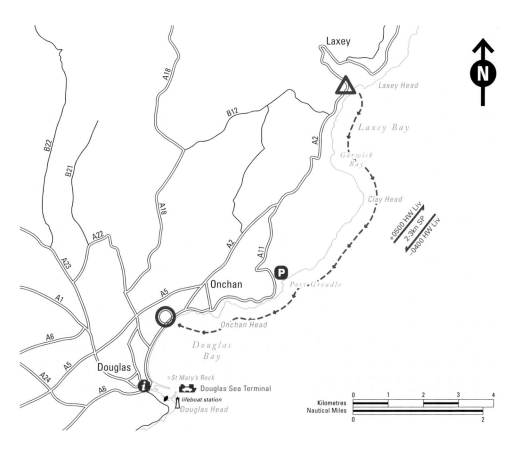

© Laxey Bay

10

Additional information

The promenade at Douglas runs the length of the seafront and is lined with hotels, bars and restaurants. Finding a car parking space close to the harbour and sea terminal requires patience at busy times. The sea terminal building has a tourist information office and short stay parking. Nearby on Lord Street, The Caff unashamedly serves high-energy food from a transport-café-style menu. This pocket of cholesterol heaven is a real hit with motorcycle TT fans due to the absence of tofu, muesli and dried apricots.

Variations

The nearest landing to the sea terminal is a set of steep steps built into the promenade wall (SC 384 755). It is possible to land upon sand at low water, but landing beside the steps once the beach has flooded would be tricky in all but the calmest of conditions. If you want to paddle into the harbour, call the port authorities on VHF channel 12. Once clearance is given, you will be able to land on the public slipway (SC 386 750) that leads up onto South Quay road.

This trip can be done in the opposite direction, but there will be significantly less help from the tidal streams.

The Cumbrian Coast

Introduction

Dramatic mountains, rivers and lakes provide Cumbria with all it needs to be the adventure capital of England. The relationship between the hilly interior and the coastal lowlands defines the scenery for kayak day-tripping along these relatively gentle shores. The sprawling coastal plains are formed of silt and shingle washed out from the glaciers that sculpted the mountains and valleys during the last ice age. The Cumbrian fells form a continuous backdrop to these free and open shores. From the Solway in the north to Morecambe Bay in the south, the Cumbrian coast is bound by areas of outstanding natural beauty. It would be impossible to explore these shores without stumbling upon Sites of Special Scientific Interest and nature reserves prized for their diversity. All of this adds up to tremendous variety and potential for adventures stretched out over more than 260km of coast.

Shifting sands and powerful tides command respect in the Solway Firth. Voyages across to Scotland often encounter unusually rough seas known as 'the White Steeds o' Solway'. The reward for making this crossing is having the beauty of the prized Galloway coast at the tip of your paddle blades.

Rich cultural heritage is very much in evidence along Cumbrian shores. Shipbuilding, exploration, mining and heavy industry have all played their part and continue to do so in some areas. Mining and ground-breaking manufacturing techniques gave rise to the early development of the harbours and towns of Maryport and Workington. Before its industrial awakening, Whitehaven was an important trading post and was also the scene of a farcical attempt at an invasion by the American navy in the late 1700s.

Towering cliffs at St Bees are the exception along the Cumbrian Coast. A tour beneath the seabird-laden vibrant red sandstone cliffs provides a sea kayakers' compact classic. Further south, the gaping valleys of Eskdale and Duddon open out into sheltered tidal estuaries perfect for a bleak winter's afternoon on the water. On Walney Island, delicate ecosystems in carefully managed nature reserves lie only a few miles from where nuclear submarines are built. The south Cumbrian estuaries of the Leven and Kent are exposed to the famous tidal surges of Morecambe Bay. Spring tides often produce tidal bores in these otherwise sedate, beautifully scenic and sheltered waters.

The Cumbrian Coast railway provides a vital transport link for tourists and residents alike. The benefit for sea kayakers is a regular and particularly scenic shuttle service that will return you to your car after a day or three of coastal touring. Good use can also be made of the Cumbria Coastal Way, which runs the length of the coast and incorporates other footpaths such as the Allerdale Ramble and the Cistercian Way.

The Cumbrian Coast

Tides and weather

Most of these areas are exposed to the prevailing winds from the southwest. Much of the coastal land is low-lying, giving little shelter other than in the middle and upper reaches of estuaries. To the north of St Bees Head, the tidal streams are governed by the might of the Solway Firth. The further north you paddle along this section, the stronger the flow.

The open coastline between Workington and Walney has tidal streams of a far more gentle nature with rates that rarely exceed 1 knot. The narrows and shallows of the southwest Cumbrian estuaries and Walney Channel have powerful flood and ebb cycles, making it relatively easy to cover long distances. With spring tides, there is usually enough water for paddling in these areas around 2 hours either side of the local time for high water.

Further information

For more information, see the following titles:

The Cumbria Coastal Way: A Walkers Guidebook, Ian and Krysia Brodie, Cicerone Press, 2007, 9781852844301.

West Coast of England and Wales Pilot, NP37, UK Hydrographic Office, 2005, 978070771880.

The Cumbrian Coast

Low tide on the Solway

The Solway

No. 11 | **Grade C** | **14 & 18km** | **OS Sheet 84, 85 & 89**

Tidal Port	Liverpool
Start A	△ Silloth, South Beach (NY 103 535)
Finish A	◎ Silloth, South Beach (NY 103 535)
Start B	△ Maryport, Maryport beach (NY 028 368)
Finish B	◎ Maryport, Maryport beach (NY 028 368)
HW/LW	Around 40 minutes after Liverpool
Tidal Times	On the English side, the NE-going (flood) stream starts around 5 hours 15 minutes before HW Liverpool and the SW-going (ebb) stream starts around 45 minutes after HW Liverpool. On the Scottish side and around Southerness Point, the NE-going (flood) stream starts around 5 hours 45 minutes before HW Liverpool and the SW-going (ebb) stream starts around 15 minutes after HW Liverpool.
Max Rate Sp	Tidal streams off Silloth and Southerness are strong and can reach 5 knots. Off Maryport they reach 3 knots.
Coastguard	Liverpool, tel. 0151 931 3341, VHF weather every 3 hours from 0130

The Solway

63

Introduction

The Solway Firth is the broad tideway that separates the North Cumbrian Lowlands from the Scottish Southern Uplands. The Criffel and Dalbeattie hills appear bold and striking and it is easy to imagine the word 'Scotland' scrawled in huge letters across their southern slopes. These tempting sights may draw you to the sea but the crossings to Southerness Point are not for the fainthearted. Flooding across shifting sandbanks, turbulent waters invade the Solway from the southwest with every rising tide. Beyond dealing with fickle waters, the ultimate skill on the Solway Firth is the art of the long-distance ferry glide. The usual points of departure to Southerness are the ports of Silloth to the east and Maryport to the south.

Description

A: SILLOTH TO SOUTHERNESS ON THE EBB

Silloth is a seaside town that still retains its Victorian charm. The wide cobbled streets, gaily painted buildings and coastal parkland fit perfectly with the bright and breezy feel of the place. The south beach can be reached by way of the old service road that runs around the south side of the harbour. There is a gritty car park and a broad path to the beach. The caravan parks and old lighthouse (NX 977 542) at Southerness should be visible 14km to the west. It is best to start around an hour before HW Liverpool. You should initially head in the general direction of Criffel, allowing the last of the NE-going stream to carry you a little higher up the estuary. The SW-going stream builds soon after the ebb begins, so it is important to line up Southerness lighthouse to transit with features among the Dalbeattie and Auchencairn coastal hills beyond. As the waters fall from the Solway, they accelerate around the approaches to Southerness Point. You should expect to go crashing through steep choppy waves in the shallows before landing on one of the sandy beaches among the rocks to the west of the lighthouse.

The return to Silloth should be completed on the second half of the rising tide, with the aim of reaching Silloth a short while after high water. As the flooding waters begin to cover the sandbanks in the middle of the Solway, conflicting currents can kick up huge, confused breaking seas with little provocation from the weather. These effects become less significant later in the flood as a greater depth of water covers the sandbanks. When approaching Silloth from Southerness, you should be aware that the tidal streams are quicker in the 'English Channel' that runs parallel to the coast around a kilometre offshore. To counter the effects of this, it is a good idea to build a few extra degrees of south into your heading. If you miss the south beach at Silloth, then the next available landing will be a slipway (NY 118 553) close to East Cote and Skinburness. It is best to avoid the stepped concrete coastal defences which run for over 2 kilometres between Silloth harbour and Skinburness, as they are steep, slippery and treacherous.

SILLOTH

The lighthouse at Southerness (NX 977 542) was built in 1748, making it the second oldest in Scotland. The old part of the village still exists as rows of low cottages sunk into hollows either side of the main street. There is no doubt that this design helps to shed the worst of the screaming gales that regularly tear across this exposed, flat promontory. The Paul Jones Hotel has a public

11

The Solway

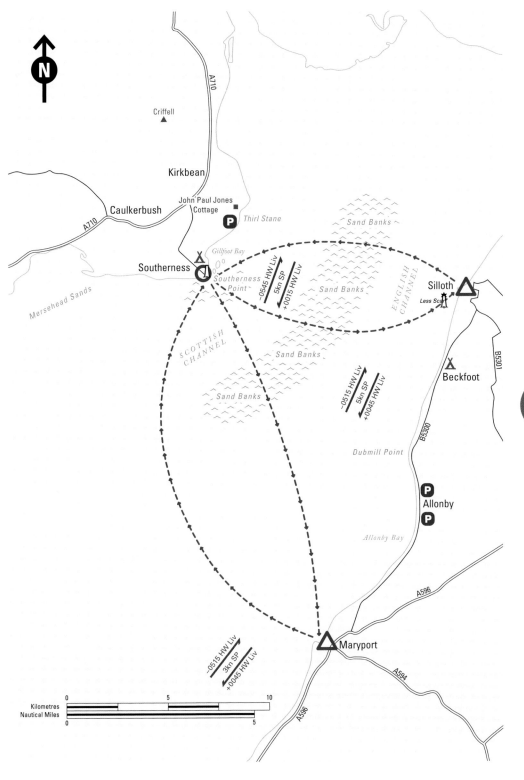

N

Criffell ▲

Kirkbean

John Paul Jones
Cottage

Thirl Stane

Caulkerbush

A710

A710

Southerness

Gillfoot Bay

Southerness Point

Mersehead Sands

SCOTTISH CHANNEL

Sand Banks

Sand Banks

Sand Banks

Sand Banks

Sand Banks

Sand Banks

ENGLISH CHANNEL

Silloth

Less Scar

Beckfoot

B5301

B5300

Dubmill Point

–0545 HW Liv
5kn SP
+0015 HW Liv

–0515 HW Liv
5kn SP
+0045 HW Liv

P Allonby
P

Allonby Bay

A596

–0515 HW Liv
3kn SP
+0045 HW Liv

Maryport

A594

A596

A594

Kilometres
0   5   10

Nautical Miles
0   5

11

The Solway

bar that serves hot drinks and snacks, but it is quite often busy with holidaymakers from the two sprawling caravan and camping sites on the inland side of the village. To the east lies Gillfoot Bay, beyond which wooded slopes tumble down to excellent secluded beaches between low rocky headlands at Thirl Stane and Borron Point.

B: MARYPORT TO SOUTHERNESS ON THE FLOOD

Maryport is a bustling town with a harbour and recent marina development. From the traffic lights where the A594 and A596 meet, follow signs to the marina and sea front. Salmoor Way runs along the west side of the marina and continues to the breakwater car park on the south side of the harbour entrance. There is easy access to the beach which is steep and pebbly at first but sandy and more gently shelving lower down.

At 18km, the crossing from Maryport is longer than the crossing from Silloth; tidal streams provide a little more help on this route, however. The best time to start is around 3 hours before HW Liverpool, with the latter half of the NE-going flood. As soon as you leave Maryport breakwater behind, it will be time to concentrate on navigating the best route to Southerness. It is always a good idea to overestimate the strength of the tide when planning a ferry glide on these waters. Even in its last hour, the NE-going stream tends to be significantly stronger near the Scottish shore as it accelerates around Southerness point.

The knobbly skyline drawn up by Criffel and the coastal hills of Dalbeattie is not just pretty to look at; the hillside features can be used as transits together with the Southerness lighthouse and other buildings in the village. If you end up being swept past Southerness Point, the secluded beaches at Thirl Stane will provide you with a suitable Plan B landing place.

The return to Maryport should be done as early as possible on the first half of the SW-going ebb. Initially, it is best to get two-thirds of the way across to the English side on an easterly heading. As you get to within a mile or two of the English shore you will be able to relax a little, run with the tide and let the ebb help you finish the journey.

Tides and weather

These routes are subject to strong tidal streams that flow over shifting sandbanks in the middle part of the Solway Firth. In calm weather this can create boils, small whirlpools and areas of choppy water. In more breezy conditions, steep and heavy confused seas known locally as 'The White Steeds o' Solway' can rear up very quickly.

Additional information

Silloth has a well-stocked Spar shop on Solway Street and a Co-op on Caldew Street. Silloth Café on Station Road does a range of home-baked delights. The fish and chips next door come in large portions and are really tasty.

The Rowanbank Caravan Park (01697 331653, www.rowanbankcaravanpark.co.uk) at Beckfoot, between Silloth and Allonby, has pitches for tents. It is a pleasant and peaceful site with good facilities and it is just a short walk through the sand dunes to the beach.

The Curzon Grill and B&B, Curzon Street (A596), Maryport is open 7 days a week and is just a stone's throw from the Co-op. They do the usual fried breakfast as well as just about anything fried or grilled with chips.

Maryport Maritime Museum is a compact celebration of Maryport's seafaring heritage. There are paintings of seascapes and a whole host of artefacts and relics, as well as displays depicting the life and times of Fletcher Christian (Muntiny on the Bounty) and Thomas Ismay (owner of the Titanic).

In Scotland, low-impact wild camping is generally accepted. For those seeking hot showers there is a large holiday park at Southerness which accepts tents. Otherwise, the Paul Jones Hotel in the village serves hot and cold drinks and bar meals.

Variations

An overnight trip can be made by starting at Silloth, crossing to Southerness on the ebb and camping for the night. The ebb crossing to Maryport the next day could be made after exploring some of these places on foot. There is even an hourly bus service along the coast road between Maryport and Silloth. These routes across the Solway need not be the journey's end but could be the gateway to further adventures at Hestan Islet, Kirkcudbright and the rest of the Scottish Solway coast.

Eroded slag heaps, Workington | Dave Brook

Cumbrian Solway Coast  12

No. 12 | Grade A | 28km | OS Sheet 89 & 85

Tidal Port	Liverpool
Start	△ Allonby Bay (NY 080 429)
Finish	◎ Whitehaven, outer harbour (NX 968 184)
HW/LW	Around 30 minutes after Liverpool.
Tidal Times	The NE-going stream starts around 5 hours 15 minutes before HW Liverpool and the SW-going stream starts around 45 minutes after HW Liverpool.
Max Rate Sp	Tidal streams reach 2–3 knots along this section.
Coastguard	Liverpool, tel. 0151 931 3341, VHF weather every 3 hours from 0130

Introduction

Views of rural life along the Cumbrian Solway coastal lowlands contrast heavily with the decaying industrial spoils at Workington. The Cumbrian coast was badly mistreated by the coal and steel industries until the mid 1980s. New developments at Maryport, as well as a general clean-up, have breathed new life into the area. The pleasant pebbly beaches are big enough to get away from it all, yet harbours and coastal villages are reassuringly close by.

69

John Paul Jones spiking the cannons, Whitehaven

Description

The village of Allonby is strung out along the B5300 coast road. Most of the houses and farms are on the landward side of the road, leaving unobstructed views across the Solway. All along the grassy seafront there are large car parks just a short walk from the beach. In the centre of the village, where the road goes over a hump-backed bridge, there is a block of houses beside the beach. The post office sells hot and cold snacks, drinks and basic provisions. The parking area extends right up to the dunes that lead to the broad sandy beach.

The effect of the strong Solway tide is hardly felt in the depths of Allonby Bay. As you make your way along the sandy shores towards Maryport, your speed will pick up. It is possible to paddle into the outer harbour and land on the public slipway two hours either side of high tide. The harbour dries close to half tide, revealing an expanse of deep sticky mud.

The steep pebbly beaches that lead southwest from Maryport dry to gently shelving sands at low tide. The chemical works at Flimby and the wind farms at Siddick dominate the coastline here and herald the approach to Workington Harbour. The last few wind turbines stand upon higher ground reclaimed from waste tips. Its industrial legacy has provided the coastline with some unexpected rocky structures. There are low cliffs, craggy pinnacles and even small caves, all of which have an unstable volcanic look.

The River Derwent enters the sea at Workington. The harbour and docks were developed during the late 1800s. To the south of the harbour entrance, the world's first large-scale steel works was built on the high ground that overlooks Moss Bay. South of this, the Cumbrian Coast railway line runs close to the shore that leads the way to the village of Harrington. The small harbour here completely dries at low water. The local sailing and fishing club building overlooks the harbour. There are three pubs, a general store and a bakery. It is possible to land on the beaches outside the harbour entrance or on the slipway just inside the outer south breakwater.

There is plenty of parking and public toilets here, making this a suitable alternative place to start or finish.

The coastline south of Harrington becomes steeper, with grassy slopes and wind turbines that dominate the skyline. The railway line manages to cling onto the foot of the slopes, precariously close to the shore. Beaches of pebbles and sand are punctuated by low rocky reefs, culminating in a low headland called Cunning Point. From here you will be able to see along the remaining 4km of coastline to the port of Whitehaven.

Lowca Beck enters the sea across shingle beaches at Providence Bay. The red sandstone cliff at Redness Point is the first sign of the rock upon which Whitehaven is built. Much of the harbour and the older surrounding buildings are constructed from locally quarried Whitehaven sandstone. The easiest and most sheltered landing is the soft sandy beach at the most southerly corner of the outer harbour. There is parking most of the way along the harbour wall, with cafés and takeaways nearby.

Tides and weather

This coast is exposed to winds from the south, west and north. Winds from the south and west give choppy conditions when wind opposes tide, especially close to the harbour entrances and around Cunning Point.

Additional information

At Allonby there is camping available at the Spring Lea Caravan and Leisure Centre (01900 881331) but it can be busy and is prone to flooding after heavy rain. Rowanbank Caravan site at Beckfoot (01697 331653) is just over 6km north of Allonby. The site is sheltered, quiet and has pitches for tents. The dunes and beach with access to the sea at high water are just across the road.

There are fish and chip shops near the harbour on Swingpump Lane and Tangier Street. The bar food is excellent value and the ales good and strong at the Weatherspoons pub near the supermarket to the east of the harbour.

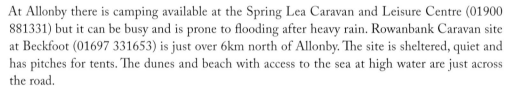

John Paul Jones

In Whitehaven, The Beacon Museum stands on the west harbour wall overlooking the marina. Exhibits include the story of John Paul Jones whose maritime career began in Whitehaven. In later life, he turned traitor by joining the American navy and leading an attack on his former home port. The raiders sneaked ashore under cover of darkness and disabled the town's defensive cannons. The invasion was however doomed to failure when the Americans entered a harbour tavern and began to drink ale of a strength to which they were quite unaccustomed. The Beacon Museum has a café on the ground floor.

St Bees Head

No. 13 | Grade B | 10km | OS Sheet 89

Tidal Port	Liverpool
Start	△ Whitehaven, outer harbour (NX 968 184)
Finish	○ St Bees Beach (NX 959 117)
HW/LW	Around 10 minutes after Liverpool
Tidal Times	North of North Head, the SW-going stream begins 45 minutes after HW Liverpool. The NE-going stream begins 5 hours 15 minutes before HW Liverpool. There is little tidal movement between North Head and South Head, but a S-going eddy forms early during the ebb between Fleswick Bay and South Head. South of South Head, the NW-going stream begins 2 hours before HW Liverpool. The SE-going stream begins 4 hours 15 minutes after HW Liverpool.
Max Rate Sp	Tidal streams are generally less than 2 knots.
Coastguard	Liverpool, tel. 0151 931 3341, VHF weather every 3 hours from 0130

© Fish and chips for lunch, Whitehaven

13

St Bees Head

Introduction

There are few places on the Cumbrian coast where tall cliffs of solid rock meet the sea. St Bees Head is the most westerly point on the coastline of Northern England. The exposed Whitehaven sandstone rises vertically from the water to heights of almost 100m in places. The only English colony of black guillemots nest among the blocky buttresses and layered shelves. The neighbouring razorbills, cormorants and kittiwakes ensure that this place is never quiet during spring and early summer. Later in the year, St Bees comes into its own as a coastal mecca for climbers. The broad sun-soaked ledges close to North Head are popular for bouldering and there are a few bolted climbing routes on the cliff itself. The finish is on St Bees Beach.

Description

The port of Whitehaven is off the A595 west lakes road. The best place to launch is the small sandy beach at the southern end of the outer harbour. The waters around the harbour entrance and the west pier can be choppy with clapotis.

Tom Hurd Rock is a reef that is exposed at low water and is marked with a small unlit beacon. The bay that lies between here and St Bees Head is Saltom Bay. On the high ground above the rocky foreshore, the Haig Colliery Mining Museum occupies the restored winding house and tells the story of mining here before the pit closures of the 1990s. A little further south, the coastline becomes steeper rising to more than 100m. As you approach North Head, tall blocky crags tower over boulder-strewn grassy slopes descending to a forbidding rocky shore.

At North Head the coastline takes an abrupt 90 degrees turn to the south and the SW-going tidal stream can generate a small tidal race here. There are broad rock ledges at the foot of the tall vertical cliff along the shore between North Head and St Bees Head. The sloping rock slabs along the foreshore present an ever-changing set of rock-hopping challenges all the way to St Bees Head and into Fleswick Bay, depending on the state of the tide. As Fleswick Beach dries, the waters reveal an array of intriguing rock sculptures. Sandstone boulders, worn smooth by the action of the sea, and a sloping wave-cut platform resemble an old rusty corrugated iron sheet strewn with pretty pebbles.

A kilometre south of Fleswick, the towering buttresses give way to a gentle rocky foreshore that leads to St Bees Beach. It is best to land as close as possible to the lifeboat slipway at the north end of the beach. At low water the beach can dry to over 300m out, which makes for a long carry to the car park where there are public toilets and a café.

Tides and weather

Whitehaven harbour entrance, Saltom Bay and North Head are exposed to winds and swell from the north and west. Winds from the south and east can generate downdraughts beneath the cliffs along the western part of Saltom Bay and in the vicinity of North Head.

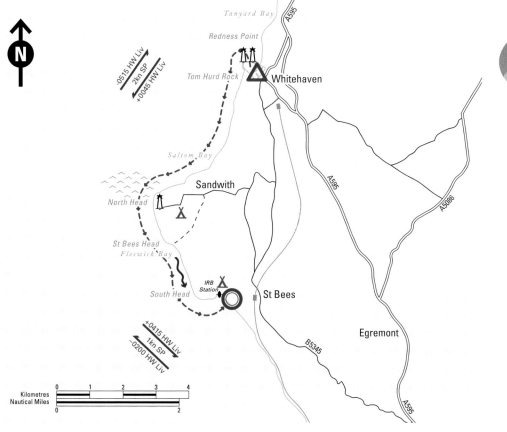

St Bega

St Bees derives its name from the story of a beautiful Irish princess called Bega, who lived in the 10th century. Bega's father arranged a marriage between her and a Scandinavian prince. As a young girl, however, Bega had promised herself to God. She wore an arm-ring, presented to her by an angel, to symbolise her betrothal to Christ. While the court was incapacitated during the pre-nuptial revelling, Bega made her escape – all locks yielded at the touch of her holy armlet. She made her way to the coast where she found a little coracle ready and waiting, paddled across the Irish Sea and landed at St Bees.

Bega then travelled over to the other side of the country and realised her ambition by taking the veil at Lindisfarne. Bega eventually returned to Cumberland, where she felt called to build a nunnery. She asked a local lord for some land, and was mockingly told she could have as much land as was covered by snow the following day (Midsummer's Day). Once again there seems to have been divine intervention as the next day brought a snow shower which covered a 3 mile plot, allowing Bega to build her convent. St Bega was to become a very influential figure in the Anglo-Saxon Church; after her death a Cult of St Bega formed, which spread throughout the North of England. The cult was particularly prominent in Whitby where her relics are interred.

By Kirstine Pearson

Additional information

Seacote Park caravan and camping site (01946 822 777) overlooks the northern end of St Bees Beach. There is a beach café and hotel that serves bar food, but the pubs and local shops in St Bees village are only 1km down the road. Whitehaven is 7km away and has supermarkets and takeaways. Another accommodation option, more suitable for small groups, is the camping barn at Tarnflatt Hall Farm on the high ground close to St Bees Lighthouse (www.tarnflattfarm.co.uk).

Variations

This trip can be paddled in either direction. The coastline to the south of St Bees Beach holds little in the way of interest to sea kayakers. There are pebbly beaches at the foot of low cliffs of boulder clay. There is also Sellafield nuclear reprocessing site and Eskmeals firing range (see Route 15).

St Bees to Isle of Man

No. 14 | Grade C | 52km | OS Sheets 95 & 89

Tidal Port	Liverpool
Start	△ St Bees lifeboat slipway (NX 959 117)
Finish	○ Port e Vullen (SC 475 928)
HW/LW	Similar to HW/LW Liverpool
Tidal Times	South of St Bees Head, the NW-going stream begins around 2 hours before HW Liverpool. The SE-going stream begins around 4 hours 15 minutes after Liverpool. Offshore, the WNW-going stream starts soon after HW Liverpool. The S-going stream starts around 6 hours after HW Liverpool, soon turning towards the SE. For Maughold Head see Route 9.
Max Rate Sp	The offshore tidal streams rarely exceed 1 knot.
Coastguard	Liverpool, tel. 0151 931 3341, VHF weather every 3 hours from 0130

Introduction

On a clear day, the shadowy silhouette of the Isle of Man can be seen from much of the west Cumbrian coastline. The closest point on the English coast is St Bees Head. The shortest crossing

© Port e Vullen Beach

is to Point of Ayre at the remote northern tip. Maughold Head is the most easterly point on the Isle of Man and is only marginally further, but provides a friendlier approach and landing. The nearby beach at Port e Vullen gives easy access to a friendly outdoor centre and the town of Ramsey. Having completed this lengthy and committing paddle, it is comforting to arrive close to civilisation.

Description

The tidal streams between St Bees Head and Maughold Head tend to run perpendicular to the route. Heading southwest from the beach at St Bees at high water will give you the best tidal advantage, because there is more of a W-going component to the flow during the middle phase of the ebb.

As you head off across the sea, don't forget to take a look over your shoulder. The view of St Bees Head from offshore is a rare perspective and provides an opportunity to see the whole length of the red sandstone cliffs with the white lighthouse perched upon the green moors above. Making a mental note of this view will stand you in good stead if you wish to return to St Bees by kayak.

During the middle stages of the crossing there is a possibility you will encounter fishing boats, larger vessels and even high-speed ferries. It is good policy to keep regular contact with Liverpool Coastguard, giving your position. They will be able to keep you updated with the position of other craft and warn you of any possible collision hazards. Later in the crossing you should pass close to the south cardinal buoy that marks the south-eastern extent of Bahama Bank. After passing Bahama Bank buoy, you will be unlikely to meet large shipping or fast ferries.

There is a steep boulder beach on the north side of Maughold Head. At low water there are shallow lagoons with flat seaweed-covered rocks beneath the cliffs known as the 'Maughold Brooghs'. If you paddle west along the Brooghs you will reach Port e Vullen after 3km. Port e Vullen is a steep pebbly beach that dries out to a gently shelving sandy shore at low water.

Tides and weather

By their nature, open crossings are exposed to weather from any direction. Although the tides tend to run across the route, there is a very slight advantage to paddling to the Isle of Man on the ebb with the E-going component of the tide.

Additional information

A steep slipway leads from the Port e Vullen to the A15 coast road. The junction with Jacks Lane is 100m to the east. If you follow Jacks Lane from here, you will reach the Lewaigue tram station and the local outdoor centre after around 1km. The tram station is part of the Manx

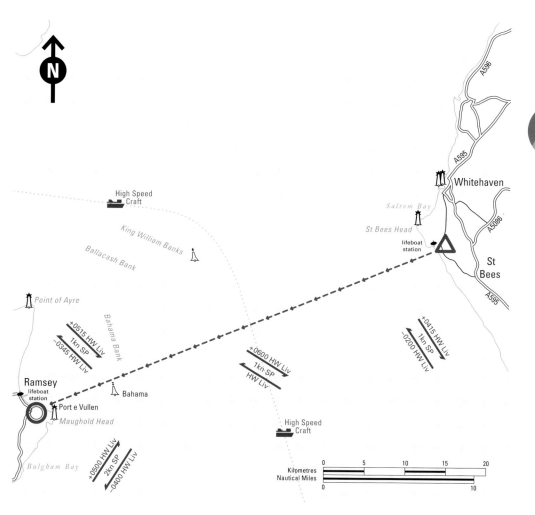

© Manx shearwater | Cormac Booth / HWDT

14

Electric Railway line that runs between Ramsey and Douglas. The outdoor centre is called the Venture Centre (www.adventure-centre.co.uk) and is run by helpful staff; it has bunkhouse-style accommodation as well as camping facilities.

The only way to return to England by ferry is on the Isle of Man Steam Packet Company services that run from the island's main port of Douglas. The paddling distance from Port e Vullen to Douglas is around 25km (see Routes 9 and 10 in the Isle of Man section). There are regular crossings from Douglas to Heysham and Liverpool.

Variations

Port Mooar is a deep and well-sheltered inlet with a pebbly beach that lies 2km along the coastline to the south of Maughold Head. There is road access, but it is much further to walk to the Venture Centre and the town of Ramsey beyond.

Muncaster bridge, River Esk at high water

Ravenglass

No. 15 | Grade A | 16km | OS Sheet 96

Tidal Port	Liverpool
Start	△ Southern end of Main Street, Ravenglass (SD 084 962)
Finish	◯ Southern end of Main Street, Ravenglass (SD 084 962)
HW/LW	Around 10 minutes after HW/LW Liverpool at Ravenglass, but can be up to 20 minutes later in the upper reaches of the Esk.
Tidal Times	The in-going stream starts around 5 hours 30 minutes before HW Liverpool. The out-going stream starts around 30 minutes after HW Liverpool.
Max Rate Sp	4–6 knots
Coastguard	Liverpool, tel. 0151 931 3341, VHF weather every 3 hours from 0130

Introduction

The pretty village of Ravenglass is set beside a tidal lagoon caught between the Drigg dunes and the rolling hills that surround the lower reaches of Eskdale and Mitedale. The River Esk meets the rivers Irt and Mite here, forming a tidal trident reaching towards the heart of the west

81

Cumbrian fells. The estuaries of the Irt and Mite can only be paddled a mile or two inland on a large spring tide, but the views and estuarine bird life make for a scenic trip. The tides of the Esk reach far beyond the sound of the open sea; it is possible to take the flooding tideway for several miles up beyond the wooded banks beneath Muncaster Castle.

Description

Ravenglass is off the A595 coast road between Bootle and Gosforth. Most of the village is clustered around Main Street, which runs parallel to the pebbly west-facing shore. At the southern end of Main Street there is a slipway that leads onto the foreshore. It is possible to unload kayaks and kit here, but you should leave your car in the main village car park off Croftlands Drive.

It is best to launch around 2 hours before HW Liverpool. If you launch much earlier, you will just keep getting stuck on sandbanks. At this time, the in-going stream can easily reach 6 knots. Some banks of sand and shingle may initially be exposed but these will soon be covered. The tidal channel heads inland from the west and soon turns sharply to the south. It is best to avoid the east side of the channel, where the remains of old fish traps can be encountered. The rows of concrete posts will be visible from the Ravenglass foreshore as you prepare to launch, but may become submerged soon afterwards. Beyond the east bank, the main Cumbrian Coast railway line runs along a stone embankment. The channel is protected from the west by the Eskmeals Dunes Nature Reserve. This area is a designated Site of Special Scientific Interest because of the rare and fragile dune habitat, which undoubtedly owes part of its isolation to the neighbouring military firing range. The 300 resident plant species include wild thyme, Portland spurge and northern marsh orchid. Birds such as ringed plover and little egret have been seen here, as well as otters and roe deer.

The flood tide begins to cover the shingle banks as the river channel turns east under the coast railway viaduct. Under the bridge a whole new view opens up towards Corney Fell to the southeast, Ulpha Fell to the east and Birker Fell hiding the upper part of Eskdale to the northeast. Trees line the north shore as you pass a chapel on the opposite bank at Hall Waberthwaite. Soon afterwards, the sides of the valley close in with rhododendrons hogging the lower slopes on the approach to Muncaster Castle. The river begins to wind and meander around Friday Point, beyond which the Castle can be seen on the lower slopes of Muncaster Fell.

The A595 crosses the river at Muncaster Bridge (SD 112 964). Beyond the bridge the river becomes narrower and more winding, with tall reeds and grasses obscuring the steep banks. The flooding waters flush bank voles from their normally dry hiding places out into the open farmland. It is in these upper reaches that buzzards and kestrels hunt patiently from low trees and posts.

The tidal limit is at Hinning House Bridge (SD 121 973). The return paddle is best done with haste to avoid running aground on sandbanks. If you arrive at Ravenglass early enough, it may be possible to land on the pebbly beach close to the Holly House Hotel. The ebbing waters can

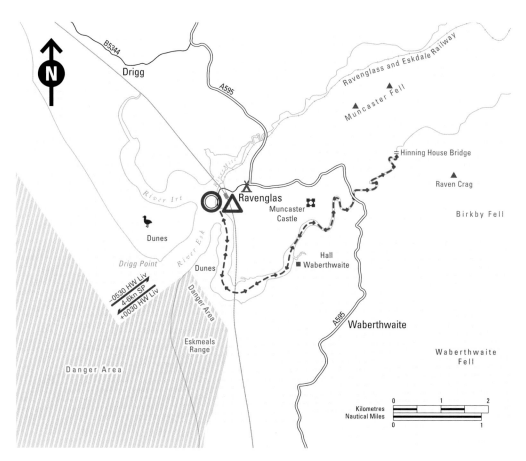

be surprisingly swift when they turn southwest away from Ravenglass towards the open sea. The resulting standing waves can provide good sport for experienced paddlers.

Additional information

Eskmeals firing range is not normally active during weekends, but it may be worth checking with range control (01229 712200).

There is a really nice (although pricey) campsite to the east of the village run by the Caravan and Camping Club, which has an onsite shop. The nearest general store is less than 4km away at the petrol station on the A595 heading north towards Gosforth. The Holly House Hotel is on Main Street, Gosforth and the Ratty Arms occupies part of the railway station buildings. Both pubs do excellent bar meals and have a fine selection of beers and real ales.

Ravenglass Seaquest

The Ravenglass Seaquest is an orienteering event for canoes and kayaks that uses the Irt, Mite and Esk estuaries. Tidal planning, navigation and paddling skills are put to the test in this annual get-together, usually held in April or May. Arrive early so you can study the locations of the control points on the provided map. Plan your route to visit as many controls as possible within the set time, while taking the tidal streams into account. Visit the website of Cumbria Canoeists (cumbriacanoeists.org.uk) for up-to-date information.

Variations

Shorter trips can be made on the lower reaches of the rivers Irt and Mite.

The coastline south of Ravenglass boasts long sandy beaches. The car park and campsite at Silecroft is around 16km along the coast; Haverigg and the western entrance to the Duddon Estuary are a further 8km beyond that. If you intend to paddle this route, then it is vitally important to contact Eskmeals range control before setting out.

The Duddon Estuary

No. 16 | Grade A | 21km | OS Sheet 96

Tidal Port	Liverpool
Start	△ Askam Pier (SD 203 776)
Finish	◯ Askam Pier (SD 203 776)
HW/LW	Around 5 minutes after HW/LW Liverpool at the entrance to the Duddon Estuary
Tidal Times	The incoming tide can be seen arriving over the sands around 2 hours 30 minutes before HW Liverpool. The out-going stream starts soon after HW Liverpool.
Max Rate Sp	2–3 knots
Coastguard	Liverpool, tel. 0151 931 3341, VHF weather every 3 hours from 0130

Introduction

The Duddon Estuary lies in the shadow of the 600m summit of Black Combe. The surrounding high ground provides good shelter for a simple trip running north with the flood from Askam Pier to the upper reaches and the villages of Kirkby-in-Furness and Foxfield. On a brisk winter's day, the view of the surrounding fells with a dusting of snow is a beautiful and inspiring sight.

Trips on the Duddon Estuary are sometimes started as far out as Haverigg and, with the help of a large spring tide, can reach the narrows of Duddon Bridge.

Description

Askam-in-Furness is on the A595 road between Barrow-in-Furness and Grizebeck. Off the southern end of Duke Street, Parklands Drive runs towards the sea through a housing estate and continues as a dirt track onto Askam Pier. Askam Pier juts out more than 500m into the estuary, providing a fine vantage point with views to the hills beyond. There is a pleasant sandy beach to the south that leads to Sandscale Haws Nature Reserve. The dunes and freshwater pools are home to natterjack toads, Britain's most vociferous amphibians. To the north there is a saltmarsh and a small creek in which a few small boats are moored. The pier itself is less pretty, built with heaped rubble and slag from the19th-century iron ore works to which Askam owes its existence. It is possible to drive right to the end of the pier, from where kayaks can be carried down a gnarly gully onto the sands below. Once the kayaks are ready on the sands, it is just a question of watching and waiting for the tide to come in.

Once on the water, brisk progress is made paddling north with the rising tide. You will shortly pass the distinct craggy headland at Dunnerholme. Very soon, the hilly scenery begins to surround you. To the west, the appropriately named Black Combe towers over the villages and woods near Millom. Looking north up the estuary, the Dunnerdale fells create a knobbly skyline that leads up towards the unmistakable pairing of Dow Crag and the Old Man of Coniston. The estuary is sheltered from the east by Bank House Moor and Kirkby Moor with its attendant wind farm. Kirkby-in-Furness lies along the eastern shore, a short way up an inlet into which a small tributary called Kirkby Pool flows. It is possible to get to the village, the Ship Inn and its bunkhouse on foot across the railway via Sand Side Marsh. The Duddon Estuary becomes narrower north of the confluence, with saltmarshes and low pastures on either side. Huge flocks of pink-footed geese gather here during the winter months, having migrated here from their breeding grounds in Spitsbergen, Iceland and Greenland.

The village of Foxfield lies between the east shore and a spur of higher ground. It is possible to land here and take a short walk to the shelter of the Prince of Wales pub if the weather prohibits alfresco dining. Otherwise, it is possible to carry on further upstream, picnic on the river bank and play in the gently swirling eddies under the railway viaduct. Substantial spring tides make it possible to paddle all the way to the tidal limit at Duddon Bridge, where you may meet whitewater paddlers coming from the opposite direction. These paddlers may have started their grade four run at Hall Dunnerdale or even higher in the gnarly gorge-bound waters above Seathwaite.

Wherever you get to, it is important to return to Askam Pier no later than 2 hours after HW Liverpool. Getting stuck on a drying sandbank is no fun and can leave you with an awfully long walk.

Tides and weather

There needs to be a tide with a HW exceeding 9m at Liverpool for this trip to be worth making. The Duddon Estuary provides good paddling when the open sea is too rough, but it is exposed to strong northerlies and southerlies.

16

The Duddon Estuary

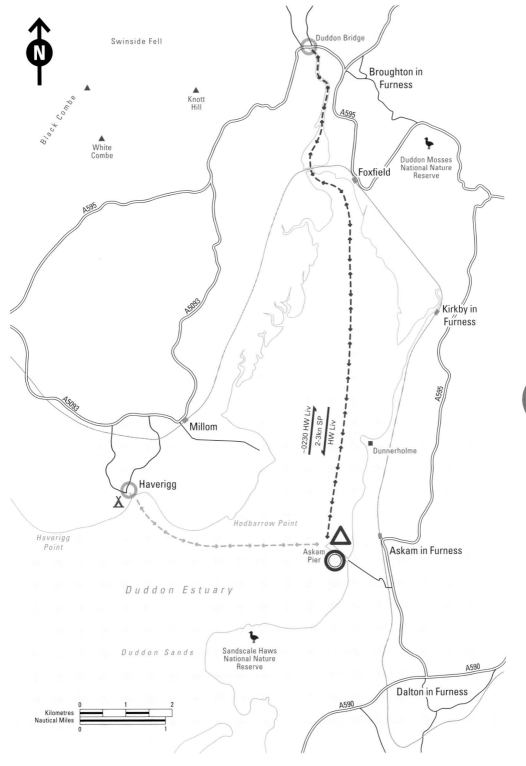

N

Swinside Fell

Black Combe

Knott
Hill

White
Combe

Duddon Bridge

Broughton in
Furness

A595

Duddon Mosses
National Nature
Reserve

A595

Foxfield

A5093

Kirkby in
Furness

A595

16

-0230 HW Liv
2-3kn SP
HW Liv

Millom

Dunnerholme

Haverigg

Hodbarrow Point

Askam in Furness

Haverigg
Point

Askam
Pier

Duddon Estuary

Duddon Sands

Sandscale Haws
National Nature
Reserve

A590

Dalton in Furness

A590

Kilometres
Nautical Miles

0   1   2

0   1

The Duddon Estuary

© Winter sunshine, Duddon Estuary

16

Additional information

Duddon Sands Hostel is next door to the Ship Inn (01229 889 454, www.theship1691.co.uk) just across the road from the railway station in Kirkby-in-Furness. The hostel is well organised and clean with excellent facilities. The Ship Inn has a small but excellent choice of ales. If you are planning a group trip then it may be worth asking whether they can order in a barrel of your favourite ale.

Variations

Haverigg and Millom stand at the southwest entrance to the Duddon Estuary. It is sometimes possible to launch into the stream called Haverigg Pool at the junction of Sea View and Bank End. The tide does not reach here until around 1 hour 40 minutes before HW Liverpool, leaving less time to explore the estuary. Sometimes local paddlers cross the mouth of the estuary from Askam to Haverigg for a visit to the nearby Harbour Hotel pub.

Walney Island

No. 17 | Grade B | 32km | OS Sheet 96

Tidal Port	Liverpool
Start	△ Walney, Earnse Point (SD 170 699)
Finish	○ Walney, Earnse Point (SD 170 699)
HW/LW	Around 20 minutes after Liverpool at Barrow-in-Furness
Tidal Times	In Walney channel, the NW-going (flood) stream starts around 5 hours 30 minutes before HW Liverpool. The SE-going (ebb) stream starts around 1 hour 45 minutes after HW Liverpool.
Max Rate Sp	Up to 6 knots in Walney Channel
Coastguard	Liverpool, tel. 0151 931 3341, VHF weather every 3 hours from 0130

Introduction

The land that divides the Duddon and Leven estuaries is known as the Furness Peninsula. Barrow-in-Furness is the main town, famous for naval shipbuilding and, more recently, nuclear-powered submarines. Barrow is sheltered from the ravages of the Irish Sea by Walney Island.

Walney is over 14km long but is less than 1km wide in most places. This low-lying island is a delight to circumnavigate. The journey includes wild beaches with surf, two pubs, a castle and surging tides. Due to the stronger NW-going flood stream in the Walney Channel, this trip is best made in an anticlockwise direction. The trip can be completed in a day, but taking a weekend to include an overnight stay on Piel Island (see Route 18 for accommodation options) makes for a better adventure.

Description

The A590 South Lakes road leads through Ulverston and into Barrow-in-Furness from the north. As you enter Barrow there are signposts for Walney Island leading over Jubilee Bridge. On the other side of the bridge, turn right and follow signs for North Walney and Earnse Point. At Earnse Point (on the west coast), there is a car park overlooking the shore with public toilets nearby. The beach is mostly sandy and gently shelving, but is steeper with pebbles close to the high water mark. There is a concrete slipway just beyond the northern end of the car park. At low water, the beach can dry out more than 500m; a kayak trolley will make the journey to the water much easier.

If you are planning to complete this trip in a day you will need to start at Earnse Point at around 4 hours before HW Liverpool, allowing plenty of time to reach Walney Meetings (north of Jubilee Bridge on the east coast of Walney) soon after high water.

If you are making a weekend of it, then you only need to paddle as far as Piel Island on the first day. It is recommended to arrive at Piel at (or before) high water; you can therefore leave Earnse Point as late as 2 hours before HW Liverpool.

South Walney Nature Reserve

The South Walney Nature Reserve includes the southern shores, the dunes and a number of shallow pools and lagoons. There can be hundreds of wading birds along the shore including redshank, oystercatcher and ringed plover. It is best to avoid landing on these beaches and disturbing the birds unnecessarily. The dunes are bound with marram grass but sea holly and sea lavender also grow here. Pyramid orchids can be found flowering on the lower ground beyond the dunes. During the spring and early summer, eider ducks come to South Walney in their hundreds to breed. The eider colony enjoys the protection of the herring gulls that also breed here in great numbers. Herring gulls are fiercely protective of their eggs and young and will attack land-based predators such as foxes, hedgehogs, cats and dogs.

Sandy and pebbly beaches line the entire west coast of Walney. Apart from the houses and caravans at Earnse Point, the only houses are at Biggar Bank where there is also a pub called the Castle House Hotel. There is a car park at the southern end of Biggar Bank Road (SD 183 662) with direct access to the beach. Another possible access point is the car park at Cross Dike Scar (SD 197 641). Hare Hill Beacon stands on a small rise along the coastline, heralding the south

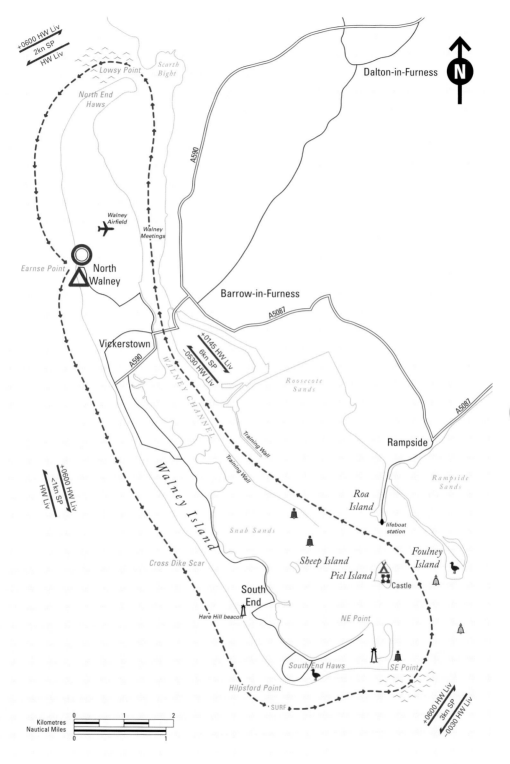

+0600 HW Liv
2kn SP
HW Liv

Lowsy Point

Scarth Bight

North End Haws

Dalton-in-Furness

N

A590

Walney Airfield

Walney Meetings

Earnse Point

North Walney

Barrow-in-Furness

A5087

Vickerstown

A590

+0145 HW Liv
6kn SP
-0530 HW Liv

WALNEY CHANNEL

Roosecote Sands

A5087

Training Wall

Training Wall

Rampside

+0600 HW Liv
<1km SP
HW Liv

Roa Island

Rampside Sands

lifeboat station

W a l n e y   I s l a n d

Snab Sands

Sheep Island

Piel Island

Castle

Foulney Island

Cross Dike Scar

South End

Hare Hill beacon

NE Point

SE Point

South End Haws

Hilpsford Point

SURF

+0600 HW Liv
3kn SP
-0030 HW Liv

Kilometres
Nautical Miles

0   1   2

0   1

17

Walney Island

91

end of the island. The remains of old groynes can be seen on the beaches, with low crumbling cliffs beyond. Surf breaks upon the sandbanks and beaches at the southwest point on all but the quietest days. Whether you relish the chance to play here, or avoid the surf by paddling offshore, you will soon find yourself paddling along Walney's southern shore. There has been a lighthouse on South Walney since 1790, originally lit for the benefit of shipping entering the River Lune bound for Glasson and Lancaster. A wooden tower was built close to the shore but it was replaced by a stone building following a fire in 1803. Over time, the sea and wind have deposited more sand and pebbles here; the lighthouse is now more than 15 metres inland.

The beaches at Southeast Point are protected by a concrete groyne. There is often a race here during the strong N-going flood into the Piel Channel. Soon after the S-going ebb begins, overfalls with standing waves develop in the vicinity of the groyne. Landing is permitted beside the groyne, but only if absolutely necessary.

If you have got the tides right, the flooding waters will lead you to Piel Island where camping is permitted in the grounds of the ruined castle and a warm welcome awaits you in the Ship Inn. Looking north from Piel, you will be able to see Roa Island and the base for the Barrow lifeboat. The rising waters flood northwest past Piel as they race into the Walney Channel. This channel is regularly dredged to maintain sufficient depth for the ships using Barrow Docks. Training walls also help to maintain the channel. These walls become submerged close to high water, but are marked by lines of posts that remain visible at all states of the tide. It is worth keeping a sharp eye out for vessels entering and leaving Barrow docks and staying clear of the marked channel if necessary. North of the dock entrance, progress will be swift past the old slipways and shipyard sheds.

The Jubilee Bridge spans the channel, linking Barrow-in-Furness with Walney Island at Vickerstown. The central span can be lifted to allow larger vessels to pass. The bridge was completed in 1908, much to the annoyance of the Furness Railway Company who ran the only ferry service to and from the island. The ferry ran from the Walney slipway known locally as the Ferry Pitching, north of the bridge. On the opposite side stands BAE Systems' Devonshire Dock Hall, otherwise known as 'the big shed', where the nuclear submarines are constructed.

Walney Meetings is the area 2km north of the bridge which dries out at low tide. Plan to pass here within the first hour after HW Liverpool. While paddling north from here, enjoy the excellent view towards Black Combe and the Lake District fells beyond. The slagheap that dominates the shore to the north of Barrow is where hot waste material was dumped from the foundries. The heap used to be much bigger than it is today, and the glow it generated could be seen from the Isle of Man on a clear night.

There are no landing restrictions at the Walney North End Nature Reserve. The sandy beaches, with dunes beyond, provide an opportunity for a final break before taking on the last stretch. Just across the water there is a jumble of sheds and huts among the dunes at Lowsy Point. The Black Huts were originally built during the Second World War for Barrow residents wanting to escape the air raids. These characteristic huts have since been inventively refurbished, extended and, in some cases, rebuilt as homes or weekend retreats.

A tide race develops in the Scarth Channel after high water; there can be standing waves and confused seas here, especially in westerly winds. As you paddle out of the Scarth Channel, Walney's western shores will come into view signalling that you only have 4km left to paddle to Earnse Point.

17

Walney Island

Tides and weather

Following a day or more of strong winds with a westerly component there will be surf breaking on the west shores of Walney, particularly at the southwest point.

Additional information

There is a general store at Earnse Point for any last-minute supplies. The Ferry Hotel at Vickerstown is a large pub that overlooks the Walney Channel; it is possible to land at the Walney Ferry Pitching slipway nearby and nip in for a bar snack or to indulge in the super-value carvery lunch.

Variations

Roa Island (SD 233 649) is often used as a start and finish point (see also Route 18). This choice saves driving through Barrow onto Walney, but makes the paddling more committing. If the conditions on the exposed west coast of Walney prevent you from completing your trip, then you will be left with a minimum of a 12km walk or taxi ride back to your car.

Piel Island

No. 18 | Grade A | 4km | OS Sheet 96

Tidal Port	Liverpool
Start	△ Roa Island public slipway (SD 233 649)
Finish	○ Roa Island ferry slipway (SD 232 647)
HW/LW	Around 10 minutes after Liverpool
Tidal Times	In the Piel Channel, the N-going stream starts around 6 hours after HW Liverpool and the S-going stream starts around 1 hour after HW Liverpool.
Max Rate Sp	3 knots in the Piel Channel
Coastguard	Liverpool, tel. 0151 931 3341, VHF weather every 3 hours from 0130

Introduction

Piel Island guards the southern entrance of the Walney Channel. This unique little island can be a real treat. The short journey includes a castle, a nature reserve, waters rich in marine life and a pub for refreshment. It is possible to camp on the island (basic facilities are provided), allowing you to stay on Piel for a couple of days and explore the nearby coastal nature reserves at a leisurely pace. Piel is an ideal place for an introduction to sea kayak camping.

18

Piel Island

Description

The closest point of departure is Roa Island at the southern end of the Barrow Peninsula. The causeway leading to Roa can be found by driving through the village of Rampside off the A5087 between Ulverston and Barrow-in-Furness. The causeway leads to Piel Street, at the end of which are the Barrow lifeboat station and the sloping jetty for the Piel ferry. The jetty and surrounding shore are ideal for launching and landing at low-to-mid tide. At mid-to-high tide, the strong flood stream can cause hazardous conditions around the jetty. In these conditions, the quieter waters around the public slipway (SD 233 649) at the eastern end of nearby Tower Street provide a safer place to launch and land. The crossing to Piel is easiest around an hour after HW Liverpool when there is plenty of water in the channel and the tidal streams are weak.

The castle ruins at the south end of Piel along with the pilot cottages at the north form a distinctive silhouette on the island's skyline. The usual landing is about half-way along the eastern shore on the stony beach beside a sloping jetty. Piel Island is only 600m long and less than 400m across at its widest.

There is plenty of space for camping on the island but it can get surprisingly busy on summer weekends. Visit www.pielisland.co.uk for news of events such as medieval banquets, hog roasts and live music in the castle grounds. The Ship Inn overlooks the jetty, and provides a simple selection of beverages and snacks. Out of the usual summer season it may be a good idea to call ahead and let them know you are coming (tel. 07516 453 784 or email shipinn@pielisland. co.uk).

Piel Island History

The red sandstone ruins of Piel Castle dominate the southern end of the island. Piel was first fortified by Savignac (later known as Cistercian) monks of the nearby Furness Abbey. The ruins that we see today date back to 1327, when the castle was used largely to house traders using Piel Harbour.

Tradition dictates that the landlord of the Ship Inn is crowned King of Piel Island.

FOULNEY AND SOUTH WALNEY

From Piel you can take short excursions along the shores of the nearby South Walney and Foulney Nature reserves. Both are managed by the Cumbria Wildlife Trust. The wardens ask paddlers not to land and to make every effort to avoid disturbing the birds. It is also best to keep a respectful distance from seals when they are hauled out on beaches. The tide races at the south of these reserves command respect. If in doubt, make your wildlife excursions at the beginning of a rising tide.

SOUTH AMERICA, ST HELENA AND THE FALKLANDS

The local 1:25,000 Ordnance Survey map shows a sandbank called South America with two small islets on either side: St Helena to its west and the Falklands to the east. Paddling out among the sand and shingle banks is a magical experience. The last of the ebbing waters of the Piel Channel will help you on your way between the exposed shingles of Foulney and South Walney. This is the best time to see wading birds at their busiest. Rounding East Scar and Foulney Twist you will find yourself among spooky shallows. Low ridges and hummocks separate pools and channels

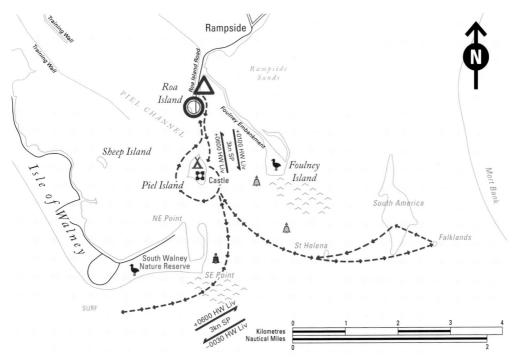

Piel Island

that form an extraordinary landscape teeming with cockles and mussels and their predators, dog whelks and starfish. As you begin to head east, you will lose the advantage of the S-going ebb and may even meet the last of the W-going ebb stream from the Leven Estuary.

St Helena becomes exposed less than a kilometre east of the southern extremity of Foulney Twist, and is around 50m long. Further to the east is South America; this sandbank shifts gently with every tide but moves more dramatically during powerful storms and floods. The Falklands is a small group of rocks to the east of South America that have been invaded, and even completely enveloped, by the sands from time to time.

The return to Piel is a simple process of retracing your outward route. It is best to head back as soon as possible after low water to avoid meeting the new E-going flood stream. Once back at East Scar, you can count on the N-going flood stream to draw you in to the Piel Channel. The round trip from Piel Island is about 10km.

Tides and weather

The shallow waters can become very choppy especially in wind against tide conditions; awkward breaking surf can develop in sustained strong winds from the south.

Additional information

The Bosun's Locker on Roa Island provides an excellent range of ice creams, snacks and meals from its traditional English café menu.

The Leven Estuary

No. 19 | Grade B | 21km | OS Sheet 96

Tidal Port	Liverpool
Start	△ Wadhead Scar car park (SD 308746)
Finish	○ Wadhead Scar car park (SD 308746)
HW/LW	HW Ulverston and in the lower reaches of the estuary is 30 minutes after HW Liverpool.
Tidal Times	Incoming tide can be seen arriving around 2 hours before HW Liverpool. The out-going stream starts around 30 minutes after Liverpool.
Max Rate Sp	4–5 knots
Coastguard	Liverpool, tel. 0151 931 3341, VHF weather every 3 hours from 0130

Introduction

The River Leven runs from the southern end of Windermere and meets the waters of Coniston via the River Crake at Greenodd. When it comes to paddling in beautiful scenery, it is difficult to surpass this estuary. It has a mysterious island, a backdrop of Cumbrian peaks and hosts thousands of ducks, geese and wading birds. Chapel Island is a small limestone outcrop in the middle of the estuary and can only be reached by a brisk ferry glide across the flooding waters.

Description

The western shores of the Leven Estuary form the Lakeland coast close to Ulverston. The A5087 runs south from Ulverston and meets the estuary shore by the village of Bardsea. There is parking at the roadside, with a pleasant grass verge above a steep shingle beach. On the other side of the road there are public toilets and a small kiosk that sells drinks and snacks, making this an ideal place to meet. However, the best launching place is at a car park beside the headland close to Wadhead Scar. This car park can be found by driving a short way north on the A5087, then east along Cooper Lane. The car park overlooks the estuary just beyond a small plastics factory building. It is best to get ready well before the surge of water gallops in across Morecambe Bay.

The initial rush of water crossing Ulverston Sands near Bardsea means that a hasty ferry glide is needed if you wish to explore the ruins on Chapel Island. In good visibility, the island can be lined up with distinctive features among the Ellerside and Cartmel fells beyond the estuary to maintain a transit. The western shore is rocky with small sharp pebbles. The southern tip ends with a sharp narrow point like a rocky dinosaur tail. Along the eastern side, limestone slabs dip towards the sea. They lead northwards to a soft sandy beach from which you can enjoy a quick stroll and explore the island. At only 400m long and 50m wide this is a bleak place, yet on a misty morning surrounded by swirling waters it is atmospheric and mysterious. Local historians say the island was once inhabited, most probably by fishermen. There was once a chapel here but the building, along with any dwellings, has long since succumbed to the powers of nature and is no longer visible. The ruin that now stands on the island's summit is actually a folly built to look like a ruined chapel.

The Leven Estuary

19

Visit the Tropics

Explore the seaward end of Chapel Island, and you will be whisked back in time 325 million years ago to when it was part of a large reef, submerged in a warm subtropical ocean.

Colonies of corals, nearly a metre across, bulged above a fine grained mud. The tiny creatures that built these structures each occupied their own space, sticking their delicate tentacles out through minute windows into the turbulent water. There were shell-fish in abundance, and a multitude of other sea creatures crawled across the surface, their routes marked by curving trails. Others burrowed into the mud, leaving holes to be later filled in by sediment. As time passed, the reef travelled north riding on its tectonic plate. The muds, shells and corals hardened into limestone rock. Eventually sea levels fell, leaving this ancient sea bed high and occasionally dry.

The coral fossils are easy to find, and careful searching will reveal shell fragments and the sinuous pathways of ancient sea-floor dwellers.

By Royanne Wilding

Thousands of wading birds roost here waiting out the high tides of short winter days. In order to minimise disturbance, it is best to stay only a short while and leave them to their island. The flooding waters will usher you north towards a railway viaduct and part of Ulverston known as Canal Foot. The Ulverston Canal was cut in the late 1700s to enable ships to berth in the heart of the town, leading to a dramatic increase in trade to the area. The canal was abandoned in 1945 but is still very much in evidence; the old sea lock gates are still intact, if a little infested with vegetation. The railway viaduct carries the west Cumbrian railway line that runs from Carnforth to Whitehaven and Maryport. The bridge spans the narrows at Plumpton, where the turbulent rising waters flood through the 48 arches. Standing waves can develop here, presenting an opportunity to play. If you wish to avoid rough water then the eastern end of the bridge will present a smoother passage.

To the north of the bridge, the upper reaches of the Leven Estuary become broader once again and the route is littered with shallows that will keep you guessing. Away from the town of Ulverston, among quieter waters, the rolling hills and woodland gradually begin to close in. The rocky tree-lined shores of Mearness Point provide excellent views and good shelter for a short break. Another kilometre further, the waters of the River Crake emerge from beneath the

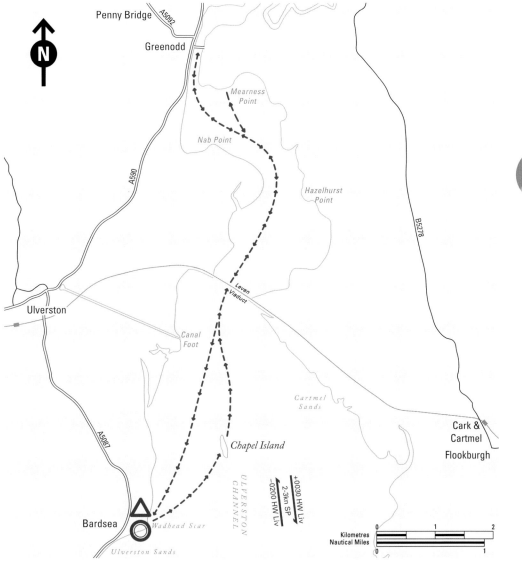

bridge that carries the A590. Greenodd Village can be found a short way up the Crake where it is possible to land beside the petrol station. The petrol station has a general store that sells snacks and drinks. There are also toilet facilities and parking, as long as you ask for permission first. You should start the paddle back down the estuary as soon as, or even before, the tide turns. There are few things worse than getting stuck on a drying sandbank or muddy shore miles from your car.

Tides and weather

There needs to be a tide with a HW exceeding 9m at Liverpool for this trip to be worth doing. Only these larger tides provide enough water for paddling for around 2 hours either side of local (Ulverston) high water. Fortunately, HW is usually around lunchtime when spring tides occur.

Additional information

The Walkers Hostel in Ulverston (01229 480 511, www.thewalkershostel.co.uk) is open all year round and provides good-quality budget accommodation for individuals or groups.

Variations

A one-way trip to Greenodd village is possible on the rising tide. In this case, you can leave a little later and launch when water arrives at the beach beside the A5087 at Bardsea (SD 304 744).

Under certain conditions the estuary can generate a tidal bore. Locals hoping to catch it put in at the end of Brick Kiln Road (SD 309 762) shortly before the start of the incoming stream.

The Kent Estuary

No. 20 | **Grade B** | **22km** | **OS Sheet 97**

Tidal Port	Liverpool
Start	△ The western end of Arnside Promenade (SD 454 787)
Finish	○ The western end of Arnside Promenade (SD 454 787)
HW/LW	Around 1 hour after Liverpool
Tidal Times	The first rush of incoming water reaches the estuary at Arnside around 1 hour before HW Liverpool.
Max Rate Sp	The flood stream regularly exceeds 8 knots; the ebb stream is less strong but may exceed 6 knots in places.
Coastguard	Liverpool, tel. 0151 931 3341, VHF weather every 3 hours from 0130

Introduction

The peaceful town of Arnside sits beside its estuary where, on a large enough spring tide, the rushing waters assume the form of a tidal wave known as the Arnside Bore. If all this sounds like too much excitement, however, the calmer upper reaches of the estuary may suit you better.

103

© Low water at Arnside

The Kent Estuary

Description

Despite the rural and 'olde England' feel to this little seaside gem, Arnside is easy to get to. The B5282 leads all the way to Arnside promenade from its junction with the A6 at Milnthorpe. When you arrive at Arnside, don't be tempted to use the main car park down by the estuary because spring tides often inundate this area at high water. It is better to use the roadside parking along the western end of the promenade, where there is a slipway leading to a sandy beach. If it is the bore that you have come looking for you need get on the water well before the wave is expected to arrive. At this point, the River Kent will be no more than a shallow channel running through the extensive sand banks. The river channel is normally conveniently close to the promenade. Paddling with the flow of the river you will soon be on your way past the coastguard station along the shores of Grubbins Wood, heading southwest for Blackstone Point. In contrast to these wooded shores, the town of Grange-over-Sands clings to the steep far side of the estuary a little over 2km away.

On a calm day you may hear the bore in the distance before you can see it. Another sign of its approach is ducks and wading birds taking flight as the bore arrives. Despite these spooky signs, the bore rarely travels at alarming speeds. In the best conditions, it is possible to ride the wave all the way back to Arnside but these conditions are rare. The Arnside Bore has been known to exceed a metre but can just as easily assume the form of a disappointing surge. The bore tends to dissipate in the deeper parts of the channel but the energy remains and the wave will re-form in the shallows on its way past Arnside promenade. Within minutes, the estuary will be inundated and all but the biggest of the sand banks covered.

The eastern or Arnside end of the Arnside Viaduct has the deepest channel where the bore eventually dies, but the fun is far from over. Soon after the flooding waters begin to run through the viaduct arches, standing waves begin to develop. As the water rises, an extensive eddy develops on the north side of the railway embankment. Depending on the strength of the 2 hour flood tide, the standing waves decay and re-form providing entertainment for sea kayakers and play boaters alike. Extreme care should be taken while playing here during the early part of the flood; the eastern and most favoured arch has some concrete and steel debris protruding from the seabed which has the potential to cause injury or entrapment.

As you leave the viaduct behind, progress up the estuary will be swift with the help of the flood tide. The next village along the eastern shore is Storth. The B5282 between Arnside and Milnthorpe meets the estuary shore and makes this a popular spot for anglers to fish for flounder. The nearby Ship Inn overlooks the water and could be a perfect lunch spot for paddlers who wish to take it easy. Others with a more adventurous spirit may wish to carry on just a little further, exploring the tributary River Bela or the upper reaches of the Kent Estuary.

The River Bela flows through Milnthorpe and Dallam Deer Park before joining the Kent from the east. Its short tidal stretch has lagoons that provide shelter to herons, mute swans and little

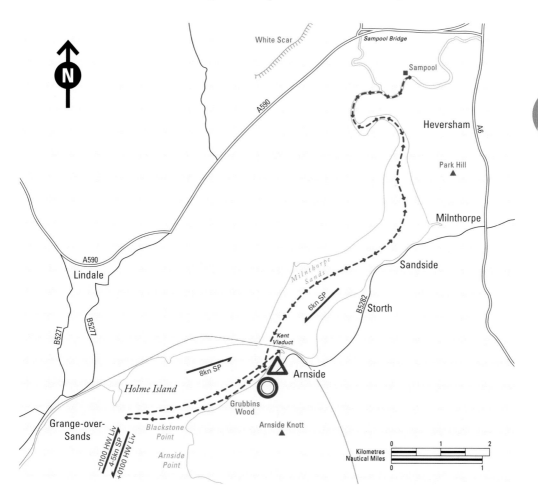

© Arnside seafront

grebes. Beyond the Bela confluence, the upper reaches of the Kent estuary gradually begin to narrow as the channel winds round to the west before a broad shallow lagoon is reached. This is a birdwatcher's paradise, often crowded with ducks, geese and wading birds. From here the flooding tide follows the river channel north in the shadow of the imposing limestone crag of Whitbarrow Scar.

It is possible to carry on even further to the normal tidal limit beyond the south-facing sandy beach beside Sampool Caravan Park. Spring tides can reach further towards the A6 bridge, beyond which lies the Levens Estate. Wherever you get to, you should start heading back at around the time of high water at Arnside. Make a hasty return to avoid being grounded.

Tides and weather

Arnside lies beside the sands that form the northeast corner of Morecambe Bay. Only spring tides provide enough water for paddling for around 2 hours before and after local high water. The surrounding land is hilly and provides good shelter from the elements, making this area great for those bad weather paddling days.

Additional information

The Arnside chip shop and adjoining Big Chip café regularly win awards for excellent food. The Bayview Bakery and café may be better suited for those with a sweet tooth. There is a popular YHA hostel at Arnside and the nearest campsite is Hollins Farm (www.holgates.co.uk).

The Lancashire Coast

Introduction

The Lancashire coast begins at its border with Cumbria and Morecambe Bay in the north and finishes at the entrance to the Mersey in the south. With the famous ports of Heysham, Lancaster, Fleetwood and Liverpool, there is no denying Lancashire of its maritime heritage. The coastline holds little in the way of obvious paddling adventures. Local paddlers are however passionate about their patch, which has given rise to some innovative ideas for trips.

This section has four trips that are unique, each with its own distinct adventurous flavour. Crossing Morecambe Bay is certainly no mean feat. This is an area where the sea holds more than a few tricks and conditions change rapidly from one minute to the next. Despite the strong tides, the Wyre Estuary is a trip for all with enough to keep seasoned paddlers entertained. With the help of a big spring tide, a trip up the Lune Estuary could float you over the tidal weir above Lancaster. From there it is possible to return to the start by canal, completing an intriguing circular route. The most unusual of all, by far, is the tour of Blackpool's famous illuminations by kayak.

Tides and weather

The land along the Lancashire coast is exposed to prevailing south-westerly winds. Much of the coastal land is low lying, giving little shelter other than in the upper reaches of Lune and Wyre estuaries.

Beaches are mostly gently shelving and there are huge areas of sand and mud exposed at low water. When the tide comes in, these areas are flooded at a phenomenal rate. This results in powerful tidal streams, especially where these advancing waters are squeezed into narrow channels and river estuaries.

Further information

For more information about kayaking in this region, see the following titles:

West Coast of England and Wales Pilot NP37, UK Hydrographic Office 2005, 978-070771880.
Sand Pilot of Morecambe Bay, Atlantic Transport Publishers 1998, 978-0906899946.

Looking north from Fleetwood across Morecambe Bay

Morecambe Bay

No. 21 | Grade C | 20km | OS Sheet 102

Tidal Port	Liverpool
Start	△ Roa Island ferry slipway (SD 232 647)
Finish	○ Fleetwood Esplanade Beach (SD 339 485)
HW/LW	HW at Piel is around 10 minutes after HW Liverpool; HW at Fleetwood is around 5 minutes before HW Liverpool.
Tidal Times	The N-going stream in the Piel Channel starts at around 6 hours after HW Liverpool; the S-going stream starts around 1 hour after HW Liverpool.
	In the open waters of Morecambe Bay, the ENE-going (in-going) stream starts around 6 hours before HW Liverpool and the WSW-going (out-going) stream starts at around HW Liverpool.
Max rate Sp	3 knots
Coastguard	Liverpool, tel. 0151 931 3341, VHF weather every 3 hours from 0130

21

Morecambe Bay

Introduction

The tides of Morecambe Bay have a well-deserved reputation. It is said that the broad sands of Ulverston, Grange and Silverdale can be inundated at a rate that cannot be outrun by a galloping horse. Some say that these claims are exaggerations, but people are frequently caught out. The tragedy in February 2004 in which the lives of at least 21 Chinese cockle-pickers were lost is well known. The 20km crossing is a serious undertaking that requires excellent navigation and paddling skills. This trip should only be undertaken in clear settled weather, ideally on a neap tide.

Description

Walney Island stands at the northern entrance to Morecambe Bay. The best place to launch is from nearby Roa Island, which is tucked inside the Piel Channel between the south end of Walney and Barrow-in-Furness. The causeway leading to Roa can be found by driving through the village of Rampside off the A5087 coastal route between Ulverston and Barrow-in-Furness.

The causeway leads to Piel Street, at the end of which are the Barrow lifeboat station and the sloping jetty for the Piel ferry. The jetty and the surrounding shore are ideal for launching at mid- to low-tide. Once on the water, follow the S-going ebb stream out of Piel Channel, past Piel Island and the SE Point of Walney and out into Morecambe Bay. You should be able to make out the Blackpool Tower from here, which lies 28km south-southeast and makes a good bearing for the next 6km of the crossing.

After this first part of the crossing, you should head southeast for the buildings of Fleetwood as the flood stream begins. This should bring you to an area known as 'Danger Patch', which is marked by a large red buoy (SD 283 516). King Scar lies just over 1.5km east-southeast, and is marked by an even larger green buoy (SD 296 509). Keep a look out for other vessels when approaching this area; all of the shipping traffic for Heysham, Lancaster and Fleetwood moves through here.

The skeletal structure of Wyre Light (now disused) stands nearly 3km to the east on the northern limit of the sandbank called North Wharf, marking the entrance to the Fleetwood channel. It is important to make good headway going south into the Fleetwood channel in order to avoid being pushed towards the River Lune by the strong NE-going flow. Once you are in the Fleetwood channel, it is just a case of following the buoys to the eastern end of the Fleetwood sea front. The Esplanade Beach is marked by a square lighthouse made of sandstone blocks known as Fleetwood's Lower Light. There is a slipway that leads from the sands to roadside parking along the Esplanade.

Tides and weather

Between Wyre Light and Fleetwood, the in-going stream follows the channel south-southwest when the sand banks are still dry. When the sands surrounding the channel become covered, the

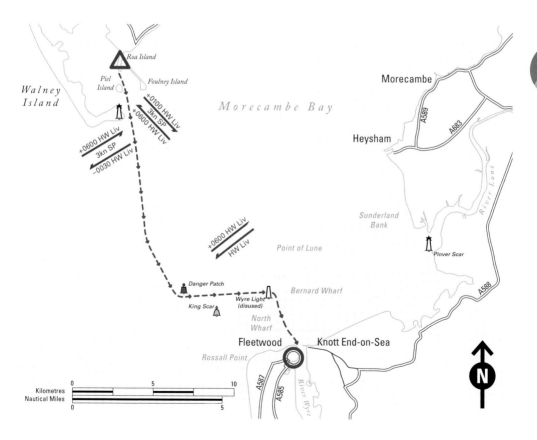

21

flow runs east across the channel. Overfalls form where strong currents rush over, around and between sand banks, which can be almost anywhere during the trip. All parts of the route are exposed to swell from the north, west and south and to winds from any direction.

Additional information

The Ferry Café is around 300m south from the Lower Light along the esplanade, located beside the ferry slipway and tram terminus at Fleetwood.

Variations

Making this crossing in reverse can be slightly easier. The best place to launch is from the beach to the south of Rossall Point to the west of Fleetwood. There is a car park and access to the beach via a path that leads over the sea wall (SD 311 455) at the junction of West Way and Fairway. In clear conditions, it will be possible to make out the lighthouse on the south of Walney Island with the buildings of Barrow-in-Furness beyond. You should allow the last of the SW-going ebb to carry you out to sea during the first half of the crossing. The NE-going flood stream will gather strength as you approach Walney Island. You should aim to pass close to Walney's SE Point to avoid missing the entrance to Piel Channel.

Historic riverside, Lancaster

The Lancaster Round

No. 22 | Grade B | 26km | OS Sheet 102

Tidal Port	Liverpool
Start	△ Victoria Arms, Glasson Dock (SD 447 561)
Finish	◯ Glasson Marina Basin (SD 445 560)
HW/LW	HW at Glasson Dock is around 30 minutes after HW Liverpool. HW at Lancaster is around 45 minutes after HW Liverpool.
Tidal Times	At Glasson, the in-going stream begins around 3 hours before HW Liverpool. The out-going stream begins around 45 minutes after HW Liverpool.
Max Rate Sp	4–5 knots in the lower parts of the estuary.
Coastguard	Liverpool, tel. 0151 931 3341, VHF weather every 3 hours from 0130

Introduction

This is a trip for when the weather might put you off paddling in areas of more open coast. Inside Sunderland Point, the estuary of the River Lune is sheltered from the ravages of the Irish Sea. The distance alone is sufficient for a long day out with a bit of a challenge. The visual contrast is terrific. The estuarine start at Glasson Dock is open and wild, but before long you will be paddling through the historical city of Lancaster. The return on the canal section brings its own special comforts, as there are plenty of pubs en route for extended lunch breaks.

Description

The isolated village of Glasson is tucked just inside the lower reaches of the Lune Estuary on its southern shore. Glasson Dock is signposted off the A6 from Junction 33 on the M6 motorway. The B5290 leads into the village from the east with the marina basin and car park on the left and the Victoria Inn on the right. While you should avoid using the Victoria Inn's car park, there is a footpath that runs alongside it which leads to the estuary shore. As the water of the incoming tide rises, it covers steep muddy banks to reach a sheltered gravel beach. It is best to launch from here around 1hr 15min before HW Liverpool. From Glasson, the estuary swings round to the north towards Lancaster amid low-lying farmland and salt marsh.

After 5km, the river bends round to the east and passes the Golden Ball Inn. Locally known as 'Snatchems', this 18th-century alehouse was frequented by smugglers and pressgangs in the days when their adversaries were Lancaster's 'hanging judges'. It is sometimes possible to paddle across the road and into the car park, where heights of the greatest floods are clearly marked and dated.

St George's Quay in Lancaster lies 2km further to the east. Lancaster's lucrative trading days are long gone and ships rarely tie up here now. The Georgian buildings and museum along the south bank tell tales of a city founded upon the triangular trade in rum, molasses and slaves.

The incoming tide floods around the bend under the Millennium footbridge and the adjacent road bridge. It then flows under the three stone arches of Skerton Bridge, before eventually heading north towards Skerton Weir. This is the usual tidal limit.

With a spring tide measuring 10m or more at Liverpool, Skerton Weir will become completely submerged. If the weir is not submerged, there can be dangerous currents around the middle part. The weir can be portaged on the east bank. Upstream of the weir, the river Lune is broad, flat and usually slow moving. The Lune Aqueduct carries the Lancaster Canal across the river and its narrow valley another 500m upstream. There is a small landing stage underneath the northwest end, from where a footpath leads steeply through woodland to the Lancaster Canal 20m above. The Lune Aqueduct consists of five arches of stone and brick and was completed in 1797; it is the second-highest aqueduct in the UK.

Looking east up the Lune valley gives views to the fells beyond the Trough of Bowland; panoramic views can also be enjoyed west across the town of Lancaster with Morecambe Bay beyond.

Paddling southeast along the canal takes you across the aqueduct, through the leafy suburbs and towards the busy centre of the city of Lancaster. A varied collection of historic buildings among modern developments lines the route through town. Canal-side pubs are a popular choice for a break. Almost as soon as the open countryside is reached, the canal runs through the 2km-long 'Deep Cutting'. The scenery here is reminiscent of a river gorge with densely wooded banks rising steeply from the water. Further south, more open scenery leads to the village of Galgate. The canal-side craft centre and its café appears on the outside of the bend just before the busy marina. Shortly after the marina, a lockkeeper's cottage and towpath bridge mark the junction

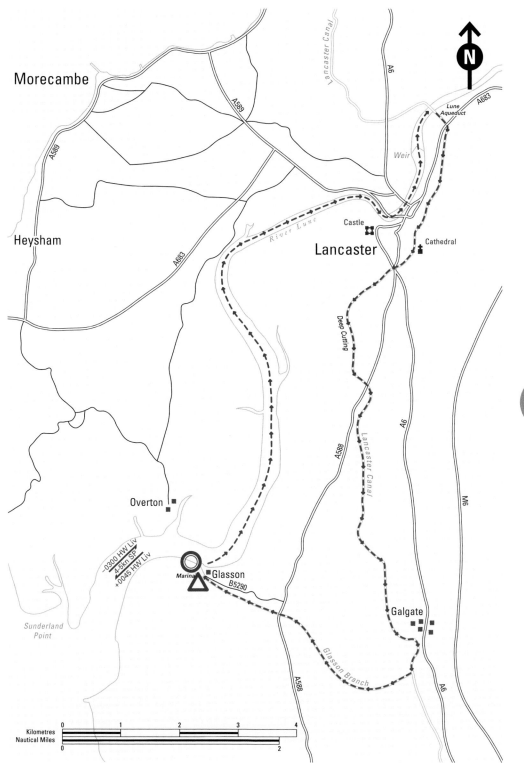

Morecambe

Heysham

Lancaster

Overton

Glasson

Galgate

Sunderland
Point

Marina

B5290

–0300 HW Liv
4-5km SP
+0045 HW Liv

River Lune

Lancaster Canal

Deep Cutting

Lune
Aqueduct

Weir

Castle

Cathedral

Glasson Branch

Kilometres
Nautical Miles

0   1   2   3   4

0   2

A589

A683

A683

A589

A588

A588

A6

A6

A683

M6

B5290

Lancaster Canal

22

© Portaging Skerton Weir

and the head of the Glasson branch. From here, the canal drops 20m through six locks over the 4km stretch to Glasson marina basin.

Tides and weather

The estuary of the River Lune is sheltered from the open sea but the surrounding land is low lying, offering little protection from strong winds. The time of HW at Lancaster can be significantly altered by the prevailing weather conditions and is notoriously variable. If the River Lune is in flood following a period of heavy rainfall, it may be difficult to reach Skerton Weir against the increased flow. In these conditions, it would be dangerous to approach the weir face.

Additional information

The Lock Keepers Rest snack van is on the east side of the tidal lock at Glasson and serves hot drinks and snacks. The Lantern o'er Lune Café can be found on the west side of the lock, and is a better option in poor weather.

Variations

If you wish to avoid the canal section, it is possible to paddle up the Lune estuary to arrive in Lancaster at HW before returning to Glasson. This provides a trip of 18km. To avoid a muddy landing, it is important to arrive back at Glasson no later than 2hr 45min after HW Liverpool.

Ships' graveyard, Fleetwood Marsh

The Wyre Estuary

No. 23 | Grade A | 22km | OS Sheet 102

Tidal Port	Liverpool
Start	△ Marine Hall, Fleetwood (SD 333 484)
Finish	○ Marine Hall, Fleetwood (SD 333 484)
HW/LW	HW Fleetwood is around 5 minutes before HW Liverpool.
Tidal Times	The in-going stream begins around 6 hours before HW Liverpool and the out-going stream begins at HW Liverpool.
Max Rate Sp	5 knots
Coastguard	Liverpool, tel. 0151 931 3341, VHF weather every 3 hours from 0130

Introduction

Fleetwood was a purpose-built town dreamt up by a wealthy Victorian landowner called Peter Hesketh-Fleetwood. The town enjoyed success as a holiday resort and seaport until the 1970s, when its deep-sea fishing fleet suffered irrevocable decline. Fleetwood retains its Victorian charm and remains popular with holidaymakers and day-trippers. Although Fleetwood no longer enjoys

23

The Wyre Estuary

the harvest of the sea, a new retail and marina development brings a different kind of harvest in the form of shopping, leisure and entertainment. The rising tide of the Wyre Estuary takes you from Fleetwood's bustling sea front, past its docks and into the pleasant countryside that surrounds its upper reaches.

Description

Fleetwood lies at the northern end of the Fylde peninsula. The A585 provides a swift route into town and leads directly to the sea front. There is limited parking along the busy road that overlooks the beach beside the 'Lower Light'. However, this beach is not ideal for launching because it is steep, has strong currents immediately offshore and is a popular fishing spot. Half a kilometre to the west, there is a large public car park between the YMCA leisure centre and Marine Hall. There are public toilets and direct access to the soft sandy beach. The beach dries out to over 3km at low water, but if you launch at around 2hr before HW Liverpool you will get away with only a short carry.

Paddling east from here will quickly bring you to the mouth of the River Wyre. The Port of Fleetwood and its busy marina are on the west bank. The best way to avoid this area is to cross the narrow buoyed channel towards Knott End-on-Sea on the east bank of the estuary. There is a sloping concrete jetty which is used for launching small fishing boats and pleasure craft. A foot passenger ferry service operates from here to Fleetwood during the summer months. The tide gathers speed as you head south up the estuary; dodging the moorings along the Knott End shore adds to the entertainment.

Once you are south of the Port of Fleetwood it is worth crossing over to the west side for deep water and to follow the best tidal flow. The area to the south of the port is dominated by Fleetwood Marsh, which is a salt marsh bursting with life and riddled with narrow channels. This offers excellent feeding and shelter for wading birds including redshank, knot and snipe. The birds find additional shelter among the skeletal remains of old ships left here to decay in their impromptu graveyard.

Barnaby's Sands is a sandbank that lies on the other side of the estuary, and is also an important refuge for wading birds. As the waters rise, huge flocks of lapwing, oystercatcher and turnstone take to the air to seek higher ground.

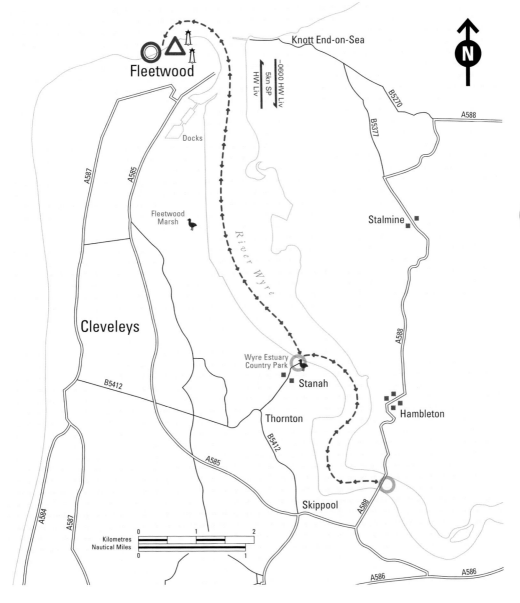

Upriver, a pair of tall pylons carries power lines high across the estuary. The Wyre Estuary Country Park lies along the west bank close to the village of Stanah. A narrow channel leads from the estuary across the salt marsh to a slipway, which in turn leads to a car park and visitor centre. The visitor centre has toilets, local information and serves hot drinks and cake. On the opposite side and just upstream lie Wardley's Pool, the yacht club and the village of Hambleton.

The river then snakes its way inland first to the west, past the numerous moorings of Little Thornton Sailing Club, then east past Skippool Marsh and Point Shard before reaching Shard Bridge. This modern road bridge carries the A588 between Skippool and Hambleton and was built in 1993, replacing an earlier toll bridge. Although the tidal limit is another 13km upstream at the village of St Michael's on Wyre, the upper reaches are shallow and hold little interest. In any case, it is best to head back as soon as there is a hint of the tide turning in order to arrive back at Fleetwood before the falling tide reveals too much of the beach at Marine Hall.

Tides and weather

The tidal streams are strongest in the lower reaches of the estuary between Knott End-on-Sea and Fleetwood Docks. The beach at Marine Hall is exposed to winds and short choppy seas from the north and west. The surrounding land in the lower reaches of the estuary is low lying and offers only limited protection from the elements.

Additional information

The Fleetwood Seaquest is an orienteering event for canoes and kayaks that uses the Wyre Estuary. Tidal planning, navigation and paddling skills are put to the test in this annual get-together that is usually held each September and organised by the local Outdoor Adventure Group.

The Ferry Café beside the ferry slipway and tram terminus serves fried breakfasts and almost anything with chips. The Thomas Drummond Pub on London Street has a reputation for good-value pub grub and a fine selection of beers. Across the estuary, the Knott End Café serves hot drinks and snacks as well as delicious locally made ice creams.

Variations

There is a small beach (SD 345 485) on the southern side of the jetty at Knott End-on-Sea, which offers a more sheltered launch. Shorter trips on more sheltered waters can be made from the slipway (SD 355 431) at The Wyre Estuary Country Park.

The Wyre Estuary

Blackpool Illuminations

No. 24 | Grade B | 11km | OS Sheet 102

Tidal Port	Liverpool
Start	△ Squire's Gate (SD 306 316)
Finish	○ Squire's Gate (SD 306 316)
HW/LW	10 minutes after Liverpool
Tidal Times	The N-going stream starts around 6 hours before HW Liverpool and the S-going stream starts around HW Liverpool.
Max Rate Sp	2 knots
Coastguard	Liverpool, tel. 0151 931 3341, VHF weather every 3 hours from 0130

Introduction

Blackpool was developed as a holiday resort for the masses and is famed for its edible rock rather than its geological interest. The Blackpool Illuminations run for 60 days from late August and provide a welcome extension to the local tourist season. This paddle along the Blackpool sea front is best started at dusk when the rising waters begin to cover the vast sands by Squire's

Gate. As darkness draws in, the millions of dazzling lights along the promenade come to life and the reflections dance and sway on the water all around. The mellow rolling hum of traffic from the promenade is punctuated by screams from fairground rides. A gentle land breeze wafts the essence of fish and chips or freshly fried doughnuts around the group.

Once the tide is in, this becomes a committing paddle with no easy landings until the end. This is a sea kayaking journey with a difference; sensory overload is a real possibility.

Description

Squire's Gate is at the western end of the A5230, which is locally known as Progress Way and Squire's Gate Lane. A concrete slipway beside the Blackpool Light Craft Club leads to a broad, soft sandy beach. Since the recent closure of the car park here, there is only limited parking in nearby streets. Sand dunes stretch away into the distance to the south. To the north, the sands are backed by an immense sea wall that extends along the entire length of the Blackpool shore. It is best to launch here at around 1hr 30min before HW. At this time, there may be a carry of 200m or more to the water's edge. A string of lights leads the way along the promenade at South Shore.

Soon afterwards, you will arrive at South Pier. The 'Adrenaline Zone' dominates the end of the pier with its collection of gravity-defying rides. The lightshow here is excellent with finely focused searchlight beams slicing through the night sky. The next part of the promenade is lined with rows of hotels drenched in a warm glow from the illuminated features that line the seafront. A giant and beautifully lit Ferris wheel dominates Central Pier and its more traditional collection of fairground amusements.

Blackpool Illuminations

The most striking feature lighting up the night sky here is Blackpool Pleasure Beach. The skyline is dominated by the UK's tallest rollercoaster ride. Known simply as 'The Big One', its twisted structure is spectacularly floodlit at night. High-speed screams, born of a heady mix of pleasure and terror, are broadcast from the heights amid the rattle and rumble of the fairground.

The most spectacular stretch is between Central Pier and North Pier, which is the most intense part of the Blackpool Illuminations. The view from the sea is especially grand with the dazzling promenade topped by the shimmering lights of the Blackpool Tower. In recent years, the tower has boasted a laser show that can be seen from 50km away. At 158m, the top of the Blackpool Tower is the highest point along the coast of northwest England. HM Coastguard takes full advantage of this, with a VHF aerial site at the top of the tower.

North Pier is quieter than the Central and South Piers and the focus here is upon its retained Victorian charm rather than hustle, bustle and bright lights. This makes it ideal for sea angling. The ends of all the piers are often used by anglers; it is best to give them a wide berth in order to avoid becoming tangled in their lines.

The area beyond North Pier is called North Shore. The view of the illuminations is less spectacular here because the promenade is raised higher and a little further back from the seafront. Ideally, you should aim to be here at local HW before heading south on the return to Squire's Gate. With so much light all around, it will be tempting to paddle underneath piers. If you do, choose your route carefully and be aware of dangling ropes, cables and semi-submerged parts of the structure.

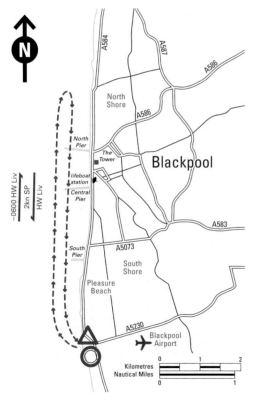

The home run between South Pier and Squires Gate is also popular with anglers. It is surprisingly dark along this stretch which makes it hard to spot any of them, let alone their lines. Remember that they will be just as surprised to see you as you will be to see them.

Tides and weather

It is important to paddle here as close as possible to local HW when the streams are less strong, which allows you to get in close to the piers and promenades. As this is a night paddle, it is especially important to make this trip in settled weather conditions.

Nightfall brings the sparkling sea front to life

24

Blackpool Illuminations

Additional information

On seeing paddlers' lights and kayaks in the darkness offshore, well-meaning on-lookers have been known to call the emergency services to raise the alarm. In the interests of avoiding an unnecessary search, it is it is vitally important to notify the coastguard of your plans before you launch.

Throughout the holiday season, including the time when the Illuminations are on, traffic can be very heavy and slow moving.

The Squire's Gate fish and chip shop is in the closest row of shops on Squire's Gate Lane. It is less than 150m from the slipway at the start/finish of this trip and has a reputation for being one of the best in the area (it might be a good idea to check when it closes before setting off).

# Trans-Pennine Network

Introduction

The hills, crags and moorland of northern England's Pennines separate the huge tidal estuaries of the Mersey and Humber. Their waters have always provided shelter for fishing boats and routes for trading vessels. During the industrial revolution, the need to transport heavy goods further inland increased dramatically. This led to the development of a comprehensive canal network. By 1816, the Pennine barrier had been breached in three places linking the Irish Sea in the west to the North Sea in the east.

The Mersey and Humber provide great paddling on relatively calm water and great distances can be covered with good use of tidal streams. However, linking these tideways via the Trans-Pennine canals presents a tough challenge. Between Runcorn and Goole, 125 locks and steep canal banks present a series of gruelling portages. This 179km route passes through some of the more unusual and hidden parts of Manchester, over the Rochdale Canal summit and through the mill towns of Calderdale.

Do we travel to paddle, or paddle to travel?

Most sea kayak voyages take place in wild and remote places far from our homes, often in different countries and sometimes on the other side of the world. Some sea kayakers who live inland use their local canals to keep paddle-fit during the winter months. However, it is actually possible to connect day trips together to form weekend trips or even longer expeditions. Running a close parallel to the Trans-Pennine Trail for walkers and cyclists, this journey passes right through the very cities and suburbs from which thousands of outdoor enthusiasts seek escape every weekend. This opens up a concept of adventures that can begin on the city doorstep and have the potential to end almost anywhere.

Further information

For more information about Trans-Pennine waterways, see:

Collins Nicholson Waterways Guide 5: North West & Pennines, David Perrott and Jonathan Mosse, Collins 2006, 0-00-721113-9.

Visit www.waterscape.com for the latest information from British Waterways.

Trans-Pennine Network

Liverpool skyline

25

The Mersey Estuary

No. 25 | **Grade B** | **37km** | **OS Sheet 108**

Tidal Port	Liverpool
Start	Crosby Beach (SD 295 004)
Finish	Wigg Island, Runcorn (SJ 521 833)
HW/LW	HW Wigg Island, Runcorn around 45 minutes after HW Liverpool.
Tidal Times	The SE-going (in-going) stream starts around 5 hours 30 minutes before HW Liverpool and the NW-going (out-going) stream starts around 15 minutes after HW Liverpool.
Max Rate Sp	5–6 knots
Coastguard	Liverpool, tel. 0151 931 3341, VHF weather every 3 hours from 0130

"Tired of golden sands, awesome cliffs vibrant with seabirds, playful dolphins and intriguing caves? Why not visit the Mersey Estuary, running through the heart of the industrialized North West. Petrochemicals, shipbuilding and scousers: the Mersey has it all."

Andy Trowler (paddler, yachtsman and expat scouser)

© Hale Head | Jean Brown

25

The Mersey Estuary

Introduction

The beginning of this journey takes you through a highly acclaimed art installation before the swift tides whisk you along towards Liverpool. Docks and jetties comprise a jumbled industrial landscape. This is Liverpool's warm-up act before the row of historical buildings forming the celebrated waterfront is revealed. The distance can be covered surprisingly quickly with a rising spring tide. After passing beneath the spectacular Runcorn-Widnes Bridge, the finish at Wigg Island brings you within portage distance of the Bridgewater Canal (giving you access to northern England's inland waterways network).

Description

Crosby is a town to the north of Liverpool that overlooks the mouth of the Mersey estuary. The A565 runs from Liverpool through the central part of Crosby and onwards to Formby and Southport. To the west of the town, a gently shelving, sandy beach runs for almost 4km from Seaforth and Bootle docks in the south to Formby Bank in the north. The easiest place to get your kayak to the water is along the northern part of the beach.

A car park overlooks the beach beside the headquarters of Liverpool Coastguard at the junction of Burbo Bank Road North and Hall Road West. Once on the beach you will find yourself in 'Another Place'. Created by sculptor Antony Gormley, 'Another Place' is an art installation that consists of 100 life-sized figures made of solid cast iron. Facing out to sea, they are spread out along the whole of the Crosby Beach foreshore at different levels between the high and low water marks. The beach dries to almost a kilometre in places, although much of this is quickly covered soon after low water has passed.

Before you launch, it is vitally important that you call both the coastguard and the Port of Liverpool Authorities (0151 949 6134, VHF channel 12, callsign 'Mersey Radio'). You should let them know your plans and follow any advice that they give you.

Soon after you launch, you will cross the main shipping lane as you head for New Brighton on the Wirral side of the estuary. The Wirral shore has a succession of beaches and is away from most of the shipping. As you approach the shores, you will encounter choppy conditions in the tide race associated with the sand banks off Perch Rock.

The New Brighton Promenades run from Perch Rock, overlooking the Mersey Estuary beaches, to Seacombe and the Mersey ferry terminal. Just over a kilometre before the ferry terminal is Egremont beach, with its slipway and the Egremont Ferry pub. This is the last practical landing place along this shore.

From this point on, the Wirral shore changes from beaches and promenades to high dock walls and jetties. The Seacombe ferry terminal consists of a bridge leading to a floating pontoon which

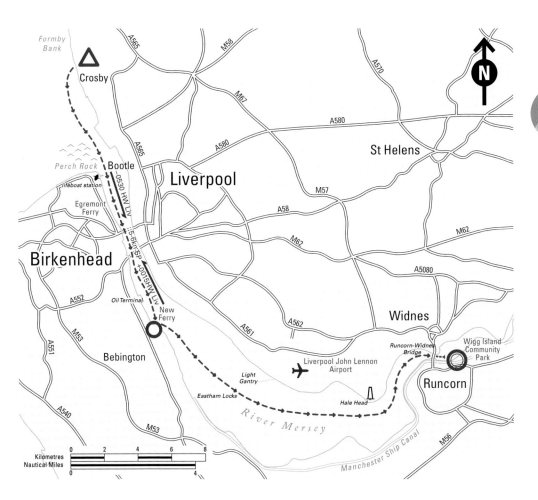

houses the waiting rooms. The tidal streams can be strong here, so it is worth giving the pontoon and the bridge a wide berth.

Soon afterwards you will pass the entrance to Alfred Dock, the first of the Birkenhead Docks. This is where the tidal heights are measured for the 'standard' Port of Liverpool. From here you will get the best view of Pier Head, the Liver Building and the rest of the Liverpool waterfront. The Birkenhead ferry terminal is much bigger than that at Seacombe. Norfolkline run their daily services to Belfast and Dublin from these colossal jetties. It is wise to give this structure and any moored ships a wide berth.

Passing the naval shipyards of Cammell Laird's, you will soon approach the Tranmere Oil Terminal. It is here that huge tankers unload crude oil, which is then taken to the Stanlow Oil Refinery via a 24km pipeline.

Eventually the industrial intensity relents with the approach to Rock Ferry. As the tide floods across the mud flats, water reaches a shingle beach with a slipway leading to a car park (SJ 339 861). This is a useful spot to stop for a break. Upstream from here, the estuary becomes shallower, wider and bends round to the east. The last of any shipping will be heading for Eastham Locks and the entrance to the Manchester Ship Canal.

Further upstream on the other side of the river, Liverpool John Lennon Airport stands on the flat ground of the north bank. Beyond the airport, Hale Head can be seen with its disused, white-painted lighthouse (SJ 472 809). There is a beach here suitable for a brief break, but no road access. From Hale Head the estuary becomes narrower, winding its way inland first north and then east once again towards Runcorn. The south and east banks are dominated by the retaining wall of the Manchester Ship Canal. The north and west banks are shrouded in dense reed beds.

The end of the trip is heralded in grand fashion by the two bridges that span the Runcorn Gap. The Runcorn Railway Bridge looks a little dull, as it stands in the shadow of the 330m steel arch of the road bridge that connects Widnes to Runcorn. The Runcorn Bridge was completed in 1959 but its capacity was soon exceeded, and by 1977 the bridge had been widened and renamed the Silver Jubilee Bridge.

The swing-bridge that connects Wigg Island Community Park and Nature Reserve to the main part of Runcorn can be seen just over a kilometre further along the south shore of the estuary. The landing is another 150m further on at the foot of a grassy bank. Ideally, you should arrive as close as possible to local HW. If you arrive too early you will be landing on a sticky muddy bank; if you arrive too late the tide will have quickly turned against you.

Perch Rock

The northernmost point on the Wirral peninsula is marked by the New Brighton or Perch Rock lighthouse. Located down by the low water mark, it was built in 1827 but decommissioned in 1973 with the advance of more modern navigational aids.

Fort Perch Rock stands at the high water mark and was built in the early 1800s to protect the Port of Liverpool. Bristling with heavy guns, the fort became locally known as 'little Gibraltar' but saw very little action through the wars. The buildings are now privately owned and feature a war aviation museum and tearooms.

Tides and weather

The tidal streams in the Mersey estuary are strong and command respect. The flow is strongest in the narrows between Liverpool and Birkenhead. The section between New Brighton and Rock Ferry is well sheltered from west and south-westerly winds. The land that surrounds the broad section between Rock Ferry and Runcorn is low lying, leaving it exposed to winds from any direction. Strong winds tend to produce gusty conditions around the Runcorn Gap, especially beneath the bridges.

Additional information

Due to the busy nature of the Liverpool Coastguard control centre, the staff are not in a position to accept visitors.

Variations

You could continue from Wigg Island to the Bridgewater Canal (which is just over 400m away) on foot, with your kayak on a trolley. Once you have crossed the swing bridge, turn right (pedestrians only) onto Old Quay Street and then turn left onto Irwell Lane. On Irwell Lane, turn left onto Wivern Place and cross the road to a footpath that leads to Canal Street and the Navigation Inn. A footpath with a few steps leads directly to the Bridgewater Canal towpath.

© 'Another Place'

The Mersey Estuary

If you plan to do the described route in reverse (i.e. Wigg Island to Crosby), you will need to complete the broad section between Runcorn and Rock Ferry quickly. The tide goes out surprisingly quickly, revealing huge areas of soft sticky mud.

If instead a shorter and more sheltered trip is sought, there are various alternative launch sites along the New Brighton shore. A popular choice among local paddlers is a trip from Crosby Beach to Egremont Ferry and back. For this trip, the best time to launch at Crosby is around two hours before HW. The return to Crosby can be started anytime soon after HW.

© Manchester YHA, Castlefield Basin | Jean Brown

 # Runcorn to the Rochdale Canal Summit

26

No. 26 | **Grade A** | **74km** | **OS Sheets 108 and 109**

Start	△ Canal Street, Runcorn (SJ 519 830)
Finish	○ West Summit Lock (SD 947 188)
No. Locks	56 (including South Summit Lock)
Access	Peel Holdings (Bridgewater Canal) and British Waterways (Rochdale Canal) license BCU members to use these canals. Proof of membership may occasionally be requested.

Introduction

This route takes you from Runcorn on the banks of the Mersey estuary to the dizzy heights of the Rochdale Canal summit in the heart of the Pennines. The scenery along the way has tremendous variety: there is rolling countryside, pleasant suburbia, industrial tangle and tall cityscapes. There are no locks along the entire length of the Bridgewater Canal. The 44km journey from Canal Street in Runcorn to Castlefield Basin in Manchester can be done in one day. However, most of

Runcorn to the Rochdale Canal Summit

© Bridgewater Canal, Higher Walton, Cheshire

this stretch is beautifully scenic and deserves a little more attention. The rigours of the Rochdale Canal are a stark contrast and will usually take more than one day. A rise of over 150m makes it necessary to portage 56 locks in the 30km from Castlefield Basin to the summit. The scenery is grotty as the canal leads out from Manchester's back streets, but improves with the steady climb into the hills.

Description

Until 1966, the Bridgewater Canal was connected to the Manchester Ship Canal and the River Mersey by a flight of locks to the east of Runcorn. Nowadays, the closest the Bridgewater Canal comes to the Mersey is on Canal Street opposite the appropriately named Navigation Inn.

Heading east out of town, the canal shares its route with the Daresbury Expressway. After 2km, more peaceful surroundings are reached as the route passes through parkland at Norton Priory. Pleasant suburban scenes lead the way to a marina on the left at Preston Brook. On the right there is a small basin and the entrance to the canal-side paddlesports shop Kayaks North West.

The canal splits two ways a little further on. The main route to Manchester heads north and the southern branch leads under the M56 towards the Preston Brook Tunnel. Following the left-hand branch north, paddle through the Cheshire countryside with its gently rolling hills, patches of woodland and quiet villages. The villages of Moore and Higher Walton have shops, pubs and cafes. Stockton Heath is a suburb of Warrington. It is more built up, but remains pleasant enough. Thorn Marine, a useful shop for spares, accessories, hot snacks and drinks, is located just before London Road Bridge.

A mixture of suburbia and countryside leads through Grappenhall and Thelwall before taking you under the Thelwall Viaduct, which carries the M6 motorway. Another 2km leads to the pretty village of Lymm, where there are plenty of shops as well as several pubs. Heading east, the canal passes Oughtrington and Agden Wharf. Soon after passing the beautiful parkland of Dunham, the outskirts of Altrincham are reached. Victorian industrial buildings are interspersed with modern factory units and ultra-modern high-rise housing.

The parks and gardens of Sale lead steadily to Stretford, into the industrial tangle of Old Trafford. Waters Meeting is a junction where the west branch heads for Wigan. The route to Castlefield Basin heads north through container storage yards and past the football stadium that is home to Manchester United. The last couple of kilometres that lead into Castlefield are a mixture of derelict land and new housing developments. Castlefield Basin is surrounded by modern dwellings and trendy bars. The Manchester YHA is beside the northern basin that can be reached by paddling under the tram bridge. Dukes Lock (no. 92) of the Rochdale Canal can be seen under the arched footbridge to the west. The paddling is all uphill from this point onwards!

The 'Rochdale Nine' is a series of locks that are mostly hidden from view by the tall buildings and busy streets of Manchester. Portaging and paddling through this underworld is both fascinating and unpleasant: this is where many of the city's homeless shelter at night. Crime can

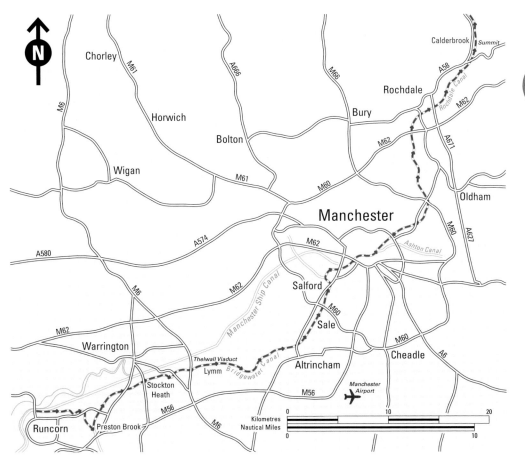

135

be a problem here, not to mention the smell. It is best to complete this section quickly and early in the day.

At Princess Street Lock (no. 87) the towpath finishes and the portage trail runs along Canal Street in the heart of Manchester's gay district. The towpath can be rejoined after Minshull Street. Soon afterwards the canal runs beneath Piccadilly station, before emerging near its junction with the Ashton Canal.

The Rochdale Canal continues to climb lock after lock through the inner city until the gradient eases at Failsworth. There are only three locks over 5km through to the north side of Chadderton; it is a relief to get some continuous time in the boat! There is an interesting low bridge that requires a spot of 'kayak limbo' in order to squeeze underneath.

From here to Slattocks the scenery opens up to countryside views but the canal rises 10 locks in just over 2km. After Slattocks, the scenery opens up with distant views across the moors as the gradient eases once again. There are no locks between Milnrow and Littleborough but there are a couple more low bridges. Littleborough is where the final push for the summit begins. There are 12 locks from here until the summit section is finally reached. Up here, you will be paddling among the crags and Pennine moors at 185m above sea level.

Additional information

Premier Inn, Runcorn is just over a kilometre from the Bridgewater Canal where it passes beneath the A56 at Preston Brook (www.premierinn.com). Manchester YHA is beside the Castlefield Basin where the Bridgewater and Rochdale Canals meet (www.yha.org.uk). Travelodge, Oldham is next to the Rochdale Canal just to the north of where it passes beneath the M60 (www. travelodge.co.uk).

Variations

Most stretches of the Bridgewater Canal have plenty of access points. There are possibilities for fitness training, day trips or paddles to any of the canal-side pubs.

26

Rochdale Canal Summit to Goole 🖼🏠📞

No. 27 | **Grade A** | **106km** | **OS Sheets 103–105 and 110**

Start	West Summit Lock (SD 947 188)
Finish	Goole Boathouse (SE 735 226)
No. Locks	69
Access	British Waterways license BCU members to use these canals. Proof of membership may occasionally be requested.

Introduction

From the Summit section, the Rochdale Canal descends steeply into West Yorkshire via the steep-sided and wooded valley of Calderdale. The descent takes you through the market and mill towns of Todmorden, Hebden Bridge and Mytholmroyd, where there are plenty of shops, pubs and places to stay.

The Rochdale Canal then meets the Calder and Hebble Navigation at Sowerby Bridge. By the time Brighouse Basin is reached, 46 of the 69 locks will be behind you and you will have descended 130m in height. Completing this section will likely take 3–4 days.

Description

The Summit section of the Rochdale Canal runs alongside the A6033 road that runs between Littleborough and Todmorden. It is little more than a kilometre in length, with Longlees Lock at its northern end. From here the canal descends steeply over 5km through 15 locks into Todmorden. Some of the locks are less than 200m apart, making paddling between them impractical. However, paddling beneath the Great Wall of Todmorden provides the perfect grand entrance to the town. This man-made cliff of 4 million bricks is the retaining wall that was built in the 1830s to carry the Manchester to Leeds railway.

After Todmorden there are fewer locks and progress is easier. Steep banks with woodland and stone terraced houses lead the way to Hebden Bridge. On the outskirts of the town, the Stubbing Wharf pub is an excellent place to stop for refreshment before portaging the two locks into Hebden Bridge itself. The Alternative Technology Centre is beside the canal and provides an entertaining distraction with its interactive models and displays. There is also a nearby Co-op supermarket as well as other local shops for supplies.

With fewer locks, the canal becomes increasingly popular with narrowboat owners; moorings line the banks for much of the way to Mytholmroyd. Along this stretch, the Calderdale valley has a mixture of farmland, housing and industrial areas that lead into Sowerby Bridge. The Tuel Lane lock now replaces the original number 3 and 4 locks. With a fall of over 6m, it is the deepest lock in the UK. The portage route is across the adjacent car park, downhill along Tuel Lane and across Wharf Street where the towpath can be re-joined. The towpath then leads past locks 1 and 2 into the Sowerby Bridge Canal Basin and the Calder and Hebble Navigation.

Heading east out of town, Calderdale is a broader valley with woodland on both sides of the canal. This is a pleasant stretch of over 3km, after which a flight of three locks is reached at Salterhebble. The busy A629 runs parallel at the top of a wooded bank. Cars and lorries roar past, temporarily shattering the rural peace.

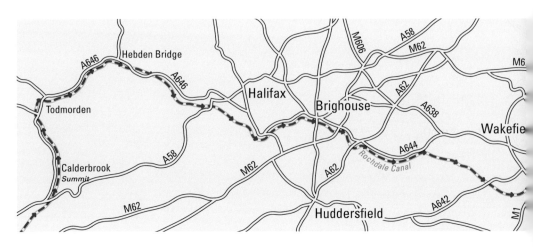

© Gorillas at Mytholmroyd | Jean Brown

After passing through Elland, the approach to Brighouse becomes quiet once again. The canal sits between wooded banks with Brookfoot Lake on one side and the River Calder on the other. Brighouse is a bustling town with a wealth of shops and pubs, and you can paddle right into the middle of town. The easiest place to land is in a small public garden area on the south bank. The food at Blakeley's fish and chip shop on Canal Street is delicious. The town's two supermarkets are close to the Brighouse canal basin.

After Brighouse Basin, the Calder and Hebble Navigation joins the River Calder in its flatter sections. Short stretches of canal with locks by-pass steeper sections of the river. When the river

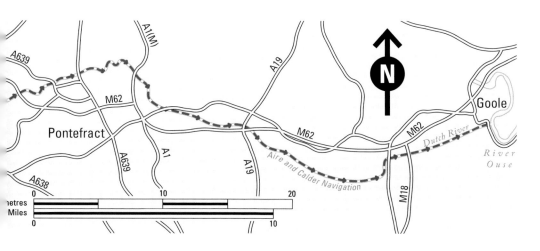

Rochdale Canal Summit to Goole

is in flood, lock gates to the canal sections are closed to protect them, effectively closing off the section between Brighouse and Knottingley. Where lock gates give access to river sections, there are colour-coded river-level gauge boards. If the level is in the green band, this indicates normal levels. The amber band indicates above-normal levels, but you should be able to proceed with caution. If the red band is showing, this indicates flood levels and the gates to the next section will be closed.

Cooper Bridge Junction near Mirfield is where the Huddersfield Broad Canal joins the Calder and Hebble Navigation. This section of waterway caters for larger craft; the landing stages also tend to be bigger. Some of the landing stages are 1–1.5m high which can make the whole process of portaging locks a little trickier than at previous sections.

Once through the towns of Horbury and Wakefield, the scenery opens up with a more rural feel. After Fall Ing Lock, the Calder and Hebble Navigation meets the Aire and Calder Navigation, which leads the way towards Castleford. Just before Castleford, Whitwood Wharf is used by industrial barges for the transportation of aggregates. It is important to keep a look out for these barges. Their skippers will be aware of smaller craft, but it is better to make way for them as they are less manoeuvrable and can create a considerable wash.

At Castleford Junction, the waterway splits into two. The north branch links with the Leeds and Liverpool Canal and the east branch leads to Knottingley and Goole. Following the course of the River Aire, the route twists and winds its way past the RSPB nature reserve of Fairburn Ings. It is common to see kingfishers and herons along the willow-lined banks.

© Rochdale Canal Summit section | Jean Brown

All too soon, the route enters the grimy industrial landscape of Knottingley with the Ferrybridge power station cooling towers in the background. At Bank Dole Junction the south fork leads onto the final 26km leg, with only 2 locks between here and the port of Goole. This last section runs across low-lying open farmland, leaving it exposed to the winds. Before entering the port of Goole, there is a grassy quayside on the south bank that leads to the Goole Boathouse Marina buildings.

Additional information

The Cross Keys Inn at Walsden is on the A6033 road between Summit and Todmorden and backs onto the Rochdale Canal. Accommodation is available as well as bar meals (tel. 01706 815185). Black Bull Inn at Brighouse is less than 100m from the Calder and Hebble Navigation. There are home-cooked bar meals as well as bed and breakfast accommodation (tel. 01484 710 493; www.blackbullbrighouse.co.uk).

The Bridge Inn is around 300m along woodland paths from Whitwood Wharf, near Castleford on the Aire and Calder Navigation. There is an excellent choice of home-cooked food and fine ales, as well as accommodation (tel. 01977 519696; www.thebridgeinncastleford.co.uk).

There is a chandlery at the Goole boathouse and marina. The helpful staff have good local knowledge (tel. 01405 763985; www.gooleboathouse.co.uk).

Portaging locks above Todmorden | Jean Brown

Variations

If you plan to continue on to the Humber, the Dutch River is just across the road that runs past the marina. The banks are steep and grassy with mud beneath, but it is possible to launch here if you are careful. From here, the Dutch River flows into the River Ouse which joins the Trent to become the River Humber.

The Humber Bridge | Jean Brown

 # The Humber Estuary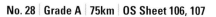

No. 28 | Grade A | 75km | OS Sheet 106, 107

Tidal Port	Immingham
Start	△ Humber Street, Old Goole (SE 750 227)
Finish	◯ Spurn Head (TA 400 111)
HW/LW	HW at Goole is 1 hour 20 minutes after Immingham and LW is 3 hours 50 minutes after Immingham. HW and LW at Humber Bridge are around 30 minutes after Immingham. HW and LW at Spurn Head are 25 minutes before Immingham.
Tidal Times	At Goole, the out-going stream begins around 1 hour 40 minutes after HW Immingham. The in-going stream begins around 3 hours before HW Immingham.
	At Kingston upon Hull, the out-going stream begins around 45 minutes after HW Immingham and the in-going stream begins around 4 hours 50 minutes before HW Immingham.
	At Spurn Bight, the out-going stream begins around HW Immingham and the in-going stream begins around 5 hours 30 minutes before HW Immingham.
Max Rate Sp	At Goole and Kingston upon Hull, the maximum tidal stream is 4–5 knots; 3 knots at Spurn Bight.
Coastguard	Humber, tel. 01262 672 317, VHF weather every 3 hours from 0150

© The Dutch River, Goole | Jean Brown

28

The Humber Estuary

Introduction

Where the tidal reaches of the rivers Trent and Ouse meet, the Humber estuary is born. The result is a huge sheltered tideway that not only serves the ports of Goole and Kingston upon Hull, but is also bristling with wildlife. A determined athlete could do the journey from Goole to Spurn Head in one day with a suitable tide. It is more usual to take two days, however, breaking the journey at either Humber Bridge or the village of Paull. This area is also popular with long-distance walkers and cyclists, as it forms part of the Trans-Pennine Trail.

Description

The industrial town and port of Goole is signposted at Junction 36 on the M62 motorway. On the south side of the port there is a bridge where the A161 crosses the Dutch River. On the south of the bridge lies the district of Old Goole. The main road runs alongside the Dutch River and then bends round to the right. The second turning on the left is Humber Street, which leads to a grassy area beside the River Ouse. It is best to launch here at HW Goole. The River Ouse is broad and steep muddy banks are revealed below dense reed beds soon after high water has passed, leaving few opportunities to get off the water.

After passing the villages of Swinefleet, Saltmarshe and Whitgift, you will reach the Blacktoft Channel. The village of Blacktoft, with its old customs jetty and pub, sits on the north bank. The south bank is occupied by the RSPB Blacktoft Sands reserve from here to the confluence with the River Trent. The place where the River Trent and the River Ouse meet is known as Trent

Falls. Downstream, a low-lying muddy and reed-infested island called Whitton Sand plays an important role as the Humber Wildfowl Refuge. With the waters of the Ouse and Trent combined, the flow becomes stronger. In the distance, it may be possible to see the Humber Bridge although it is still more than 12km away. From here onwards, the best flow tends to be in the channel off the north bank.

The beach beneath the north end of the Humber Bridge is the only place along these shores where it is possible to land without sinking up to your knees in sticky mud – 31km after the starting point. The Humber Rescue boat and other water users frequently use the pebbly shore and slipway. There is a car park with toilets as well as a modern pub and restaurant set among the grounds of the Humber Bridge Country Park.

Downstream, the green suburb of Hessle sweeps down to the shore with gardens and playing fields. The first of the Hull quays is St Andrews Quay. There are no ships these days, and the surrounding land has been regenerated with a modern trading estate. The entrance to Albert Dock heralds the approach to Kingston upon Hull and its modern waterfront. The wedge-shaped building that stands beside the confluence with the River Hull is an aquarium complex known as The Deep.

Humber Bridge

Construction of the Humber Bridge began in 1973, and by the time it was open to traffic in 1981 this mighty structure dwarfed everything in sight. The two supporting towers are 155.5m high and stand nearly 1.5km apart. With a total length of 2.2km, this was the longest single-span suspension bridge in the world until 1989.

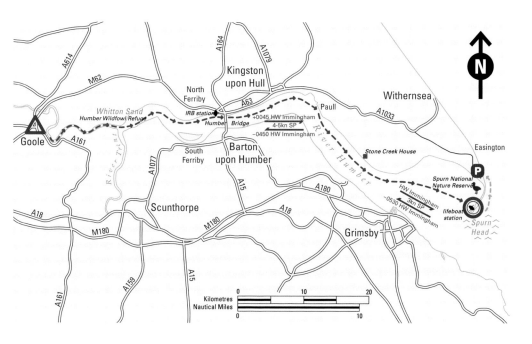

The River Ouse near Trent Falls

Further on, as the Humber turns to the south, huge car ferries and container ships operate from King George Dock and the adjacent jetty. Keeping an ear out for chatter on VHF channel 12 will keep you informed of any vessel movements in this area. The Salt End petrochemical jetties herald the village of Paull.

The beach to the south of the old Paull lighthouse is made up of shingle and pebbles, but dries to mud below half tide. This is the easiest landing between Humber Bridge and Spurn Head. The old lighthouse was built in 1836 by Trinity House but was decommissioned within 40 years to be replaced by a pair of newer lights on nearby Thorngumbald Clough. There are three pubs in Paull which all serve excellent food. There is parking in the nearby village streets and at the southern end of the playing field.

As you continue south from the village shore, broad beaches of sand and mud stretch into the distance towards Hawkins Point. This is the beginning of the 12km-wide south-facing bay of Spurn Bight. It is common to completely lose sight of the surrounding low-lying land while crossing this expanse.

Spurn Head forms the eastern side of the bay at the mouth of the estuary. The lighthouse and nearby buildings will be visible before the thin strip of land comes into view. Spurn Head, including the foreshore down to the low water mark, is a nature reserve that is owned and managed by the Yorkshire Wildlife Trust. If you wish to land on the sandy beach between the old lighthouses and the Humber Pilot jetty, seek permission first from the Yorkshire Wildlife Trust (tel. 01964 659570; www.ywt.org.uk); it may not always be possible or appropriate for permission to be given.

There is a car park from which a road leads off the reserve and through the village of Kilnsea.

Tides and weather

The out-going ebb stream tends to be stronger and longer lasting than the in-going flood. This is increased with high river levels after heavy rain.

Winds from the east and southeast tend to funnel up the river making progress difficult. Strong winds from any direction cause gusty conditions around the Humber Bridge.

Additional information

In addition to contacting the coastguard, it is important to contact Vessel Traffic Services (VTS) Humber before launching and to follow any advice they give with regards to vessel traffic on the river. Telephone 01482 212191 or call on your VHF radio (call sign 'VTS Humber') on channel 12, 14 or 15 for sections Humber Bridge to Spurn Head, Goole to Trent Falls and Trent Falls to Humber Bridge, respectively.

Whitgift Hall Caravan and Camping site is quiet with basic facilities. The site is 8km from Goole through the villages of Swinefleet and Reedness (tel. 01405 704283). Country Park Inn and Lodge overlooks the river in the shadow of the Humber Bridge. There is a café/bar and pub-style food is served. There is also good-quality budget accommodation in the lodge (tel. 01482 640526; www.countryparkinn.co.uk).

Variations

Starting at Goole and finishing at Paull is the best way to make the most of the area, and can be done in one day. Another popular day trip starts at the Humber Bridge: paddle with the flood to the Trent Falls area for some bird watching before returning with the ebb.

The Yorkshire Coast

Introduction

From Flamborough Head to Saltburn-by-the-Sea, this coastline is dominated by monstrous cliffs. The Yorkshire Wolds and North York Moors meet the erosive persistence and might of the restless North Sea at England's eastern fringe. The North Sea grinds and gnaws its way into relatively soft chalk and Jurassic shales. The result is a steep, gnarly coastline of high cliffs that are footed by boulder beaches, jagged reefs and wave-cut platforms. Where the coastal landscape relents, there are long sandy beaches with attendant Victorian holiday resorts such as those at Bridlington, Filey, Scarborough and Whitby. These seaside towns have their historical foundations set deeply in seafaring, with exploration, trade, fishing and smuggling forming essential building blocks.

Parts of the east Yorkshire coast are receding at alarming rates that can exceed a metre per year. In some places this leads to landslides. Larger landslides of historic importance are well documented near Runswick Bay; along the Holderness coast, entire villages have disappeared beneath the waves. The seaside town of Robin Hood's Bay has recently benefited from an award-winning civil engineering project that has stabilised almost 1km of steep cliffs.

As the cliffs are eroded, reefs known as wave-cut platforms are left behind. Huge expanses of these reefs are exposed at low water revealing a world full of rock pools among seaweed-smothered rocks. Some of these reefs extend more than a kilometre offshore beyond the low water mark; in all but calm seas, these areas can become dangerous when swell breaks heavily on them.

There are relatively few sandy beaches along this part of the east coast of England. Access to the sea for even a small group of paddlers can be a significant challenge in the planning of any voyage. The steep, winding and narrow streets of Staithes and Robin Hood's Bay are not at all suitable for cars and trailers laden with long kayaks. The larger seaside towns such as Scarborough, Whitby and Saltburn are better because they have grown up around the needs of seaside tourism. In the busy summer months, timing your trip with the traffic can be almost as important as tidal planning. Yorkshire's seaside resorts expanded rapidly following the development of the railways, making it possible to plan overnight trips and extended voyages along this coast using the train or coastal bus services instead of shuttling cars.

Tides and weather

The tidal streams along this section are not generally all that strong and it is possible to make progress against them in all but a few places. The flood stream runs generally southeast and the ebb northwest, giving rise to the saying 'flood to Flamborough, ebb to Edinburgh'. The streams do not coincide with the timings of high and low water. Sustained winds from the north can extend and strengthen the SE-going tidal streams.

Local weather and tidal streams are comparatively easy to predict in comparison to the ocean swell that influences this coast. The North Sea is restless and relentless. From the Dutch coast in the south, this expanse of water extends far to its permanently frozen state at the North Pole. Arctic storms with hurricane-force winds generate phenomenal sea states. The fallout from this weather reaches England's east coast in the form of ocean swell that makes rocky reefs and headlands hazardous and long sandy beaches a surfer's paradise.

Gentle summer sea breezes can bring thick fog locally known as 'sea fret'. This fret can develop in a matter of minutes without warning and dissolve just as quickly; more often than not, however, it will last for hours until early evening. The skies over the Yorkshire coast can be biblically dramatic. The prevailing south-westerlies drag wrung-out remains of rain clouds out to sea. This leaves the sky with the classic Yorkshire coast look of dark broody patches sliced by piercing shafts of brilliant sunlight.

Further information

For more information, see:

Forth, Tyne, Dogger, Humber: A cruising guide from Blakeney to St Abbs, Henry Irving, Imray 2002, 0 85288 578-4.

For surf and swell forecasts, see www.surf-forecast.com and www.magicseaweed.com.

Spurn Head at dusk

 # Spurn Head

No. 29 | Grade A | 14km | OS Sheet 107

Tidal Port	Immingham
Start	△ Kilnsea Beach (TA 419 159)
Finish	○ The Crown and Anchor, Kilnsea (TA 409 158)
HW/LW	Around 15 minutes before Immingham
Tidal Times	On the seaward side of Spurn, the S-going stream begins around 6 hours before HW Immingham and the N-going stream begins around HW Immingham. In the entrance to the Humber, the incoming stream begins around 5 hours 30 minutes before HW Immingham and the outgoing stream begins around 30 minutes after HW Immingham.
Max Rate Sp	2–3 knots on the seaward side of Spurn; 4 knots in the entrance to the Humber
Coastguard	Humber, tel. 01262 672 317, VHF weather every 3 hours from 0150

Introduction

Spurn Head is a fragile spit of land comprising sand and pebbles bound together with marram grass and sea buckthorn. This 6km long spit is less than 50m wide in places. Spurn protects the

29

Spurn Head

Humber like a huge breakwater, keeping the North Sea at bay. It also provides shelter and food to thousands of migrating birds, making this a birdwatcher's paradise. This Site of Special Scientific Interest (SSSI) is owned and managed by the Yorkshire Wildlife Trust, who discourage landing upon any of the beaches that are part of the nature reserve. You should aim to finish the trip at the Crown and Anchor pub at (or shortly before) high water – but not much later than that!

Description

The village of Kilnsea is at the southernmost tip of the Holderness peninsula. As you drive through you will pass the Crown and Anchor pub just before a sharp left-hand bend where the road runs beside the Humber Estuary. The car park at Kilnsea Beach is only 750m further on. There is a car park, toilets and the restored café. Erosion regularly exposes the steep face of the low cliffs formed of glacial clay. Carrying kayaks down this steep slippery drop can be a little awkward.

Steep shingle beaches littered with skeletal remains of groynes arc away to the south. Although the beaches along the spit seem remote, they are often well attended by sea anglers, birdwatchers and other folk out to enjoy a brisk walk in the sea air.

As you approach the end and draw level with the lighthouse you may notice the agitated waters over Stony Binks, a bank of sand, shingle and pebbles that runs to the east from Spurn Head and dries at low water. It has formed where the south-going offshore tidal stream meets the east-going ebb stream from the Humber estuary. When heavy swell or strong winds are from the southeast, this area can kick up threatening and chaotic seas. On quieter days, it can be a pleasure to play here among the gently surging standing waves. It is usually possible to find smoother waters between Stony Binks and Spurn Head.

Rounding Spurn Head and its steep pebbly beaches will bring you to the strangely calm waters of the Humber Estuary. If the Humber Lifeboat is at its mooring then it will come into view shortly before you see the end of the pier used by the Humber pilots. Looking southwest, you will be able to spot the Bull Sand Fort 2.5km across the water.

The warren at the end of Spurn is occupied by The Pilot station, Humber Vessel Traffic Services (VTS), and is the only permanently manned lifeboat station in the UK.

The most recent of the lighthouses at Spurn is known as the High Light and stands among the dunes north of the lifeboat station. It was built in 1895 as the foundations of the previous structure began to crumble away. The lighthouse was decommissioned in 1985. The lighthouse tower that stands on the adjacent foreshore is known as the Low Light and was built in 1852.

The inner shore forms a huge bay that is rich in birdlife. Wading birds feed here at low water and roost among shingles and vegetation at the high water mark, where they are vulnerable to disturbance.

With good timing you will arrive on the small shingle beach just across the road from the brightly painted Crown and Anchor pub. Arrive too early or too late and you will have a squelchy walk across smelly, sticky Humber Estuary mud.

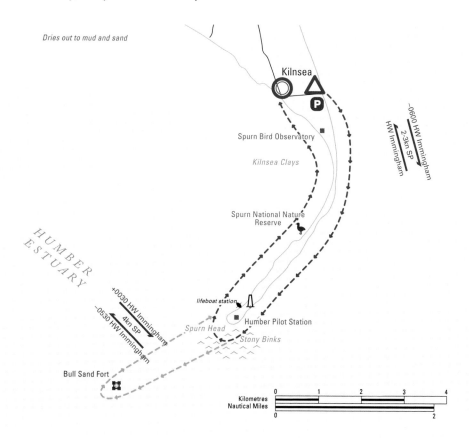

Tides and weather

The seaward side of the headland is exposed to winds and swell from the northeast, east and southeast with dumping surf on the steep shingle beaches. South-easterlies can give rise to confused breaking seas at Stony Binks. A spring tide will be needed to completely cover the mud flats beyond the sandy beach at The Crown and Anchor pub.

Additional information

The Spurn Heritage Coast tea room and exhibition is an old house adjacent to the car park at Kilnsea Beach. The homemade cakes, pies and puddings that are sold here are excellent. The proprietors also run the Farmhouse Bed and Breakfast nearby (telephone 01964 650 528).

The Crown and Anchor pub serves good-value bar meals and a range of fine ales. The management are particular about cleanliness and behaviour, so remember to bring clean, dry clothes.

The only campsiite in the area is the Driftwood Caravan and Camping site (01964 650 208).

Variations

This trip can be done in reverse as long as you are confident that you can land safely through the surf on Kilnsea Beach. For additional interest, you might consider including a visit to Bull Sand Fort (TA 370 093). This will add an extra 5km to the trip, but there is nowhere to land. It is vitally important that you contact VTS Humber (telephone 01482 591 825, VHF channel 12) before crossing the shipping lanes to get to and from the fort.

Flamborough Head

Flamborough Head 🪨🔲🔷🌊

30

No. 30 | Grade C | 24km | OS Sheet 101

Tidal Port	North Shields
Start	△ Flamborough South Landing (TA 231 692)
Finish	◯ Filey Beach (TA 121 809)
HW/LW	Around 1 hour 15 minutes after North Shields; around 1 hour after North Shields at Filey
Tidal Times	Off Flamborough Head, the NW-going stream starts around 3 hours after HW North Shields. The SE-going stream starts around 2 hours 30 minutes before HW North Shields.
Max Rate Sp	Along the exposed sections of the headland, rates can reach 2–3 knots (1–2 knots is more typical for the rest of the route)
Coastguard	Humber, tel. 01262 672 317, VHF weather every 3 hours from 0150

Introduction

This is where the tough chalk layers of the Yorkshire Wolds finally yield to the power of the North Sea. Flamborough Head juts out over 8km beyond the gentle shores of Bridlington and Filey. The seas here are rarely calm and the regular surges and explosive swell have carved gullies,

arches and huge caves into the dazzlingly white cliffs. As if nature's architecture were not enough, this is home to thousands of seabirds that nest among the cliffs each spring. In flight, their sheer numbers create aerial displays of Hitchcock proportions.

Description

The pretty village of Flamborough can be found by driving east from Bridlington along the B1255 or southeast from Filey along the A165 and then the B1229. Once in the village the street names give vital clues: South Sea Road leads to South Landing, North Marine Road leads to North Landing and there are few prizes handed out for guessing where Lighthouse Road leads. At the foot of South Sea Road there is a lifeboat station with limited parking for crew. Boats can be unloaded here but you must park your car at the top of the steep hill in the Pay & Display car park beside the Boathouse Café. The beach at South Landing is formed of large white rocks and pebbles, with sand lower down. South Cliff rises to almost 40m from the sea as it leads the way to High Stacks and Flamborough Head. The pebbly beach at the foot of South Cliff is built upon a gently sloping wave-cut platform.

As you approach High Stacks, the wave-cut platform extends eastwards into reefs. Any North Sea swell will make itself known in the shallows here. High Stacks is a complex network of chalk towers, reefs and arches with a couple of secluded pebbly beaches thrown in for good measure. Although a delightful cruise on a calm sunny day, this could become a demolition derby for kayaks when swell is running from the east or southeast. The sounds of wading birds at South Cliff are now replaced by the distinctive call of kittiwakes squabbling over real estate. Beyond this point stands Flamborough Head itself, the most easterly point in northern England. This mighty headland guards the depths of Selwicks Bay from the south. Once in Selwicks Bay, you will be able to view the lighthouse and radio mast.

The old lighthouse was constructed in the early 1670s. Thanks to restoration work arranged by local volunteers, the chalk tower remains the oldest lighthouse still standing in Britain. The new lighthouse was built in 1806 and stands over 26m tall. This gives the light an elevation of 65m over the sea, so it can be seen from over 40km away.

The cliffs astride the shingle beaches of Selwicks Bay can be a kayakers' mystery tour. Some gullies lead round blind corners to a dead end and some lead into caves and blowholes. While some caves may lead into another opening, others are seemingly endless and dark. Continuing along from Selwicks Bay you will engage the north-facing shores of Flamborough. The cliffs are higher and rougher, supporting squadrons of razorbills and guillemots. Keep an eye out for anglers: lines are cast from the 40m cliff tops to over 100m out and can be difficult to see. One such popular fishing spot is the promontory known as Breil Nook. This area is often the most exposed to swell and the waters here are rarely smooth. On the rare occasions when the sea is calm enough, paddling into the deep gullies and caves is awe-inspiring as the rising cliffs loom over you.

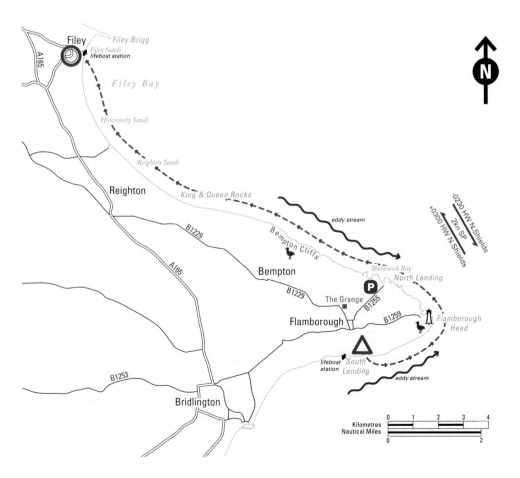

North Landing (TA 239 721) is a cosy spot for a break. This deep bay is well protected from the prevailing weather by high cliffs and from the swell by reefs at its entrance. There is also a car park, toilets and a café. South Landing is a little over 3km away by road or 6km by way of the coastal footpath, so a walk back to the car at this stage might appeal if the conditions are not favourable.

Surf's up at Filey

I've always had fond childhood memories of Filey but my keenest memory is of the day I finally got my surfing together. I'd been working too hard for too long and took the day off for a little mid-week solo paddling. I headed south for Flamborough but never got there as I was seduced by the waves near Hunmanby Gap. It all came together: mental rehearsal; feel the lift and the acceleration as the boat catches the wave and the nose dips; stern rudder; edge the boat. I felt the power from the blade through my arms all the way down my body to the footrests – I was part of the sea for run after liberating run. In my rapture I didn't notice the squall come in, but suddenly found myself on bottle green water drenched by rain which was backlit by the sun. Perhaps I should have got off the water when I saw the lightning offshore, but it was too precious. More runs, laughing and whooping. I imagine anyone who saw a grinning, exhausted, solitary, salty madman emerging from the rain to land at Filey that afternoon must have wondered what on earth he had been up to. But they would have known from my face that it had been very, very good.

By Bob Mark

Thornwick Bay lies just next door to the west of North Landing and has a wider, more open, feel. Looking west from Thornwick, the cliffs begin to take on a more solid appearance as they rise vertically to over 80m from the sea. After 2km, North Cliff runs into Bempton Cliffs. These towering northern edges are home to hundreds of thousands of nesting seabirds. The rock arch of Scale Nab at Bempton has the only gannetry on the British mainland coast.

The further west you paddle, the higher the cliffs rise. At the point where Buckton cliffs run into Speeton cliffs, the tops reach 135m in height. All too soon, however, the drama is over. The coastline at last becomes gentler as you approach the King and Queen Rocks, with steep grassy slopes descending to a sandy beach known as Reighton Sands.

The Reighton Sands Holiday Village commands a glorious view from above, but sadly provides no road access to the sea. The surf between here and Hunmanby Gap can be great sport. As you head further along the sprawling beaches, the surf tends to peter out due to the shelter afforded by Filey Brigg. Easier, happy landings can be found on the beach beneath the Victorian promenade, beside the lifeboat station 5km away at Filey.

Tides and weather

The shores of Flamborough Head are exposed, committing and vulnerable to winds from any direction and swell from north, east and south. South Landing and Filey Sands are well sheltered from the prevailing north-easterly swell.

At the peak of the tidal flows, east-going eddies develop between South Landing and High Stacks and between Bempton Cliffs and Breil Nook. This results in an almost constant east-

going stream along both these shores that rarely exceeds 1 knot.

Additional information

The hope is that the Boathouse Café (burnt by vandals in 2009) at Flamborough will be re-built very soon. There are also cafés at North Landing and the lighthouse car park. The lighthouse is open to the public for guided tours.

Thorpe Hall Caravan and Camping site at Rudston is several kilometres inland but is quiet and sheltered with a shop on site (01262 420 393, www.thorpehall.co.uk). The Bosville Arms in Rudston village does good food and B&B accommodation.

The Grange campsite on Bempton Lane is just outside the village of Flamborough and is a little more basic (01262 850 207).

Variations

This trip can easily be done in reverse. Filey is a busy summer resort and parking is difficult in the congested streets. Starting here early in the morning can make for a more pleasurable experience; by paddling south, the trip builds to a natural crescendo as you round Flamborough Head 3km from the finish.

A popular variation is to paddle from South Landing to the Bempton Arch to see the gannets before heading back to either South Landing or North Landing.

Filey to Scarborough ⚲📘⛱

No. 31 | **Grade B** | **15km** | **OS Sheet 101**

Tidal Port	North Shields
Start	△ Filey, Coble Landing (TA 120 808)
Finish	○ Scarborough Lifeboat Station (TA 047 887)
HW/LW	At Scarborough, 50 minutes after North Shields
Tidal Times	The NW-going stream starts around 3 hours after HW North Shields. The SE-going stream starts around 2 hours 30 minutes before HW North Shields.
Max Rate Sp	2 knots around the end of Filey Brigg
Coastguard	Humber, tel. 01262 672 317, VHF weather every 3 hours from 0150

Introduction

Filey and Scarborough are two typically British but very different seaside resorts. Filey is quiet and has a Victorian elegance. Scarborough is the biggest and most brash holiday resort on the Yorkshire coast. The coastline between could hardly be in greater contrast. Tall gnarly cliffs, sheltered rocky inlets and surf breaks will keep anyone paddling this coast entertained.

Description

The town of Filey can be found off the A165 coast road between Bridlington and Scarborough. If you arrive on a quiet day or early in the morning, there may be spaces in the Pay and Display parking beside the lifeboat station at the northern end of the sea front. There are also public toilets, cafés and a RNLI shop. Additional parking is usually available nearby on Ravine Road. The gently shelving, sandy beach either side of the main slipway becomes completely submerged at high water. At the north end of the promenade just beyond the cafés and shops, there is a more sheltered slipway. This is Coble Landing, from which small fishing boats called cobles are still launched. This slipway is higher up the beach, more sheltered and can be used at any state of the tide.

Once on the water head for Filey Brigg and get exploring, but don't forget to take a look over your shoulder at the pretty seafront and Victorian terraces. Filey Brigg is a natural breakwater that provides shelter to the bay from the north. The Filey Brigg Ornithological Group has a hide on the headland and this area is also popular with anglers. The south side is lined with boulders and shingle thought to be the remains of a medieval or Roman landing stage. Tidal streams around the end rarely exceed 2 knots but can develop into overfalls in wind against tide conditions. This is the most exposed part of this route. The north side consists of angled slabs of sandstone and limestone, housing deep and clear kelp-infested lagoons.

As you paddle east, the blocky cliffs rise sharply from the sea with intriguing gullies and a stunning rock arch. Filey's North Cliff leads along towards Cunstone Nab with boulders, steep pebbly beaches and deep water below. The rocky layers are overlaid with boulder clay and the cliff tops rise steadily to an impressive 80m.

At Cunstone Nab there is a definite change: there are shallows at high water and swell breaks explosively offshore upon Old Horse Rocks and Castle Rocks. These reefs extend over 500m out to sea and are the remains of ancient cliffs eroded over time. These expansive wave-cut platforms are common along the Yorkshire coast. As the tide goes out, kelp-infested gullies and sandy-bottomed lagoons provide happy hunting for seals and exploratory fun for paddlers.

A weakness in the reef beyond Yons Nab allows swell from the northeast to break more grace-fully upon a broad sandy beach in a relatively sheltered bay. This is the popular surf beach of Cayton Bay. There are good reef breaks at either end of the bay, and it is wise to take care here as the water can be alarmingly shallow. The proximity of several holiday parks gives Cayton broad appeal despite the steep descent from the road above. As the bay sweeps round to the north, tree-lined slopes offer the first splash of greenery along this coast. The steep wooded slopes are prone to landslips and a Second World War pill box that was on the cliff now squats awkwardly on the sands. This area of the bay known locally as Johnny Flinton's Harbour was once an official naturist beach but the local council have since rescinded this designation.

As you approach Osgodby Point, or Knipe Point as it is sometimes known, the sandy beach is replaced by boulders and layered rocks that continue around into the next bay. Clear views across the water to Scarborough can be enjoyed on rounding the point. Cornelian Bay also has slopes with plenty of greenery. The slopes cascade down to a small sheltered beach beyond which there is a shallow lagoon hemmed in by rocky reefs.

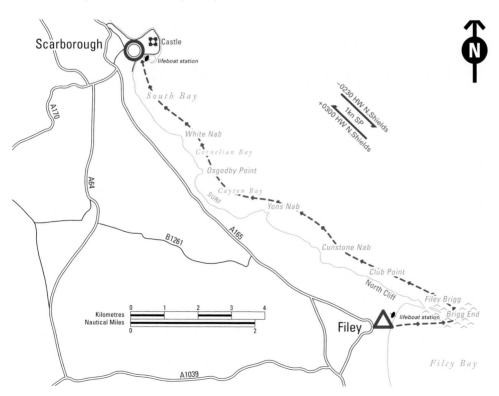

© Gristhorpe Cliff and North Cliff

White Nab and the aptly named Black Rocks herald the southern extent of Scarborough's South Bay and soon the wilderness is replaced with Victorian splendour. A promenade runs along the shore beneath South Cliff Gardens leading to the popular South Sands. Landing is usually most sheltered beside the lifeboat station where there is Pay and Display parking along the old harbour wall.

Tides and weather

Tidal streams are relatively weak along this section. Streams can exceed 2 knots at Filey Brigg, however, and overfalls can develop especially when the wind direction opposes that of the tide.

Additional information

There is a convenience store on Murray Street, Filey (near the promenade) and the butcher's shop opposite does excellent bacon butties. The bakery next door has a whole host of sticky treats.

There is a pleasant campsite at Saxdale House Farm outside the nearby village of Hunmanby (01723 892346). The village has three pubs, a village store and a fast food takeaway.

Variations

This trip can easily be done in reverse. For a longer day, you could paddle to Scarborough for a fish supper before paddling back to Filey.

 Looking north from Scarborough's headland

Scarborough to Robin Hood's Bay

32

No. 32 | Grade C | 20km | OS Sheet 101 & 94

Tidal Port	North Shields
Start	△ Scarborough Lifeboat Station (TA 047 887)
Finish	◯ Boggle Hole (NZ 955 040)
HW/LW	Around 45 minutes after North Shields
Tidal Times	The NW-going stream starts around 3 hours after HW North Shields. The SE-going stream starts around 2 hours 30 minutes before HW North Shields.
Max Rate Sp	2 knots around the Scarborough headland
Coastguard	Humber, tel. 01262 672 317, VHF weather every 3 hours from 0150

Introduction

You only have to paddle a short distance along this trip before Scarborough's towering headland and castle grab your attention. Once away from Scarborough, the low cliffs and rolling landscape

32

gradually build to a crescendo as you arrive beneath the towering crags of Ravenscar. This is where the North York Moors meet the North Sea. A geological weakness has allowed the sea to take a huge bite at the landscape, leaving rocky scars and shallow lagoons with crumbling cliffs beyond. This bight forms the Jurassic amphitheatre that is Robin Hood's Bay.

Description

Scarborough is a bustling seaside holiday resort. There is a handy car park between the lifeboat station and the harbour on Foreshore Road that runs along the South Bay promenade. Keep your eyes and ears open as you pass the harbour entrance, which can be surprisingly busy with fishing boats and pleasure craft. The ruined Scarborough Castle stands high upon the gently sloping ground on top of the headland.

Scarborough's North Bay is popular with surfers when the swell runs from the north and east. The Sea Life Centre, with its distinctive pyramid roofs, stands just to the south of Scalby Ness Rocks. Along the next 3km beyond Scalby Ness, there is a series of shallow lagoons bound by small reefs that offer delightful rock-hopping all the way past Cromer Point to Long Nab. Between the lagoons and the low cliffs are steep beaches of shingle and pebbles and, in places, access to the Cleveland Way coastal path above. The coastline grows in stature as you pass Long Nab and Hundale Point, becoming steeper and blockier as Cloughton Wyke is reached.

Along the Yorkshire coast, the name 'Wyke' is typically given to a sheltered place where a small boat can be landed and its goods offloaded; the near vertical cliffs at Cloughton Wyke have slab ledges at the bottom that descend like amphitheatre steps to a beach of pebbles and boulders.

Paddling north from the small bay, the vertical cliffs back away to reveal steep grassy slopes topped with tall crags. A landslip in the distant past has left a grassy boulder-strewn platform called Rodger Trod slumped beside the sea. A little further to the north is Hayburn Wyke. The slopes of this small bay are lined with dense woodland from which a stream cascades onto the pebbly beach. Mossy streamers dangle precariously from ledges where the cliffs are too steep to support trees.

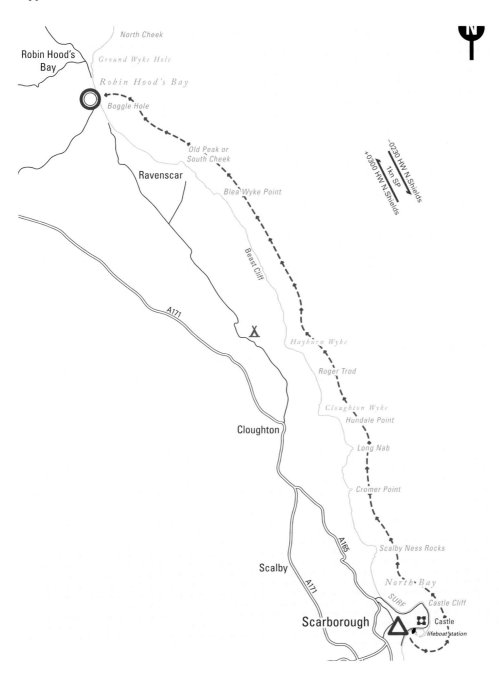

Who knows what horrors lurk high among the thickly vegetated slopes of Beast Cliff? Once you round the steep arête of Blea Wyke Point, the tallest of these towering cliffs leads the way to the headland of Old Peak and the reefs that mark the southern entrance to Robin Hood's Bay.

Boggle Hole lies another 3km along the bay from the headland (see Route 33). Robin Hood's Bay is backed with terrific rolling hills that are typical of the North York Moors. This bay becomes really intriguing at mid–low tide when a series of long curved reefs of Jurassic Mudstone, carved flat by wave action, are revealed. It is hardly surprising that seals from the nearby Ravenscar colony frequently come here to feed.

Tides and weather

With the exception of the start of this trip, this section is exposed to wind and swell from the north and east. As you paddle around the headland at Scarborough you will be exposed to winds from all directions. Between Scalby Ness and Blea Wyke Point there is good shelter from winds from the south and west, but you should beware of downdraughts from the cliffs. Winds from the west and southwest funnel out from Robin Hood's Bay, which can make the last few kilometres a hard slog.

Additional information

Lowfields Caravan and Camping Site (TA 001 975, tel. 01723 870574) is situated just over a kilometre inland from Hayburn Wyke. This quiet site is close enough to the sea for a stroll along the cliff-top path or down to Hayburn Wyke, and is conveniently close to Scarborough, Robin Hood's Bay and Whitby. The nearby Hayburn Wyke Inn does fine food and ales and welcomes outdoor types.

Variations

This route can be paddled just as easily in the opposite direction. Scarborough's North Bay can also be used as an alternative place to start, but it can be crowded with surfers and most of the main beach beneath the promenade completely floods at high water.

Scarborough Castle

Scarborough's prominent headland is recognised as having been of strategic importance since Roman times. The castle was originally built by William Le Gros, Earl of Yorkshire and Lord of Holderness, in the middle of the 12th century. Henry II seized the castle following his ascension to the throne in 1176, claiming that its construction was unauthorised. During the English Civil War Scarborough Castle changed hands a number of times through a series of dramatic sieges, and was further damaged when the German Navy shelled Scarborough during the First World War. The castle and the site of the Roman signal station are now managed by English Heritage (www.english-heritage.org.uk). The castle is open every day from April until the end of September (limited opening during the winter months).

 # Robin Hood's Bay to Whitby

No. 33 | Grade B | 13km | OS Sheet 94

Tidal Port	North Shields
Start	△ Boggle Hole (TA 955 040)
Finish	◎ Whitby Marina Slipway (TA 900 105)
HW/LW	Around 40 minutes after North Shields at Whitby
Tidal Times	The NW-going stream starts around 3 hours after HW North Shields. The SE-going stream starts around 2 hours 30 minutes before HW North Shields.
Max Rate Sp	Around 1.5 knots
Coastguard	Humber, tel. 01262 672 317, VHF weather every 3 hours from 0150

Introduction

You will be committed to these forbidding shores after leaving the shelter of Robin Hood's Bay. North Sea swell breaks upon the reefs at the foot of huge 70m cliffs. When the sea rests, it is possible to get closer and explore some of the exposed Jurassic foundations of the North York Moors. As you approach Whitby the cliffs ease and the drama fades away. The silhouette of Whitby Abbey and the welcoming arms of the harbour entrance signal the approach of calmer waters.

Description

A minor road leads from the A171 Scarborough to Whitby coast road to the Boggle Hole car park. From here, the road descends steeply to the beach through woodland alongside Mill Beck. This road is mostly used by the Youth Hostel Land Rover for bringing in supplies, but can also be used for launching and retrieving boats. Where the road meets the beach it is steep and narrow, allowing only limited space for turning. If you are not well practised at hill starts or have a dodgy handbrake, it may be best to carry your kayaks from the car park.

Paddling north from Boggle Hole gives a wonderful view of Robin Hood's Bay village and the rolling hillsides beyond. As soon as you leave the village behind, the cliffs along the northern shores of the bay become steep and imposing. These cliffs are constantly crumbling away and the resulting debris of boulders and huge broken slabs make a forbidding foreshore. It is upon this shore, just beyond North Cheek, that the 54 foot trawler Sarb J ran aground early in 1994. The nets became entangled in her propeller, leaving her adrift and at the mercy of the wind, tide and reefs. Attempts to tow her away failed so the crew were airlifted to safety. The vessel has remained perched high upon the rocky foreshore ever since.

To paddle beyond North Cheek is to paddle beyond the protection that it, and its associated reefs, give to Robin Hood's Bay. If there is a swell running then this is where you will begin to experience its true might. Breakers will form at the seaward edge of any reefs and crash violently at the base of the cliffs. In these conditions this is a truly committing paddle, because the next safe landing will not be until you reach Whitby Harbour. The cliffs are overhanging in places and the blocky nature of the rock makes this place truly overpowering. In calmer conditions it is possible to get more intimate with these shores (like sneaking a close look at a sleeping giant).

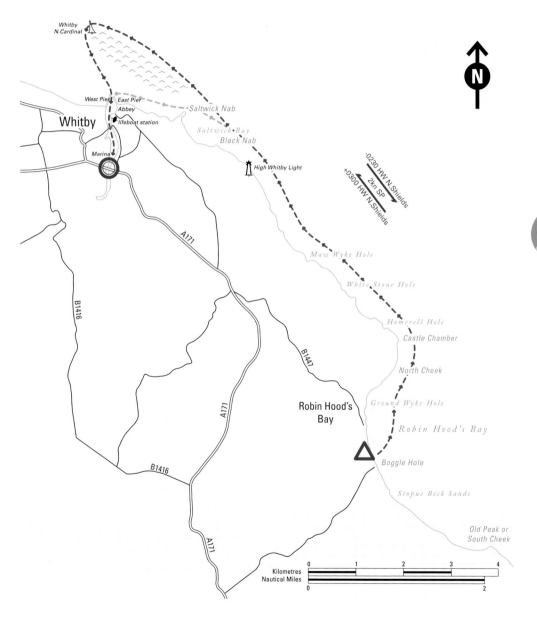

Robin Hood's Bay to Whitby

© High Whitby cliffs

The water at Maw Wyke Hole is deeper and calmer and, in settled conditions, can provide a welcome landing for a brief leg stretch. There is no escape route along this coast but it is amazing to see the descent routes sometimes taken by sea anglers. You might spot one of these paths by looking out for a fixed rope anchored high up the cliff. Steeper craggy sections sometimes have fixed ladders.

With the approach to Whitby Light and Fog Station, the coastline begins to take on a more westerly direction. The stacks and reefs of Black Nab and Saltwick Nab will come into view. When heavy swell runs from the north or east, it breaks explosively along these reefs which run continuously to the Whitby north cardinal mark. On a calm day, it is possible to pick your way into Saltwick Bay and land on the sandy beach for a rest. The East Pier at Whitby can be seen from Saltwick, a little under 2km to the west.

Staying outside of the Whitby north cardinal (NZ 896 135) will keep you away from the chaotic breakers and open up a path of smoother water due north of the harbour entrance. In calmer conditions you can take a route between the reefs and the shore. It is then possible to paddle through a gap between the inner and outer East Pier. The water in and around the harbour entrance can be surprisingly choppy, with waves bouncing off the tall vertical walls and pleasure boats coming and going. Once into the harbour, you can relax a little and take in the panoramic view of the old town. As you paddle on towards the swing bridge, stone buildings with terracotta roofs are gathered tightly along the narrowing river. As the town closes in around you, the unmistakable smell of freshly fried fish and chips will undoubtedly spur you on to the end of your trip. The marina slipway is less than a kilometre up the river beyond the 100 year old swing bridge on the west side.

Anatomy of a trashing

A thorough trashing on the reef break at Black Nab led to the loss of my spare paddles, the contents of my buoyancy aid pockets and my camelback water carrier. Tip: don't play chicken with a substantial reef break while admiring the scenery. I like views along the coast with some breaking surf in the near foreground, but it is important to keep watching out for freak sets of waves. A glimpse of a large incoming wave was my cue to turn and paddle into it. My relief at reaching the crest didn't last for long; a second wave of similar size was right behind and, over the top of it, I could see a third wave that was even bigger and already starting to break. I made it over the second wave but lost all my speed. The third wave looped me over backwards as I tried to climb the vertical face.

The ensuing bongo slide was a washing machine experience: repeatedly rolling and then getting power-flipped. It took most of my strength just to keep hold of my paddles. The sixth roll pushed me out of the breaking water onto the green face of the wave, where control could be regained. Thankfully, I was still about 15–20 yards from the pinnacle of rock that marks the reef and had time to get off the wave and turn the boat back out to sea.

I rode out a few smaller waves while I got my breath back and looked around, unsuccessfully, for my missing possessions. A nice little rip going out alongside the reef took me back out beyond the break: my respect for the sea had been restored.

By Sean Jesson

Tides and weather

This coast is exposed to wind and swell with any northerly or easterly component. Winds from the southwest tend to funnel out of Robin Hood's Bay. Strong south-westerlies cause unsettling downdraughts and swirling winds along the cliffs.

The tidal streams that run in and out of the entrance to Whitby Harbour are generally weak. However, following a period of heavy rain there can be an out-going stream of 2-3 knots. During extreme flood or spate conditions in the river Esk this can be as much as 5 knots.

Additional information

Hooks House Farm campsite (01947 880 283) is just outside the village of Robin Hood's Bay. Boggle Hole Youth Hostel is perfectly situated but is often fully booked over a year in advance. Robin Hood's Bay village is a maze of narrow streets and cobbled alleyways clinging to the sides of a deep gorge. There are galleries, shops and a collection of pubs.

Variations

If you arrive early in the morning or outside the holiday season, it is possible to drive to the slipway in Robin Hood's Bay to drop boats off. There are car parks a short walk up the hill overlooking the village. Launching from the steep cobbled slipway at high water would be very tricky, even in the slightest swell. The best time to launch from here is mid-tide, to avoid having

© *The wreck of the trawler Sarb J. North Cheek*

to carry kayaks too far over seaweed-covered rocks. At low water or in heavy swell, consider using the fisherman's slipway to the north of the village known as Ground Wyke (NZ 953 052). It tends to get the best shelter and there is a shorter distance to the water's edge when the tide is out. Unfortunately, there is no public road access and the path to the slipway is steep. A trolley would be handy.

This trip is often done the other way round starting from Whitby or, to avoid a car shuttle, paddle there and back in the same day.

 Runswick Bay

Whitby to Runswick Bay 34

No. 34 | Grade B | 13km | OS Sheet 94

Tidal Port	North Shields
Start	△ Whitby Marina slipway (NZ 900 105)
Finish	◯ Runswick Bay slipway (NZ 811 159)
HW/LW	Around 40 minutes after North Shields at Whitby
Tidal Times	The NW-going stream begins around 3 hours 30 minutes after HW North Shields. The SE-going stream begins around 3 hours before HW North Shields.
Max Rate Sp	Usually less than 1 knot
Coastguard	Humber, tel. 01262 672 317, VHF weather every 3 hours from 0150

Introduction

Whitby is a popular tourist destination and a cultural Mecca for Goths because of its associations with Bram Stoker, the author of the famous 1890s horror novel *Dracula*. The trip from the marina begins by taking in the scenic architecture of the old town of Whitby. Once away from the harbour entrance, there is plenty of time to play in the surf along Whitby Sands on the way

to Sandsend. Here the shale cliffs rise steeply from wave-cut platforms, which provide plenty of scope for rock-hopping all the way to Runswick Bay.

Description

Whitby owes much of its early existence to fishing and whaling. James Cook began his seaman training here in the mid 1700s, later becoming Captain Cook. Another of Whitby's sons, William Scoresby Junior, was mapping East Greenland and other Arctic regions in the early 1820s. The River Esk runs through the town and provides sheltered waters for a small fishing fleet, a variety of pleasure craft and a lifeboat station.

Whitby is just off the main A171. Whitby Marina and its expansive car park are at the end of Langbourne Road, which leads south from the roundabout beside the bus and rail station. There is a Co-op supermarket that is handy for snacks and supplies. Parking can be paid for at the marina office and the fee includes the use of the marina showers and toilets. The marina has a wide slipway with a pebbly beach on either side. As you leave the marina behind, there is a warm-up of over a kilometre before you reach the entrance to Whitby Harbour. This is a great opportunity to feast your eyes upon the old town buildings crowded along the steep river banks. On the high ground to the east of the harbour entrance stands the Church of St Mary and the famous Whitby (or St Hilda's) Abbey.

After leaving the harbour entrance, the gently shelving sandy beach that leads west to the village of Sandsend can provide fun in the surf. Sandsend is a pretty village, parts of which are strung out along the coast road. There are plenty of cafés, shops and a couple of pubs. The quieter streets are nestled in the shelter of narrow valleys along the banks of East Row Beck and Sandsend Beck. At the west end of the village, there is a car park with public toilets. There is a concrete ramp that leads to the sandy beach. This makes for a good sheltered lunch stop, or an alternative place to start or finish.

The coastline between here and Runswick Bay is dominated by the shale cliffs of Sandsend Ness and Kettleness. The soft shales are readily eroded by the sea, leaving extensive wave-cut platforms. These rocky ledges extend up to 250m out to sea and are exposed at low tide interspersed with shallow lagoons teeming with sea-life. Coated in barnacles and rusting among the reefs are two boilers from a shipwreck from an era fuelled by mining and quarrying.

The long sandy beach and lush green slopes make Runswick Bay a welcoming sight to a weary paddler. The eastern end is wild with steep ground and cliffs that play host to breeding fulmars and other sea birds during the spring and summer. The village is tucked away at the western end, where there is a beach café, public toilets and a Pay and Display car park.

Tides and weather

These shores are exposed to winds and swell from the north and east, especially around the headland of Kettle Ness. Strong southerly or westerly winds tend to funnel out of Sandsend and Runswick Bay. These winds can also deliver downdraughts from the cliffs between Sandsend Ness and Kettle Ness.

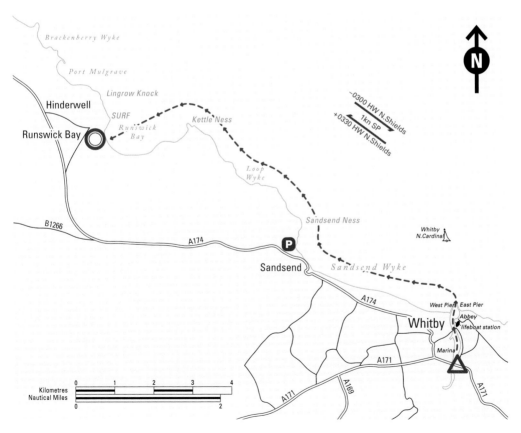

Additional information

The Runswick Beach café has everything you would expect and more. The Royal Hotel is a charming real ale pub tucked away in the old part of Runswick Bay village that clings to the steep slopes at the western end of the bay. The Runswick Bay Camping and Caravan Park (01947 840997) is just outside the higher part of the village (worth booking in advance during the busy summer months). East Barnby Outdoor Education Centre (www.outdoored.co.uk/EastBarnby, 01947 893333) provides accommodation as well as instruction and guiding in a number of outdoor activities, including sea kayaking.

Variations

Runswick Bay is an excellent place to stay for a weekend. If the sea is calm then nothing can be more satisfying than exploring the coast by sea kayak. In rougher weather, the beaches at Saltburn, Skinningrove and Runswick all have good surf. This trip can also be completed in the opposite direction, or Sandsend could be used as an alternative place to start or finish.

St Hilda

Hilda was quite a woman. She was born into a rich and influential family and in 657 was one of the first English women to build and head her own religious institution. What's more, by combining a nunnery and a monastery on the same site, it became the first dual-sex establishment in England. Legend has it that when Hilda found her preferred site on the cliff top above Whitby, she found it infested with snakes. Undeterred, she drove the snakes over the cliff edge with her staff. As the snakes tumbled to the sea, Hilda called to the heavens and sliced off their heads with her whip. This caused them to coil up and petrify. Their remains can be seen as the ammonites which are frequently seen in the cliff base hereabouts.

By Kirstine Pearson

 Boulby Cliff

Runswick Bay to Saltburn-by-the-Sea

No. 35 | Grade B | 19km | OS Sheet 94

Tidal Port	North Shields
Start	△ Runswick Bay slipway (NZ 811 159)
Finish	◯ Saltburn Beach (NZ 667 217)
HW/LW	Around 25 minutes after North Shields
Tidal Times	The NW-going stream begins around 3 hours after HW North Shields. The SE-going stream begins around 3 hours before HW North Shields.
Max Rate Sp	Usually < 1 knot
Coastguard	Humber, tel. 01262 672 317, VHF weather every 3 hours from 0150

© Staithes harbour

Introduction

The name 'Cleveland' is derived from Norse and loosely translates as 'land of cliffs'. These tallest cliffs of northern England form an imposing and forbidding coastline. The villages of Staithes and Skinningrove occupy the only gaps and provide oases for those travelling along this section of coast. The finish at the popular resort of Saltburn-by-the-Sea often has surf, which can make landings entertaining even on average days.

Description

The village of Runswick Bay is off the A174 road that runs from Whitby to Saltburn-by-the-Sea. As you drive into the village, the beach is signposted down an alarmingly steep road to the right opposite the Runswick Bay Hotel. On all but the busiest days, it should be possible to drive down the concrete ramp that leads to the sandy beach. Kayaks and kit can be unloaded here before parking your car in the nearby Pay and Display car park.

The small red-roofed cottages loom over your route out of the bay. Swell from the north breaks impressively in the shallows at Cobble Dump on the western edge of the bay. This area and other nearby reef breaks are popular with some of the more experienced local kayak and board surfers. The Lingrow Cliffs begin to rise to over 70m, heralding the deeper waters off Port Mulgrave.

Before its development in the 1850s, Port Mulgrave was called Rosedale Wyke. The small harbour was built to take locally mined iron ore by sea to Jarrow, to be turned into steel for shipbuilding. A narrow gauge railway brought ore from the mine by way of a tunnel. The tunnel entrance can still be seen part of the way up the steep slopes at the back of the bay. The nearest mine had become unproductive by the early 1900s and other mines had access to the local coast railway. Port Mulgrave fell into disuse and the processes of nature gradually began to reclaim the bay. Finally, in the early part of the Second World War the Royal Engineers destroyed the remaining piers and infrastructure amid fears of a German invasion. These days Port Mulgrave is more famed for its Jurassic origins and is frequented by geologists and fossil hunters.

The approach to Staithes harbour can be intimidating in any height of swell. There are reefs everywhere and waves seem to break all around, but the delightful glimpses of picture-box village through the harbour entrance will draw you in. As you get closer you will be able to make more sense of the confused waters and the route to the harbour entrance will quickly unfold. At low tide, Staithes harbour dries almost all the way to the entrance; at high water, however, you will be able to paddle all the way in and land on the small sandy beach inside the east breakwater.

Tall terraced cottages with tiny windows loom over the network of narrow cobbled streets and ginnels (narrow walkways between houses) beyond the harbour. There are a handful of shops that sell souvenirs, trinkets and antiques. Working your way up the village streets, a couple more pubs and The Captain Cook and Staithes Heritage Centre (www.captaincookatstaithes.co.uk) – dedicated to the life and times of Captain Cook – provide further distractions. It is worth setting a good part of the day aside to explore this village trapped in time between the sea and the cliffs.

Paddling east from the layered cliffs of Staithes, you will soon find yourself in the shadow of the mountainous Boulby Cliff that rises to a colossal 200m. The impregnable coastline relents before long to reveal Skinningrove beyond rocky scars nestled in a deep ravine. It is easiest to land to the east of the old pier beside the village, where Kilton Beck meets the shore. A number of traditional fishing boats known as cobles operate from here, and the locally popular pastime

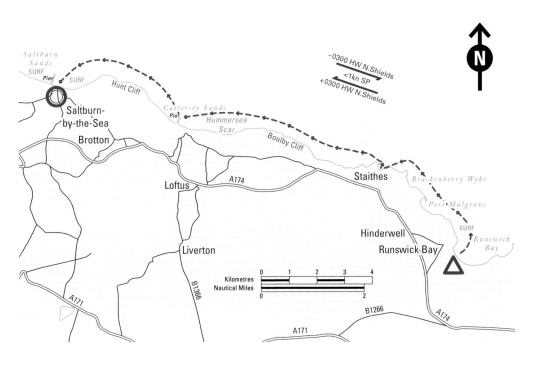

© Left: stone snake; right: devil's toenail; middle: frozen thunderbolt | R Wilding

Runswick Bay to Saltburn by the Sea

of pigeon fancying is apparent from the string of lofts clinging to the steep village fringes. The village has a fish and chip shop, a general store, a pub-come-coffee house and a winery that uses locally farmed produce and foraged wild fruits. This small isolated community owes its existence largely to ironstone mining. The Tom Leonard Mining Museum (run solely by enthusiastic local volunteers) tells the story of the skills and customs that built Cleveland's Ironstone heritage.

Stone snakes

The crumbling cliffs of Yorkshire's Jurassic coast reveal the ancient myths that surround havens such as Whitby, Robin Hood's Bay and Port Mulgrave. Once the home of devils that regularly shed their toenails, the wrath of the Gods culminated in Thor hurling his thunderbolts at the cliffs where the cold muds froze them solid. Then came a plague of snakes, but the pious Hilda (of Abbey fame) took pity on the poor people of the area and turned all the hideous reptiles to stone.

No less intriguing are the geological explanations of these fossils representing life from about 150 million years ago. The Devil's Toenails are the shelly remnants of creatures that resembled modern mussels found around the tide lines. During their time, squid-like belemnites (with their bullet-shaped internal skeleton) and ammonites (that used the air-filled chambers in their coiled shells as a kind of personal flotation device) would have been found dashing around in the surface waters.

By Royanne Wilding

Surf can dump heavily at Cattersty Sands, to the west of the Skinningrove pier, at high tide. The old slagheaps up above the pier give the cliff tops a surprisingly natural craggy look. Beyond Cattersty Sands is Hunt Cliff, which is tall and dominating. Hunt Cliff is somewhat reminiscent of Boulby Cliff, but actually much smaller. As you make your way through or around the shallows beneath the cliff, a broad sandy surf beach and Victorian pier come into view.

Overlooking the northern extent of the steep Yorkshire coastline is Saltburn-by-the-Sea. This was the centre of smuggling in the 1700s. It was the Victorian era that brought a more honourable identity to this splendid location as a holiday resort. Nowadays, the seafront promenade cafés and gently shelving beach are popular with holidaymakers as well as those taking an introductory surfing lesson from the Saltburn Surf School.

The beach can be busy with surfers and bathers so it important to choose your landing spot carefully. There is access to the road via a concrete ramp beside The Ship public house. There is also access to the popular beach car park to the east of the pier.

Tides and weather

This section is exposed to wind and swell from the north and east. On rougher days, swell can break heavily at the entrances to Runswick Bay, Staithes harbour and Skinningrove. Large swell also breaks explosively upon the wave-cut platforms and reefs beneath the cliffs that dominate this section. The tidal streams are weak and rarely reach 1 knot.

Additional information

Runswick Bay Camping and Caravan Park (01947 840997) is a pleasant site close to the Runswick Bay Hotel. The beach is just a short drive down the hill.

Sea Drift Café at Staithes is a must: their coble cake washed down with a steaming cappuccino or hot chocolate will impress those with a sweet tooth. The Cod and Lobster pub is just across the road and is more for those with a savoury appetite and an unsavoury thirst. The Beach Road Fisheries fish and chip shop has a terrific reputation for excellent food, but it can be difficult to catch them open.

Variations

Paddling this route in the opposite direction may make sense if the swell is forecast to increase throughout the day, as Runswick Bay is less exposed than Saltburn. Skinningrove and Staithes can be used as alternative places to start and finish, but driving through and parking at Staithes can be difficult.

The Tyne-Tees Coast

Introduction

Following the Industrial Revolution, the bold, proud industrial heritage of northeast England came with plenty of grease and grime. This is when mining, foundries and heavy engineering formed the backbone of the economy and beaches were black with waste from the collieries. The heavy industry that defined this coast slowly collapsed following the pit closures of the late 1980s. This left harbours and factories idle; whole communities were stunned into the unfamiliar task of looking for new careers.

The great thing about the Tyne-Tees coast is the effects of its renaissance. Among the disused buildings and quaysides are gradual beginnings of new, cleaner modern industries including tourism. A great deal of effort has been put into rediscovering the coastal heritage and reviving its natural history. With drastically reduced pollution, wildlife is recovering at a pleasing rate among new nature reserves and along cleaner shores. The practice of tipping coal waste along beaches stopped in the 1980s and, with every tide, these shores are returning to a more natural, healthy state.

The Tyne-Tees coast has a never-ending chain of special places waiting to be explored. Some of these places have a remote and wild feel, despite being conveniently close to major towns and cities. Other waters may bring you right into the heart of urban culture among artwork and architecture both ancient and modern.

When journeying through wild and remote places, prudent explorers make good use of resources and features that they find along the way. Urban sea kayaking need not be any different; there are regular rail and bus services along this coast. A public transport alternative often provides a new and different aspect and, without the hassle of traffic jams, can sometimes be just as quick as shuttling by car.

Accommodation will need a fresh approach. You can forget camping, but there can be excellent weekend deals in B&Bs and backpacker's hostels. For long weekends, the holiday parks and static caravan sites along this coast can provide excellent short-notice deals. While exploring the inner city and urban areas in this section, you should take a little extra care with your belongings. There is no need for paranoia, but it is simply better to be aware that petty criminals ply their trade hereabouts.

Rocky shores around Hartlepool, South Shields and Whitley Bay are riddled with intriguing nooks and crannies tailor-made for rock hopping on hazy days with gentle swell. On rougher days, when rock hopping would be out of the question, the powerful North Sea swell produces excellent surf at Saltburn, Whitburn and Long Sands. The only really sheltered waters are those of the Tyne. The illuminated bridges and riverside buildings at Newcastle and Gateshead set the scene for a spectacular evening paddle. The journey from Derwenthaugh to Tynemouth provides a full and varied day out. These are easy-to-reach places within a couple of hour's drive of many northern towns and cities, and well worth a weekend or two of urban sea kayaking adventures.

Tides and weather

Tidal streams are generally weak at less than 2 knots. They mostly run parallel to the coast and there are no overfalls. Although the tidal streams do not coincide with high and low water, the saying 'flood to Flamborough, ebb to Edinburgh' gives the general idea.

This section is exposed to wind and swell from the north and east. Sustained winds from the north can extend and strengthen the SE-going tidal streams. Following a period of unsettled weather, the North Sea takes a number of days to settle down. Winds from the southwest generally leave these waters calm, and the shores in the lee of high ground will be sheltered.

Where the Tyne-Tees coast may lack the grandeur of the Yorkshire coast, it does have a few quiet corners that provide sheltered paddles for those days when the open sea is too rough. The obvious choice is the tidal Tyne, but there are also possibilities on the Tees between Yarm and Stockton (which was tidal until the construction of the Tees Barrage and the whitewater course).

Further information

For more information on kayaking in this area, see:

Forth, Tyne, Dogger, Humber: A cruising guide from Blakeney to St Abbs, Henry Irving, Imray 2002, 0 85288 578-4.

A Canoeist's Guide to the North-East, Nick Doll, Cicerone Press 1991, 1-85284-066-8.

Guidelines for Recreational River Users, Port of Tyne Authority.

Visit the following websites for further information:

www.durhamheritagecoast.org - Durham Heritage Coast

www.portoftyne.co.uk - Port of Tyne authorities

www.magicseaweed.com - surf and swell forecasts

© Seaton Sands

Crossing the Tees

No. 36 | Grade B | 20km | OS Sheets 93 & 94

Tidal Port	North Shields
Start	△ Saltburn Beach (NZ 667 217)
Finish	○ Hartlepool Fish Sands (NZ 527 336)
HW/LW	HW and LW for this section are around 15 minutes after North Shields.
Tidal Times	In Hartlepool Bay and at the River Tees entrance, the N-going stream begins around 1 hour after HW North Shields. The S-going stream begins around 5 hours before HW North Shields.
	Between Saltburn and the River Tees entrance, the SE-going stream begins around 3 hours 30 minutes before HW North Shields. The NW-going stream begins 3 hours after HW North Shields.
Max Rate Sp	Generally weak but can reach around 3 knots at the entrance to the River Tees.
Coastguard	Humber, tel. 01262 672 317, VHF weather every 3 hours from 0150

36

Crossing the Tees

Introduction

The Victorian seaside resort of Saltburn-by-the-Sea, complete with pier, promenade and pubs, holds court along the northern reaches of the Yorkshire coast. The gentle expanse of surf-strewn Marske Sands leads the way from the tall cliffs and rolling hills into a more open landscape and the sinister industrial tangle of Redcar and Teesside. After crossing the mouth of the Tees, Hartlepool Bay and its historic headland will offer you its mysteries, myths and chips.

Description

Most of the Saltburn's streets and parades are high above the sea. The route to the beach is by way of a short steep road that twists and winds its way onto a busy seafront with cafés and car parks. There is excellent access to the beach here, but the car parks soon fill up on sunny weekends and the waters become crowded with surfers. At these busy times, it may be better to launch at a couple of quieter places accessible from car parks along the A1085 coast road between Marske and Redcar.

There is a subtle interruption to the seemingly endless sands on the coast at Redcar: Redcar Rocks and Coatham Rocks are low-lying reefs that stand just off the sands and are exposed at low water. These reefs offer a degree of protection and shelter from the swell here at mid-to-low water. Across Coatham Sands, the South Gare Breakwater with its lighthouse can clearly be seen a little over 4km away to the west, marking the entrance to the mouth of the River Tees.

The mouth of the Tees is a busy shipping lane bound by sand dunes, overshadowed by the dominating structure of the Redcar steelworks. It is this scenery of pipes, towers and chimneys swirling with menacing vapours that is thought to have inspired the film set for the classic sci-fi movie Bladerunner. Entering or crossing the mouth of the Tees should be done with care to avoid shipping traffic. You should contact the Tees port authorities by VHF radio (channel 14) or telephone (01642 277205).

It is possible to land along the shore of South Gare close to the old lifeboat station, but be aware that the slipway here is privately owned by the South Gare Marine Club. The club has an old-style weekend café that serves a traditional range of greasy delights for cold and hungry yachtsmen. Kayakers are welcome too, but don't expect to find muesli on the menu. The café has an upstairs lounge that commands a grandstand view to the south across a small fishing harbour to a shallow bay. The harbour is called Paddy's Hole, and is home to a handful of small boats whose skippers tend pots for crab and lobster along the shores of Teesmouth and Hartlepool Bay. The shallow bay beyond of Bran Sands is popular with local windsurfing and kite sports enthusiasts.

Daring to wander beyond the 'Do Not' signs among the eclectic collection of huts and sheds is the only way to explore the South Gare headland thoroughly. It is all pretty shabby and in a precarious existence, built upon the decaying WW2 concrete breakwater among the shifting dunes.

After passing the mouth of the Tees you will be able to see Seaton Sands and the suburb of Seaton Carew beyond. This heralds the southern extent of Hartlepool Bay. People of these shores are all too willing to impart witty tales and banter relating to John 'The Canoe Man' Darwin.

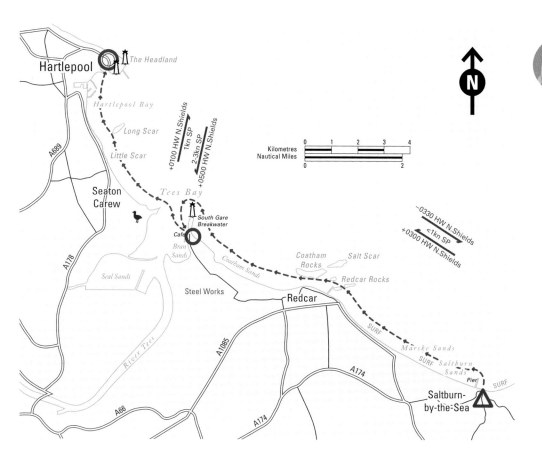

After faking his own death in early 2002 in a canoeing accident, Darwin became a cult figure in this area (and in the life insurance industry).

The surf tends to break more gently on these shores than at Marske and Saltburn. This is largely due to shelter provided by Headland at Hartlepool, but there is also a rocky reef called Long Scar in the middle of Hartlepool Bay which bears the brunt of the swell. Even if you can't see the reef itself, there will almost certainly be waves breaking along the eastern edges.

The *Seaton Carew* wreck

The Industrial Revolution during the late 18th century brought about an increasing need for coal. This 'black gold' was carried from the major coalfields of northern England in vessels known as colliers, often bound for London but sometimes northern Europe. Many came to grief during the winter storms, often with the loss of all hands; the *Seaton Carew* wreck is believed to be one of those.

In September 1996, following a period of unseasonably stormy weather, the skeleton of an old wooden collier of unknown origin was revealed by the receding sands of Seaton Beach. The wreck measures 25m in length and 7m across the beam, and lies upright between the high and low water marks. The remarkably well-preserved timbers of oak and elm periodically appear and disappear beneath the shifting sands, giving this wreck an added air of ghostly mystery.

The Hartlepool Headland with its churches and gaily painted Georgian houses lies less than 2km to the north of Long Scar. Fish Sands lies just inside the entrance to the Victoria Harbour. The small sandy beach is tucked away between a short breakwater at the southwest point of the headland and the old town wall. Once you have landed, the easiest way to the road is through the sandstone archway and up a short flight of steps.

Tides and weather

The tidal streams along this section are generally weak except in the immediate vicinity of the entrance to the mouth of the River Tees. Swell from the north and east tends to break most heavily along the exposed shores between Saltburn and Seaton Carew. There can be some limited shelter gained from the reefs at Redcar close to low water. There are landings with better shelter inside the entrance to the mouth of the River Tees, along the shore of South Gare close to the old lifeboat station.

Additional information

The Harbour of Refuge pub can be found close to the sandstone archway at Fish Sands. A bronze statue of comic-strip character Andy Capp stands in the open ground next to the building. If you feel hungry from a hard day's paddling, you may wish to visit the area's best takeaway. Verril's fish shop, standing in the shadow of the local parish Church of St Hilda, is within sight of the Old Town Wall. People come from miles around to devour the succulent cod and haddock with chips fried to perfection.

Big ships, small ships

Parts of the Church of St Hilda date back to Norman times, but most of the building is from the late 12th century. St Hilda's is open to visitors on Wednesday, Saturday and Sunday afternoons for fascinating tours and a welcoming cup of tea. One possible camping option is the Whitewater Caravan Club site beside the Tees Barrage Whitewater Course at Stockton-on-Tees (tel. 01642 634880).

Variations

This trip can be done in reverse, but be sure to check the surf forecast. While conditions may be benign in Hartlepool Bay, an increasing sea state may leave you with a pounding in the surf at the end of your trip at Saltburn. If in doubt, you could always paddle to the entrance of the River Tees and explore South Gare and Seaton Carew before returning to Hartlepool. If you are planning to use the regular local rail service to get back to Saltburn, the nearest landing to Hartlepool station is on the beach beside the Tees and Hartlepool Yacht Club in the West Harbour (NZ 518 329).

Hartlepool to Seaham 37

No. 37 | Grade B | 22km | OS Sheets 93 & 88

Tidal Port	North Shields
Start	△ Hartlepool Fish Sands (NZ 527 336)
Finish	○ Seaham North Beach (NZ 426 505)
HW/LW	HW and LW at Hartlepool occur around 15 minutes after North Shields.
Tidal Times	The NW-going stream begins 1 hour 30 minutes after HW North Shields and the SE-going stream begins around 4 hours 30 minutes before HW North Shields.
Max Rate Sp	Around 1 knot.
Coastguard	Humber, tel. 01262 672 317, VHF weather every 3 hours from 0150

Introduction

Hartlepool is steeped in maritime history. Despite the proximity of industry and suburbia, this area has a wild, gnarly and committing coast that is largely isolated from the trappings of modern life by the Durham Coast railway line. Having been recently released from the grip of heavy industrial pollution, the wildlife is recovering at a pleasing rate and the shores are returning to a more natural, healthy state.

Steps leading to Fish Sands

Description

Upon the historic headland along the Old Town Wall, a set of steps leads through a sandstone archway to Fish Sands in the jaws of the old fishing harbour. A bronze statue of Andy Capp propping up the bar, pint in hand, overlooks the south-facing harbour entrance.

Brightly coloured Georgian houses line up along the sea front. The harbour was little more than a haven for a few fishing boats until the industrial revolution. The Heugh lighthouse and First World War gun battery stand on the most easterly point. The reefs here are good for a little rock hopping. An old wooden pier juts out from the shore at North Sands and Hart Warren Dunes Nature Reserve is located a little further on. The rolling sand dunes are host to rare coastal flora such as the burnt tip and pyramidal orchid. Despite the close proximity of urban life and heavy industry, there is a breeding colony of little terns here. The colony has had better success since areas were fenced off during the breeding season.

Crimdon Beck flows out across the beach at Crimdon Dene, beyond which the coastline becomes steeper. The local Magnesian limestone starts to assert itself and the cliffs take on a rugged look at Blackhall Rocks. This small headland stands surrounded by pebbly beaches, interspersed with rock pools and small lagoons at low water. The headland is so riddled with caves it seems to be almost completely hollow. Pebbly beaches reach through multiple archways into a central cavern which is large enough to house a couple of double-decker buses.

When paddling along these shores, it is hard to imagine that this was once one of the most heavily polluted coastlines in Europe. The practice of dumping coal slack and cinder stopped in

Featherbed Rocks

Seaham

Seaham Harbour

Liddle Stack

Nose's Point

A182

Chourdon Point

Hawthorn Hive

B1432

Shippersea Bay

Easington
Colliery

Fox Hole

Horden Point

~0430 HW N.Shields
1kn SP
+0130 HW N.Shields

A1086

Peterlee

P

Denemouth

37

Blackhall Rocks

B1281

A1086

A19

North Sands

Pier

A179

Parton Rocks

A19

Hartlepool

The Headland

Marina

Yacht Club

A689

Hartlepool Bay

Kilometres
Nautical Miles

| 0 | 1 | 2 | 3 | 4 |

| 0 | | | 2 |

Long Scar

195

the 1980s. Ironically, the high volumes of waste stemmed the rate of coastal erosion for over 100 years. Erosion has returned with a vengeance in places, so be careful when selecting which cliffs to sit beneath when choosing your lunch spot.

Castle Eden Burn meets the sea at Dene Mouth between Blackhall Colliery and Horden. There is a car park (NZ 454 407) near the beach which can be used as a bad-weather escape or as an alternative start/finish. The Durham Coast railway line comes close to the cliff tops near Shippersea Bay and crosses the deep ravine at Hawthorn Hive by way of an elegant brick viaduct. A short walk from the beach will take you into the dense woodland of Hawthorn Dene. These sheltered woods are teeming with songbirds and pungent with wild garlic at springtime.

Seaham harbour is just another 3km further along steep shingle shores, among more limestone outcrops and an entertaining sea arch at Nose's Point. Huge confused seas can develop around the harbour walls in bad weather or big swell. There is an escape route via steps from the beach south of Nose's Point, but the best landing is just over 1km to the north of the harbour where there is a car park above Seaham beach and promenade.

Tides and weather

The tidal streams along this coast are generally weak and rarely exceed 1 knot. While conditions may be benign in Hartlepool Bay, an increasing sea state or onshore winds may leave you with difficult landings through dumping surf on steep shingle beaches. The isolation provided by the Durham Coast railway line leaves little practical road access for bad-weather escape routes. The outer walls of Seaham Harbour reflect waves and swell back out to sea, creating clapotis and tricky confused seas.

Additional information

Heugh Gun Battery museum occupies the original structures built to defend Hartlepool since Napoleonic times on the east side of the headland. Original weaponry and other wartime exhibits occupy this substantial site both above and below ground. The Museum of Hartlepool is also well worth a visit for its exhibits depicting local maritime history.

This is urban sea kayaking, so forget camping. Just to the north of Hartlepool, Park Resorts run an extensive caravan park at Crimdon Dene which overlooks the coast. Visit www.park-resorts.com for off-season caravan breaks that won't hurt the pocket.

Variations

There are advantages to paddling this trip in the opposite direction: the exposed beach and harbour walls at Seaham can be dealt with first, leaving a sheltered landing at Hartlepool for the end. For shorter trips there is a car park (NZ 454 407) at Dene Mouth, which is around half-way between Hartlepool and Seaham.

 Seaham to Sunderland

No. 38 | **Grade A** | **10km** | **OS Sheet 88**

Tidal Port	North Shields
Start	△ Seaham North Beach (NZ 426 505)
Finish	○ Roker Beach (NZ 409 587)
HW/LW	HW and LW along this stretch are similar to North Shields.
Tidal Times	The NW-going stream begins around 1 hour 30 minutes after HW North Shields and the SE-going stream begins around 4 hours 30 minutes before HW North Shields.
Max Rate Sp	Around 1 knot.
Coastguard	Humber, tel. 01262 672 317, VHF weather every 3 hours from 0150

Introduction

This is a relatively short journey along a straightforward but scenic stretch of coast. The journey connects the town of Seaham with Roker at the mouth of the river Wear in Sunderland. The shingle beaches are drawn out between rocky headlands and backed by cliffs of Magnesian limestone overlaid with glacial deposits.

38

Seaham to Sunderland

Description

The town and harbour of Seaham can be found just off the A19 from which a new coastal bypass leads into the town centre. There is a car park off the B1287 from which a footpath leads down to a low promenade and the beach.

The rocky cliffs are overlaid with sand and crumbling boulder clay and there is always recent evidence of collapse along the coast. After heavy rain, softer pockets of the boulder clay become saturated with water and begin to liquefy. The gradual motion of collapse leaves brown muddy streaks down the face of the sea-washed Magnesian limestone cliffs. Where the cliffs are overlaid with sand and gravel deposits, there are frequent mini-avalanches leaving telltale heaps at the head of the beach.

In at least one area close to Pincushion Rocks, where the ground is more stable, sand martins burrow small tunnels into the cliff in which to lay their eggs and raise their young. There is also a headland where a tougher patch of limestone has resisted the power of the sea. The rocky sea stack and reef, which extend a short way offshore, provide some rock-hopping entertainment. The shore continues with steep beaches at the foot of the cliffs. The beaches here are submerged at high water and the cliffs are undercut leaving small buttresses, caves and arches.

The coastline arcs round, forming a bay which gathers up to a headland at Salterfen Rocks. As you approach the rocky point the different tones of undulating sandy layers appear to form a wave in the cliff above the headland. The rocky point at Salterfen Rocks provides one last opportunity for some rock hopping before the coastline and landscape beyond become dominated by the industries surrounding Sunderland Docks. The cliffs become lower and soon recede into a gentle slope, on which a new promenade has been built. There is a slipway at the southern end of the promenade, but landing or launching here would be tricky in anything but the calmest conditions or close to low water.

Sunderland Docks are protected by high concrete and stone sea walls beyond which little can be seen. After passing the most easterly point along the dock walls, you will be able to see the banded lighthouse marking the entrance to Sunderland Harbour. Roker Beach lies inside, protected by Roker Pier.

The slightly more adventurous may wish to carry on beyond the harbour entrance, bypassing Roker Beach for a landing through surf at Whitburn Bay. Parsons Rocks are marked by a conspicuous disused lighthouse on the shore, beyond which Whitburn sands can be found. Access to the roadside parking from the gently shelving beach is easy via steps either side of the shelter building on the promenade.

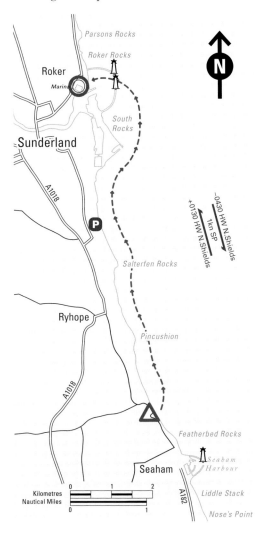

Tides and weather

The outer walls of Sunderland Harbour and the docks reflect waves and swell back out to sea, creating clapotis and confused seas. There is a sand bar at the entrance to the harbour where tricky confused seas can develop, especially when easterly winds meet a falling tide. Despite the protection of the harbour walls, strong easterly winds can bring swell into the harbour entrance. Surf of up to 2m is not unheard of at this usually sheltered spot.

Additional information

The Sunderland Marine Activities Centre is part of the Marina development and provides a wide range of outdoor activities. They provide courses in sea kayaking and surf kayaking from beginners to more advanced levels (www.marineactivitiescentre.co.uk).

The Roker Refreshments café beside the beach provides plentiful pies, pasties and other hot food and drinks. The Smugglers pub beside Roker Pier is a nice spot for that après-paddle pint with a view across the bay, but the nearby Harbour View pub specialises in locally brewed ales. Pullman Lodge is a distinctive B&B with its railway carriage eatery overlooking Whitburn sands (tel. 0191 529 2020).

© Crumbling cliffs, near Seaham

Variations

This trip can be done in either direction, with the beach at Whitburn Bay making a perfectly suitable alternative start or finish point.

 © Souter Lighthouse overlooking rocky shores

Sunderland to South Shields ▨▨▨

No. 39 | Grade A | 11km | OS Sheet 88

Tidal Port	North Shields
Start	△ Whitburn Sands (NZ 407 606)
Finish	○ South Shields Beach (NZ 380 672)
HW/LW	HW and LW along this stretch are similar to North Shields.
Tidal Times	The NW-going stream begins 1 hour 30 minutes after HW North Shields and the SE-going stream begins around 4 hours 30 minutes before HW North Shields.
Max Rate Sp	Around 1 knot.
Coastguard	Humber, tel. 01262 672 317, VHF weather every 3 hours from 0150

Introduction

This is a short stretch of coast, but it is highly concentrated with all the ingredients that make up a classic sea kayaking trip. There are sea arches, caves and limestone cliffs surrounding secluded

© Souter lighthouse, Lizard Point

Sunderland to South Shields

beaches. There is even a lighthouse painted red and white, straight out of a children's storybook. The caves and arches along this section are at their best around mid-to-high water. With its sea bird colonies, this stretch of coastline is as inspiring and intriguing as any shore in the UK.

Description

There is roadside parking along the A183 coast road that runs between Sunderland and South Shields. Access to Whitburn Sands is easy via steps that lead down to the beach. Paddling north from Whitburn Sands, the shores soon become rocky with low cliffs and reefs riddled with gullies and rock arches. The architecture of the Magnesian limestone here is generally blocky; however, a natural process known as 'concretion' has led to rare spherical formations in places, referred to as 'cannonball limestone'. On calm days with little swell, the rock hopping here is excellent. The steep shoreline blocks the view of suburbia, giving an unexpected wild feel to this area.

A military firing range, normally active during weekdays, is located on the land above Souter Point. When firing is in progress, red flags are flown on the cliffs nearby indicating that you should not proceed any further. It is possible that by the time you can see the warning flags you will be able to hear the sound of gunfire. The coast beyond continues with similar rock architecture right the way round Souter Point, to where you can see the Souter Lighthouse.

If you wish to visit the lighthouse, the best place to land is a small pebbly cove around 400m south of Lizard Point called Byer's Hole (NZ 410 639), from which there is a path along the cliff tops to the lighthouse. Those of a nervous disposition should stay to look after the boats however, as the lighthouse buildings are said to be haunted.

Souter Lighthouse

Souter Lighthouse actually stands on the high ground above Lizard Point and was first put into operation in 1871. The need for a lighthouse was clear when in 1860 alone there were 20 shipwrecks upon the reefs here. The twin diaphone foghorns are reputed to be the loudest in the country and are angled in order to be heard up and down the coast. They can be heard as far south as Sunderland, as far north as Whitley Bay and as far inland as Jarrow. Both the foghorns and the lighthouse were decommissioned in 1988, but the horns are still in working order and can be heard on special occasions.

The site is now a museum run by the National Trust, and is open to the public from mid-March until the end of October. There is a charge for entering the main lighthouse building, but entry to the tea rooms and souvenir shop are free.

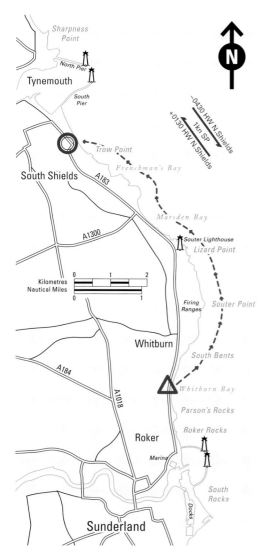

Marsden Bay is hemmed in by tall cliffs and adorned with tall stacks. The largest stack is Marsden Rock which is home to hundreds of breeding fulmars and kittiwakes. Another rock feature of the bay is Marsden Grotto, a unique pub and restaurant housed in a sea cave (www.marsden-grotto.co.uk). Access to the grotto and its open-air beach terrace is either via the pebbly beach or by descending the cliffs using its dedicated lift.

The limestone coastline continues with more calcareous nooks and crannies as you pass Frenchman's Bay and finally Trow Point, until the sands and promenade of South Shields Beach are reached. Easy parking, ice creams and plentiful café food await tired, hungry paddlers upon their arrival.

Tides and weather

This coast is exposed to wind and swell from the north and east, but there is good shelter beneath the cliffs from south-westerlies.

Additional information

Whitburn Range is normally active Monday–Friday during the hours of 09:30–16:30, when red flags are flown on the cliffs at the boundaries. Firing times are normally published in the Shields Gazette. Further information

© Magnesian limestone features

can be obtained by contacting the Whitburn Range control (tel. 0191 239 4261) or Humber Coastguard.

Variations

This trip can just as easily be done in the opposite direction to the route described above, and is also short enough to be paddled there and back.

The Tyne

No. 40 | **Grade A** | **21km** | **OS Sheet 88**

Tidal Port	North Shields
Start	△ Derwenthaugh Marina (NZ 203 633)
Finish	◯ Herd Beach (NZ 370 680)
HW/LW	HW and LW at Derwenthaugh Marina are around 10 minutes before North Shields.
Tidal Times	The E-going ebb stream begins at around HW North Shields. The W-going flood stream begins around 5 hours before HW North Shields.
Max Rate Sp	1.5 knots in the River Tyne, but the ebb can be greater after heavy rain.
Coastguard	Humber, tel. 01262 672 317, VHF weather every 3 hours from 0150

Introduction

This is a sheltered trip on the tidal stretch of the River Tyne through the heart of Newcastle, Gateshead and Jarrow and into the North Sea at Tynemouth. The rich and varied architecture of the Tyne Bridges and the riverside buildings is amazing. The lower reaches have varied scenery with rolling parkland, tangled industrial docklands and the jumble of buildings and moorings that surrounds the fish quays.

Description

There is access to the south side of the river via a slipway at Derwenthaugh Marina, which is the home to the Powerhouse Marine watersports shop and TS Northumbria Sea Cadets. This location is tricky to find by road as it is at the end of a warren of industrial units, but it is the only access to the water in the area. Derwenthaugh Marina is at the eastern end of Tundry Way which is off the eastbound carriageway of the A695 locally named Chainbridge Road. It is best to launch here at or very shortly after high water to take full advantage of the ebbing waters, and to avoid getting muddy feet.

After less than 3km you will reach the old wooden jetty on the right bank where the River Team enters the Tyne. This is Dunston Coal Staithes and, at over 500m long, is reputedly the largest wooden structure in Europe.

Leaving Dunston behind, the famous Tyne bridges that connect Gateshead with Newcastle will come into view. The grand stone buildings of Newcastle upon Tyne tower over the north bank and the humdrum of busy city-centre life rumbles all around. Down on the river in your kayak you can appreciate the quiet waters, mindful of the sentiment 'Go placidly amid the noise and haste'.

Beneath the bridges and despite the city's hustle and bustle there is a breeding colony of kittiwakes. Their distinctive call serves as a reminder that this is a city built upon maritime trade and this is urban sea kayaking. As with the more remote coastal colonies, these fish-eating sea birds take their penultimate place in the food chain. The increasingly successful city-centre peregrine feeds well among the bridges and tall buildings during spring and early summer. Newcastle's trendy quayside bars and modern arts venues of Gateshead astride the Millennium Bridge give rise to a dramatic setting comparable to any wild coastal scenery.

The river becomes more open as it winds on past St Peters Marina and the Friars Goose watersports club. There is a floating jetty and slipway leading to their clubhouse, where paddlers are welcome.

The old tar works at St Anthony's has been demolished and the land put to good use as a local park. The slipway here may look like a good spot to sit and eat your packed lunch, but the foreshore is contaminated with chemicals from the site's industrial past. A far better place would be just after the river turns north on the broad grassy slopes of Hebburn's Riverside Park (on the right).

The river turns east once again after the park at Hebburn, initially revealing the scene of an exposed desolate place. Broad slipways and old wooden jetties are punctuated by redundant buildings decaying through neglect since heavy industries left these shores.

Spare a thought for the hundreds of thousands of commuters driving their cars beneath the river through the smoky Tyne Tunnel; the conical ventilation shafts are easily distinguished along the skyline of each bank. Passing Jarrow, you will see the Tyne Dock on your right and the Royal Quays on your left. The advice from the Port of Tyne authorities is to let them know of your plans before paddling through the busy areas around the docks and shipyards. They can be contacted by telephone (0191 257 0407) or VHF radio (channel 12). Keep a sharp eye out for the small quick ferries that carry foot passengers on the route that connects South Shields with North Shields.

The last bend before the mouth of the Tyne sees buildings old and new crowding along both shores, overlooking a mixture of quayside moorings. The north bank hosts the old Fish Quay and the Tynemouth Lifeboat station. The south shore runs into the Herd Groyne with its distinctive red light beacon. The groyne protects the Herd Beach to its south, which marks the end of this

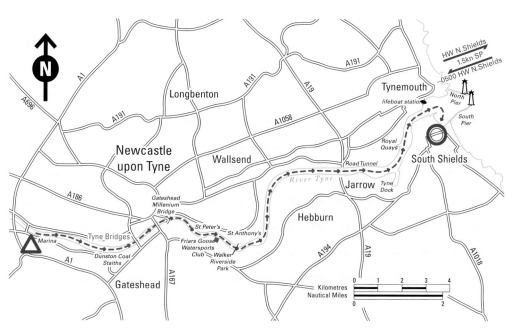

journey down the tidal Tyne. There is a huge car park at the top of the beach which is just a short drive from South Shields town centre.

Tides and weather

Although there is good shelter for most of this section, there can still be surf on the beaches that are protected by the breakwaters. Following periods of heavy rain, the E-going ebb stream can run stronger and for longer than usual.

Additional information

At the launch site for this trip there is a watersports shop called Powerhouse Marine (tel. 0191 414 0065). The shop sells kayaking accessories and spares, and the staff can provide up-to-date local knowledge.

Friars Goose watersports club (NZ 278 633) is located on the south shore of the river around 2km downstream of the Tyne Bridges (tel. 0191 469 2545). A warm welcome awaits cold, thirsty and hungry paddlers, especially if you call ahead to let them know you will be coming.

Advice and information on traffic movements along the busy part of the river can be sought from Port of Tyne authorities (tel. 0191 257 0407; VHF channel 12).

Variations

It is possible to paddle this trip in the opposite direction, but the incoming flood stream is weaker so greater effort will be required upstream. If you just want a short paddle to view the Tyne bridges, it is possible to start at Friars Goose watersports club. The paddle upstream with the last of the flood can be an atmospheric trip as night falls. The bridges and town centre buildings are beautifully lit at dusk, but remember to bring head torches and light sticks for the return to the club slipway with the early ebb.

The Tyne

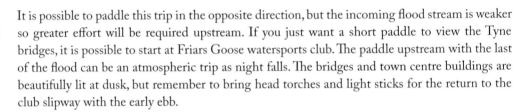

Dunston Coal Staithes

Built in 1890 by the North Eastern Railway Company, the Staithes was used for loading locally mined coal for export onto ships. The Staithes heyday was in the 1920s when over 140,000 tons of coal was handled. They remained in use until the 1970s but, following pit closures in the 1980s, the structure fell into disuse and was partially dismantled. The Dunston area played a central role in the Gateshead Garden Festival in 1990, when the Staithes were restored and used as a landing stage for pleasure boats. The wooden structure has sadly been damaged by fire and is no longer accessible to the public, but the Dunston Coal Staithes remains a striking feature on the River Tyne and is a grade 2 listed building.

Tynemouth to Blyth

No. 41 | Grade B | 16km | OS Sheet 88

Tidal Port	North Shields
Start	△ Low Lights Beach (NZ 364 687)
Finish	○ Blyth, South Beach (NZ 322 793)
HW/LW	Times of HW and LW are similar to North Shields.
Tidal Times	At the entrance to the River Tyne, the E-going ebb stream begins at around HW North Shields and the W-going flood stream begins around 5 hours before HW North Shields.
	Along the coast between Tynemouth and Blyth, the S-going stream begins around 4 hours 10 minutes before HW North Shields and the N-going stream begins around 2 hours 20 minutes after HW North Shields.
Max Rate Sp	Weak and generally less than 2 knots.
Coastguard	Humber, tel. 01262 672 317, VHF weather every 3 hours from 0150

© Seaton Sluice harbour

Tynemouth to Blyth

Introduction

As you leave the sheltered waters in the shadow of Tynemouth Priory, sturdy Victorian terraces stand above and beyond the craggy shores upon which relentless swell crashes. When conditions are suitable, this is a fun journey that combines rock hopping with a little surfing. The trip begins in the heart of Tynemouth and continues along the beaches of Long Sands and Whitley Bay before finishing at the Northumbrian port of Blyth.

Description

A pay-and-display car park can be found at Low Lights at the foot of Tanners Bank, a narrow street that runs down the hill south off the main A193 Tynemouth Road in North Shields. There are public toilets and access to the beach is a couple of straightforward steps from your car down to the sand.

Paddling east from Low Lights takes you to a rocky reef called Black Middens. These rocks were the scene of many shipwrecks before the protective North and South Piers were built in the mid-to-late 1800s to provide a smoother passage into the river and docks. The Tynemouth Volunteer Life Brigade was established in 1864, and still plays an important role in search and rescue in the area. Visit the museum dedicated to the brigade's history, located on the headland overlooking the Black Middens in the watch house beside the Spanish Battery.

Tynemouth Priory stands guard 30m above the northern entrance to the Tyne. This headland has been an important defensive position since Napoleonic times, but spectacular reinforcements to the cliffs were made during the First World War when heavy artillery was installed. Tynemouth Sailing Club is based immediately to the south of the priory, in the sheltered cove of Prior's Haven. The waters in the immediate area around the end of the breakwater can be surprisingly choppy and confused, and in heavy swell the area to the north of the breakwater can be quite chaotic. Immediately to the north of the priory headland is King Edward's Bay and a small beach called Short Sands. The beach is set among a steep rocky shore with Sharpness Point at the northern entrance.

Beyond Sharpness Point lies the gently shelving surf beach of Long Sands. There is easy access from the streets above making this a popular spot with locals; the shallow waters can be congested during sunny weekends. The shore becomes rockier at the northern end of Long Sands, and the jagged reefs around Cullercoats Bay hide a smugglers cave and a small beach harbour. There has been a lifeboat station here for over 150 years. The elegant Victorian boathouse has a bell tower and an impressive gable end to the main roof which displays the inscription 'So when they cry unto the Lord in their trouble he delivereth them out of their distress and bringeth them unto the haven where they would be.'

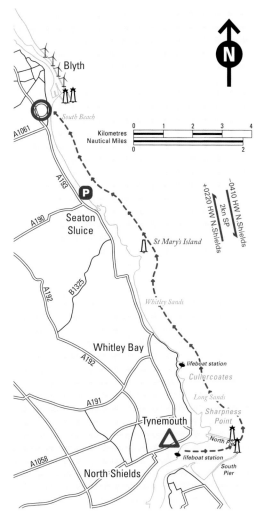

The reefs beyond Cullercoats and around Brown's Point herald 3km of sand and shingle at Whitley Bay. These beaches dry out to rocky reefs at low water. The northern extent of Whitley Bay is marked by the lighthouse on St Mary's Island, which is linked to the mainland by a natural causeway at low tide. The lighthouse was decommissioned in 1984 but has since been restored and opened to the public.

The shore continues with craggy cliffs, small bays and semi-submerged reefs that keep you guessing the route all the way to the harbour at Seaton Sluice. This small harbour was developed in the late 1600s for shipping coal and to support the developing local glass trade. A fine view can be had looking north from the harbour entrance along the sand dunes and sparkling surf towards Blyth and Newbiggin and the southern reaches of the Northumberland coast. The nearest possible landing is around 300m along the beach, where there are paths through the dunes to a car park beside the A193 coast road. Surf dumps awkwardly close to high water here, but landings are easier when the tide is out. Landing conditions are often more sheltered on the beach 2.5km further at Blyth, where there is a visitors centre, café and paved access to the car park.

Tynemouth to Blyth

Breakwaters at Blyth

Tynemouth to Blyth

Tides and weather

The ideal time to start this trip is around an hour after high water in the Tyne. By launching then, you will not have far to carry your kayak at the beginning and the gentle tidal streams will help you along your way. Check the surf forecast and conditions before setting out: there is nothing worse than coming to the end of a trip to be faced with an unexpectedly heavy surf landing.

Additional information

Crusoe's Café at Long Sands Beach gets busy at weekends, but their sugar and cholesterol-loaded hot chocolate is a must. The Boardwalk Café beside the beach at Whitley Bay is also well worth a visit.

Variations

This trip can be done from north to south, and it is also possible to start or finish at a number of different places. There is road access to the beach at Long Sands but the parking is very limited. Cullercoats is another possibility, but The Links car park at Whitley Bay may be better for space. The nearest access to Seaton Sluice is the car park by the roundabout at the junction of the A193 and the A190, but there is a long carry over soft sands.

The Northumberland Coast

Introduction

From the industrial harbour town of Blyth in the south to the craggy shores of the borders in the north, Northumberland attracts a whole host of outdoors enthusiasts. Kite surfing, horse riding and walking are all popular pursuits along this Area of Outstanding Natural Beauty. The sea kayaking along these shores is excellent. When Northumberland was styled, it was painted in broad strokes. Rolling hills lead to spreading shores where the swollen seas surge among the rocks and crash upon the surf beaches. The paddling takes you along great stretches of rocky coast, out to off-lying islands and up the tidal estuaries.

In the past, promontories and headlands were vehemently defended. The chain of ancient castles that link the shores from Warkworth to Lindisfarne tell of an embattled and violent history. On a clear day, two or three of these monumental structures can be seen standing out against the crystal skies at any one time. These strongholds loomed over the battlegrounds from high upon outcrops of Whin Sill, an igneous rock fundamental to Northumbrian geology and most famously exposed at the Farne Islands. It is here and at the nearby Holy Island of Lindisfarne that northeast England proudly presents its two coastal National Nature Reserves. From marine mammals to wildfowl, cliff-nesting sea birds to rare orchids, the sheer number and variety of species that can be seen along these shores is staggering.

Northumberland has its own unique culture and independent identity. The county flag is conspicuous throughout the area and can be seen flying from official buildings, as well as printed on signposts and car bumper stickers. Folk music is popular here, with the traditional Northumbrian pipes playing an important role. There is even an annual sea shanty festival held in Seahouses each June. Craster kippers are the most memorable local delicacy. There is a range of locally brewed fine ales, but the most distinctive tipple is the recently resurrected and uniquely warming Alnwick Rum.

Tides and weather

With the exception of the Farne Islands and the estuaries of the Coquet and Tweed, tidal streams along the coast are generally weak. Although the saying 'flood to Flamborough, ebb to Edinburgh' is sometimes useful, it is worth remembering that the coastal streams do not coincide with the timings of high and low water. The prevailing south-westerly winds are offshore, which gives the seas a deceptively calm look. The only places that are well sheltered from these winds are between Berwick and Eyemouth and near Craster.

Further information

For more information on kayaking in this area, see:

Forth, Tyne, Dogger, Humber: A cruising guide from Blakeney to St Abbs, Henry Irving, Imray 2002, 0 85288 578-4.

Embleton Bay and Dunstanburgh Castle

Surf and swell forecasts can be studied at www.surf-forecast.com and www.magicseaweed.com. For access and other local information, visit the local paddlers' website www.john_rae.dsl.pipex.com. Active4seasons (www.active4seasons.co.uk), based in Berwick-upon-Tweed, provide coaching and guided trips in the area.

 Blyth to Druridge Bay ▨▨▨

No. 42 | Grade B | 18km | OS Sheet 81

Tidal Port	North Shields
Start	△ Blyth, South Beach (NZ 322 794)
Finish	○ Druridge Bay Car Park, Cresswell (NZ 290 940)
HW/LW	High and low water at Blyth is similar to Tyne. High and low water at Druridge Bay is around 10 minutes before Tyne.
Tidal Times	The S-going stream begins around 4 hours before HW Tyne and the N-going stream begins around 2 hours after HW Tyne.
Max Rate Sp	Less than 1 knot.
Coastguard	Humber, tel. 01262 672 317, VHF weather every 3 hours from 0150

Introduction

Paddling this stretch of coast will deliver you from the last of the industrialised northeast coast and into the unspoilt reaches of Northumberland. Leaving Blyth behind you, the proudly revamped seafront of Newbiggin-by-the-Sea will beckon you across the mouth of the River Wansbeck. The power station and aluminium plant give Lynemouth Bay a grimy air. Finally, all

© 'Couple', Newbiggin-by-the-Sea

will be forgotten with the approach to the rocky shores of Cresswell that herald the soft sands and nature reserves of Druridge Bay.

Newbiggin Bay

In 2007 an insular breakwater was built across the mouth of the bay as part of a £10 million regeneration and coastal protection scheme. Half a million tonnes of sand were brought in to replenish the badly depleted beach. The finishing touch was the sculpture at the northern end of the breakwater. 'Couple' depicts a man and woman looking out to sea. The 5m high figures stand upon a raised platform, out of reach of all but the biggest waves.

Description

South Beach is off the junction of the A1061 and A193. There is a large car park, information centre, fish and chip shop and ice cream parlour. It is easiest to get to the water from the southern end of the car park using the track that passes the Blyth Battery Museum. There is a broad concrete ramp that leads down to the sandy beach from the promenade.

Paddling northeast from the beach, you will soon pass the entrance of Blyth Harbour with its skeletal breakwater and wind turbines. Sow and Pigs is a group of rocks that form the end of the reef which protects the harbour. The breakwater is built upon the inner edges of the reef. Swell

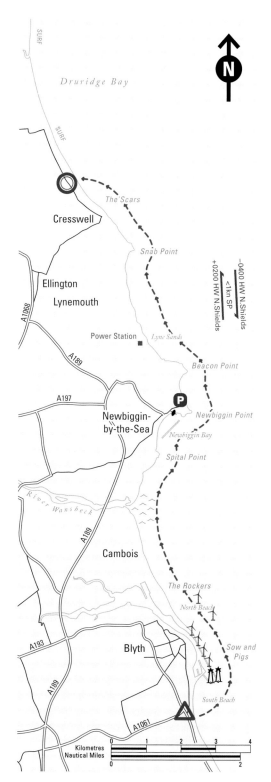

surges into channels along the outside edges and there is good rock-hopping all the way to Cambois Beach, where there is road access via three car parks. The sandy beach and dunes extend northwest for over 3km to the mouth of the River Wansbeck. The river mouth is clogged with sand bars that kick up steep waves and create awkward currents, especially close to low water.

North of the river, the Sandy Bay caravan site stands upon level ground above the low cliffs that rise gently from the sands. Towards the northern end of this bay, the cliffs become a little higher with distinct dark layers that are seams of poor-quality coal. Fragments of coal washed out from seams on the seabed or cliffs are found along nearby beaches. Spital Point is where the cliffs end, marking the southern entrance of Newbiggin Bay.

The northern entrance to the bay is marked by Newbiggin Point; the southern part of this rocky headland is occupied by St Bartholomew's Church. Church Point Caravan Park sprawls out along the northern shore between the churchyard and the Newbiggin Golf Club. The golf course covers the land above rock ledges and lagoons for over 2km to Beacon Point, as well as the southern reaches of Lynemouth Bay. Spoil heaps and industrial waste line the shores in the shadow of the power station that supplies the adjoining aluminium smelting plant.

Snab Point signals the approach to the village of Cresswell. Low cliffs, rocky ledges and reefs are interspersed with shallow lagoons and sandy coves. There is a surf break at The Scars, but the biggest of the waves can often be avoided by paddling a little further north into Druridge Bay where landings are easier upon the soft sands.

The Cresswell car park has a low barrier (6 feet 6 inches) at the entrance, meaning that kayaks will have to be loaded onto cars at the roadside.

Tides and weather

This section is exposed to winds and swell from the north and east. The coastline is mostly low and rocky, giving little protection from strong offshore winds.

Additional information

The Blyth Battery Museum (blythbattery.org.uk) celebrates the defence of the Port of Blyth throughout the two world wars, and is open to the public at weekends during April to September.

Wansbeck Riverside Park Caravan and Camping site is pleasantly located beside the river and run by the resident park wardens (tel. 01670 812323). The caravan parks at Sandy Bay, Newbiggin-by-the-Sea and Cresswell are run by Park Resorts (www.park-resorts.com). Weekend caravan breaks can be excellent value for small groups.

Variations

This route can be paddled just as easily in the other direction. There may be some benefit in starting at Druridge Bay if the swell is from the north or east and is forecast to increase during the day.

At high water, it is possible to paddle 4km or more up the River Wansbeck. Just upstream of the road bridge, there is a weir that becomes completely submerged an hour or so either side of high water. Upstream, the river is slow moving with easy paddling, sheltered from the weather all the way to Wansbeck Riverside Park and beyond.

Coquet Island

No. 43 | Grade A | 9km | OS Sheet 81

Tidal Port	North Shields
Start	△ Togston Links (NU 281 015)
Finish	◯ The Braid, Amble (NU 260 050)
HW/LW	High and low water at Blyth are similar to North Shields. High and low water at Coquet Island are around 15 minutes before North Shields.
Tidal Times	Around the island and along the coast, the S-going stream begins around 4 hours 40 minutes before HW North Shields. The N-going stream begins around 1 hour 20 minutes after HW North Shields.
	In the River Coquet and the harbour entrance, the in-going stream begins around 6 hours before HW North Shields and the out-going stream begins around HW North Shields.
Max Rate Sp	Around the island and along the coast, the tidal streams are generally weak and rarely exceed 1 knot. The streams are stronger in the River Coquet and the harbour entrance, and can exceed 3 knots.
Coastguard	Humber, tel. 01262 672 317, VHF weather every 3 hours from 0150.

Introduction

A trip along this stretch of coast is a delight for wildlife lovers. Flocks of wading birds feed along sandy coves between fingers of rock that extend out to sea. Coquet Island is one of several nature reserves in the area. During spring and early summer, its surrounding skies swarm with noisy seabirds. The surrounding waters are home to hundreds of inquisitive seals all year round. Nearby, the shelter of Amble Harbour and the Coquet estuary suit paddling of a gentler nature. However, the exposed beaches along this stretch are excellent for surfing.

Description

The minor road to Togston Links runs east from the A1068 between Druridge Bay Country Park and High Hauxley. There are no obvious road signs. If you turn north where the road reaches the shore, after about 500m you will find a small parking area with easy access to the beach. The broad, surf-soaked sands of Druridge Bay stretch away to the south. The chimneys of Lynemouth and wind turbines of Blyth can be seen silhouetted beyond the rocks of Hadston Carrs. To the north are the reefs of Bondi Carrs. In calm seas, these and the rocks around Hauxley Haven are a rock-hopping wonderland of gullies and lagoons. When swell runs in from the east, there are a series of reef breaks and the surfing here is excellent.

Coquet Island lies just over a kilometre to the north, and your arrival here is likely to be attended by a number of inquisitive grey seals. This rugged, low-lying island is less than 500m long and no more than 300m across at its widest. The surrounding waters are shallow with kelp-infested reefs. South Steel is the reef that extends from the southern end of the island. The east-facing shore is steep with rock ledges that lead to the reefs and gullies of North Steel. The inner, west-facing shore is more sheltered from the elements and has a small sandy beach with a path that leads to the lighthouse.

Just over a kilometre to the west, the rocky shores and sandy coves of Amble are reassuringly close. The coastline here comprises steep sand dunes propped up by low outcrops of sandstone. The mostly sandy beaches are littered with small reefs that form sheltered lagoons as the tide goes out.

Amble Harbour is marked by two light towers, each standing at the end of a breakwater (one to the north and the other to the south of the harbour entrance). There are occasionally choppy conditions here due to a sand bar, which can be exacerbated by clapotis from the breakwaters.

The River Coquet descends into its tidal reaches in the shadow of Warkworth Castle before it meets the sea at Amble. The ebbing tide runs strongly past the marina and the fish quay and out to sea between the harbour breakwaters.

Tides and weather

The tidal streams can exceed 3 knots in the River Coquet and the harbour entrance, especially when a strong ebb tide is combined with a strong flow from the river following a period of heavy rain.

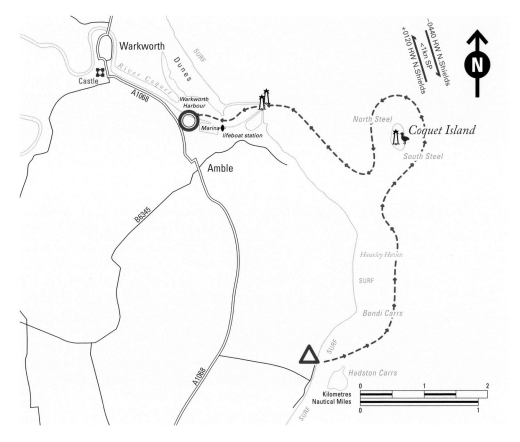

Coquet Island

Additional information

The Coquet Canoe Club is based just upstream of the harbour and makes good use of the sheltered shores for their training and introductory sessions. The club hosts the Coquet Island race every June. The route starts (and finishes) in the lower reaches of the estuary before leaving Amble Harbour to circumnavigate the island. The scenic 5 mile course, coupled with an informal atmosphere, attracts a broad range of paddlers. In recent years the event has been competed more vigorously and has been won in well under an hour.

Variations

This trip can easily be made in either direction, or kept shorter by starting and finishing a circumnavigation of Coquet Island at the Braid.

Sandy beaches lead to the secluded estuary of the River Aln and the picturesque village of Alnmouth 5km north of Amble. During the last hour before high water, it is possible to paddle into this pretty estuary and explore the salt marsh and sand dunes.

Coquet Island Bird Sanctuary

The island itself is a bird sanctuary that is owned and managed by the RSPB. In the spring, over 35,000 sea birds – including eider ducks, Arctic terns and puffins – arrive here to breed, but Coquet Island is most prized for its rare roseate terns. During the spring and summer months, wardens take up residence in the lighthouse buildings. Their duties include managing and maintaining the island's habitat as well as performing scientific studies and protecting the birds. Landing on the island (unless in a genuine emergency) is not permitted at any time of the year.

 # Alnmouth to Craster

No. 44 | Grade B | 12km | OS Sheet 81

Tidal Port	North Shields
Start	△ Alnmouth Bay (NU 251 106)
Finish	○ Craster Harbour (NU 258 200)
HW/LW	High and low water along this section are around 25 minutes before North Shields.
Tidal Times	The S-going stream begins around 4 hours 40 minutes before HW North Shields. The N-going stream begins around 1 hour 20 minutes after HW North Shields.
Max Rate Sp	The tidal streams rarely reach 1 knot.
Coastguard	Humber, tel. 01262 672 317, VHF weather every 3 hours from 0150

Alnmouth to Craster

Introduction

The first part of this trip is characterised by intimate sandy coves drawn out between rocky reefs. For the final stretch, the shores are more gnarly with jagged headlands and reefs which lead to a harbour sheltered behind treacherous rocks.

44

Alnmouth to Craster

Description

The village of Alnmouth is signposted off the A1068 east of Alnwick. The B1338 leads over the River Aln and onto Northumberland Street, from which a car park is signposted down the first turning on the left (The Wynd). This leads directly to the broad sandy beach at the northern end of Alnmouth Bay.

Heading north, the first feature is the reef known as Marden Rocks at the northern end of the sands. The rocks divide Alnmouth Bay from Fluke Hole, where there is a small sheltered beach overlooked by Foxton Hall and the Alnmouth Golf Club.

The next set of rocks is Seaton Point, which marks the beginning of a complex network of low-lying rocky reefs that dominates the next 4km of coastline. At low tide, the rocks extend over 500m from the high water mark.

There is a shallow lagoon in the southern part that is almost 1km long and over 200 metres wide, backed by a pleasant sandy beach. This is the natural harbour of Boulmer Haven; even when high water covers the rocky reefs, they absorb the power of the sea leaving the waters of the haven calm. Local fishermen work their traditional fishing boats (cobles) from here, often bringing the catch ashore to the Fishing Boat Inn. This pub overlooks the haven and has gained a reputation for delicious local seafood.

To the north, the fading remains of these reefs divide the pretty beaches of Sugar Sands and Howdiemont Sands. The quality of the surf here is outstanding. Iron Scars separates Sugar Sands from a small beach where Howick Burn enters the sea. If you want to avoid the surf, this beach

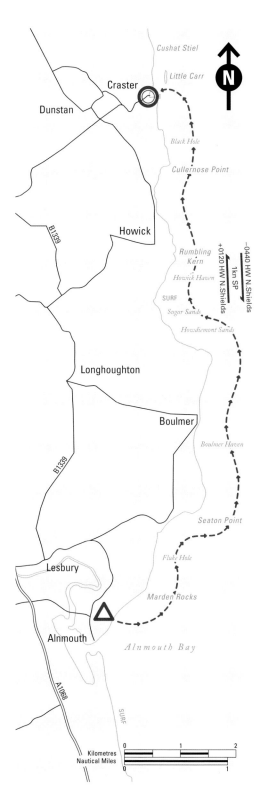

is often slightly more sheltered from the swell. There is also a pleasant woodland walk along the burn.

A substantial stone house overlooks these rocky shores. The house was built by Charles, the 2nd Earl Grey (of Earl Grey tea fame), as a family retreat.

Further north, Howick Haven is an even smaller sandy cove that faces southeast. It can provide another option for a sheltered landing, as the off-lying reefs keep the worst of the swell away. The next stretch of coastline is excellent for rock hopping in calmer conditions, and the remains of a shipwreck provide extra interest.

As the tide rises, the swell surges into deep gullies and blowholes among the rocks to the north of Howick Haven. The booming sound resembles that of awkward digestion and has no doubt given rise to the local name 'Rumbling Kern'.

Further north, a beach formed of boulders and pebbles known as Swine Den shelters in the shadow of Cullernose Point. The south-facing cliff plays host to a small nesting colony of kittiwakes.

As soon as you round the point, you should be able to see the off-lying rocks of Little Carr and Muckle Carr (the more southerly and larger of the two) that provide shelter to the harbour entrance and village of Craster. These rocks are only just covered at high water. The channel between Muckle Carr and the shores of Craster dries at low water. Despite these rocks, winds and swell from the north and east can conspire to create awkward, choppy conditions in the narrow harbour entrance.

The village and harbour were built by the Craster family in 1906. Their main business was quarrying local stone, much of which was used as kerbstones in London. There is limited parking in the village streets and around the harbour; the visitors' car park is just a short walk from the harbour at the site of the old quarry.

Tides and weather

This section is exposed to any wind and swell with an easterly component. The land around Boulmer Haven is low lying and provides little shelter from winds from any direction. The tides are weak and progress can be made against the flow throughout this section.

Additional information

Proctors Stead is a charming family-run caravan and camping site around a mile inland from Craster (www.proctorsstead.co.uk). A walk up the main street of Craster will take you to the smokehouse of L Robson & Son, producers of the famous Craster Kippers. The Jolly Fisherman pub is just across the road and serves a range of fine ales, but is particularly famous for crab sandwiches and crab soup.

Variations

This trip can be paddled in either direction. It is also possible to start or finish at Howdiemont Sands (NU 262 156). There is parking on the farmer's land that overlooks the beach; fees can be paid by means of an honesty box beside the road at Low Stead Farm.

 # Craster to Beadnell

No. 45 | Grade B | 12km | OS Sheet 75 & 81

Tidal Port	North Shields
Start	△ Craster Harbour (NU 258 200)
Finish	○ Beadnell Haven (NU 233 296)
HW/LW	High and low water along this section are around 40 minutes before North Shields.
Tidal Times	The S-going stream begins around 4 hours 30 minutes before HW North Shields and the N-going stream begins around 1 hour 30 minutes after HW North Shields.
Max Rate Sp	1 knot
Coastguard	Humber, tel. 01262 672 317, VHF weather every 3 hours from 0150

Introduction

With jagged headlands, broad beaches awash with surf and off-lying rocky reefs, this section typifies the Northumbrian coast.

Description

The village of Craster is signposted off the B1339 between Longhoughton and Embleton. There is limited parking in the village streets and around the harbour, so it is best to unload kayaks and kit before parking. The visitors' car park, public toilets and tourist information are just a short walk away on the site of the old quarry, off the road that leads into the village.

The beach within the harbour is steep and pebbly at high water with more gently shelving sand at low water. The rocky reefs of Muckle Carr and Little Carr that lie 100–200m offshore, popular with seals, are only covered at high water. The coast between here and Dunstanburgh Castle consists of rolling grassland that descends gently to rocky slabs that slope steeply into the water.

As you approach the castle, there is a broad cove with a boulder-strewn beach called Nova Scotia. Beyond the cove, the shore rises steeply up to the flatter ground upon which stand the ruins of Dunstanburgh Castle, built by Earl Thomas of Lancaster in 1313. Dunstanborough played a more significant role in the Wars of the Roses than in any Anglo-Scottish border conflict.

Castle Point and its north-facing cliffs of Whin Sill form the southern entrance to Embleton Bay. The southern part of the bay has boulder-strewn rocky shores, but before long the rocks give way to a kilometre-long broad sandy beach with dunes. There is excellent surfing right the way along the bay. There are a series of rocky reefs further north extending offshore which provide shelter to, and almost separate, the northern part of the bay. This area is known as St Mary's or Newton Haven. Tucked away in the west corner of the bay is the pretty village of Low Newton-by-the-Sea. It is here, among the whitewashed fisherman's cottages, that the owners of the Ship Inn dispense a small selection of ales from their microbrewery.

Newton Point is a low rocky headland that leads to a semi-circular bay called Football Hole. The back of the bay has a sandy beach with sand dunes. Snook Point is a narrow rocky headland that juts out over 600m into the North Sea and separates Football Hole from Beadnell Bay.

Beadnell Bay is reminiscent of Embleton Bay, with similar gently shelving beaches backed by tall sand dunes. Halfway along the bay, Tughall Burn enters the sea forming a small isolated sand spit. This is Newton Links, a nature reserve owned and managed by the National Trust. This natural barrier offers some protection to the breeding colony of arctic terns and little terns. It would be best to avoid surfing or landing in this area of the bay.

Beadnell Harbour, with its distinctive 18th-century limekilns, is situated at the northern end of the bay and is well sheltered by the rocks that lie to the east. This is the only harbour on the east coast that has a west-facing entrance. The adjoining beach can be a good place to land and has good car parking and toilet facilities. This beach is also excellent for surfing. When swell runs in from the east or southeast, the area closest to the harbour normally has only gentle surf. The further you move away from the harbour, the bigger the surf becomes.

The coastal scenery beyond the harbour and Beadnell Point is too tempting to miss and makes an excellent finale to the trip. A series of finger-like reefs extends out to sea, forming a number of intriguing coves along the eastern shores of Beadnell village. Nacker Hole is one of the larger coves; it is rocky at low water, with a steep pebbly beach that leads up to the road. The easiest landing for all tidal conditions is another kilometre further at Beadnell Haven. The rocks here act as groynes, protecting a narrow sandy beach. A short footpath leads up from here to the road beside the village Post Office.

45

Craster to Beadnell

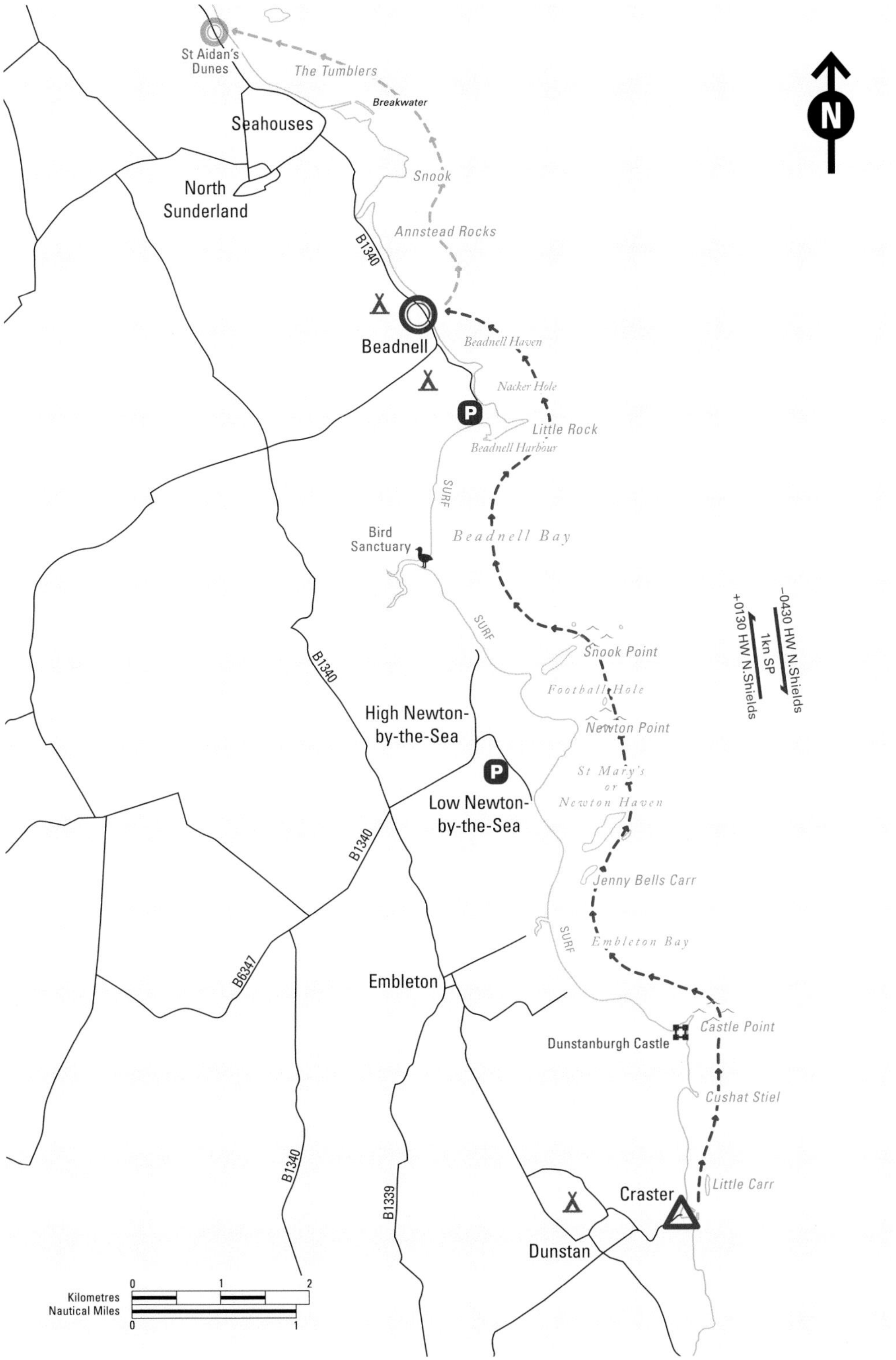

St Aidan's Dunes

The Tumblers

Breakwater

Seahouses

Snook

North Sunderland

Annstead Rocks

B1340

N

Beadnell

Beadnell Haven

Nacker Hole

Little Rock

P

Beadnell Harbour

SURF

Bird Sanctuary

Beadnell Bay

SURF

Snook Point

–0430 HW N.Shields

1kn SP

+0130 HW N.Shields

Football Hole

B1340

High Newton-by-the-Sea

Newton Point

P

St Mary's or Newton Haven

Low Newton-by-the-Sea

Jenny Bells Carr

SURF

B1340

B6347

Embleton Bay

Embleton

Castle Point

Dunstanburgh Castle

B1340

Cushat Stiel

B1339

Craster

Little Carr

Dunstan

Kilometres
0   1   2

Nautical Miles
0   1

45

Craster to Beadnell

© Eider ducks, locally known as 'Cuddy ducks'

Tides and weather

This section is exposed to wind and swell with an easterly component. Any swell at Craster is reflected off the harbour wall and nearby rocks, which can make the first part of this trip a little choppy. Tidal streams are generally weak and it is possible to paddle against the flow. Small overfalls can sometimes develop off Castle Point when wind opposes tide.

Additional information

Beadnell village has two pubs: the Beadnell Towers Hotel and the Craster Arms. Both have a range of fine ales and serve good pub grub.

The Beadnell Bay Caravan and Camping Club site is outside the village, just across the road from the beach close to Beadnell Haven (tel. 01665 720 586). Farne Diving Services has lodge-style B&B accommodation as well as a sheltered camping area within in a walled garden (www.farnedivingservices.com).

Variations

This trip can be easily paddled in either direction. It can also be extended by an additional 4km of coastline north of Beadnell to Seahouses and its harbour entrance. The harbour takes its name from the nearby village of North Sunderland. At the time of writing, landing fees are £5 per kayak and parking costs £4. St Aidan's beach lies another 1km north where both landing and parking are free, but there is a long carry through the dunes to the nearest road.

The Inner Farne Islands

No. 46 | **Grade B** | **10km** | **OS Sheet 75**

Tidal Port	North Shields
Start	△ St Aidan's Beach (NU 212 327)
Finish	○ St Aidan's Beach (NU 212 327)
HW/LW	High and low water along this section are around 1 hour before North Shields.
Tidal Times	The SE-going stream begins around 4 hours 30 minutes before HW North Shields. The NW-going stream begins around 1 hour 30 minutes after HW North Shields.
Max Rate Sp	The tidal streams run at up to 2 knots in open water but this increases to 4 knots through The Kettle, around headlands and in narrow stretches between islands.
Coastguard	Humber, tel. 01262 672 317, VHF weather every 3 hours from 0150

Introduction

The Farnes are a chain of between 15 and 28 rocky islands, depending on the state of the tide. Of the 15 that remain visible at high water, several are big enough to have thin soils that support sparse grassy areas ideal for ground-nesting birds such as arctic terns, eider ducks and puffins. The

St Aidan's Dunes and beach

cliffs that run along the south-eastern edges support breeding colonies of razorbills, guillemots and kittiwakes.

The whole chain lies 2–7km from the sandy beaches of Seahouses and Bamburgh. The island of Inner Farne is the most frequently visited; tourist boats operate from Seahouses bringing day-trippers to see the nesting seabirds, seals and other marine wildlife at close quarters. This route described here is best used during the last couple of hours of the NW-going ebb stream.

Description

The roadside lay-by at St Aidan's Dunes can be found beside the B1340 at the northern edge of Seahouses. A path runs over 100m through the dunes and onto the broad, gently shelving sandy beach. A kayak trolley would be useful for getting your boat and kit down to the water's edge. Even in settled weather, you should expect to launch through surf here.

Once you have paddled beyond the break, it's worth having a look over your shoulder to see what the beach and surrounding dunes look like for when you return. You will be able to gauge the NW-going tidal stream from here, by using the red-coloured Shoreston buoy as a transit against the islands in the distance. The Shoreston buoy lies just over one-third of the way across to Inner Farne. It marks the end of Shoreston Outcarrs and shows the port hand for boats heading north through the inner sound. As you approach the islands you will become increasingly aware of the seals and bird life that inhabit this archipelago.

The white buildings of the Farne lighthouse are perched on top of the vertical cliffs at the southern end of Inner Farne. The grass-topped, rocky islands immediately to the east are called

West Wideopen and East Wideopen. The channel that divides Inner Farne and these islands is called Wideopen Gut. The Wideopens are quite substantial, rising to over 10m, but the islets of Little Scarcar and Big Scarcar that lie immediately to the east are barely exposed at high tide. The channel between the Wideopens and the Scarcars is called Scarcar Gut. If you paddle through here, you will enter a bay that is sheltered from the north by Knoxes Reef. This is a strip of rock running east–west almost 1km long, with a small patch of grass and shingle at the highest point. The eastern end is called Knocklin Ends; Solan Rock marks the western end.

South of Solan Rock is a stretch of water sheltered from the weather but potentially turbulent with tidal movement, known as The Kettle. The area immediately northwest of the landing stage on Inner Farne is Farne Haven. The only place for kayakers to land is on the gently shelving seaweed-covered rocky foreshore. Landing on the sandy beach to the south of the jetty – or anywhere else on the Inner Farne archipelago – is not permitted, but touring around them by kayak is an excellent way of getting close to the abundant wildlife.

There is no charge for landing on the rocks, but there is a charge for walking above the high water mark and entering the nature reserve that occupies the island.

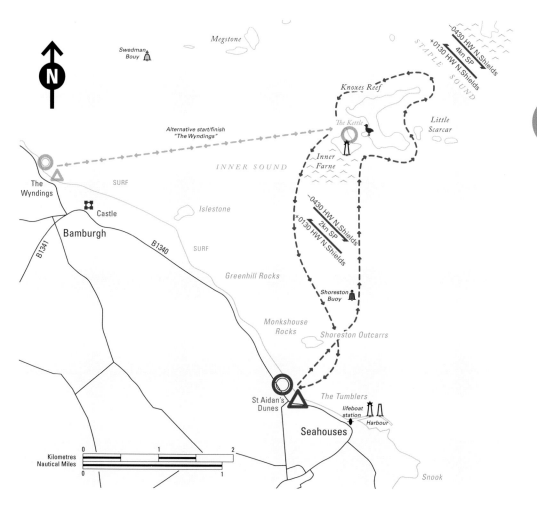

The Inner Farne Islands

Tour boats loaded with enthusiasts swarm around these islands on busy weekends in late spring and early summer, making this wild place seem more like a zoo or theme park attraction. A steep path leads from the jetty up to St Cuthbert's chapel, the pele tower and associated outbuildings. The pele tower was built around 1500 as a defensive structure against a feared invasion by the French. Until the lighthouse was built in 1809, the only light marking these islands was a fire lit in a brazier on the roof of the pele tower. It now serves as accommodation for the wardens. The outbuildings have been converted into a visitor's centre where information about the island's cultural and natural history is on display.

St Cuthbert's Chapel

St Cuthbert lived here as a hermit during the 7th century and made great efforts to protect the eider ducks that were exploited for their downy feathers. St Cuthbert's Chapel was built in his memory during the 14th century and remains open to visitors. One particular point of interest in the chapel is a memorial stone inscribed with the story of Grace Darling's heroic rescue of 1838. Her family were the keepers of the then new lighthouse on Longstone. She and her father rowed over a mile through heavy seas to help survivors of the SS *Forfarshire* that had run aground on the rocks of Big Harkar. There is a museum dedicated to this story run by the RNLI heritage trust in the village of Bamburgh.

From the chapel there is a circular walk that takes people around the edge of the grass-topped island. Terns and eider ducks nest on practically every patch of spare ground. If you get too close to any of the terns' nests, they will dive-bomb you while emitting a piercing screech. They may even strike you on the head, and you will be lucky to avoid a smattering of bird poo. The best advice is to wear a durable (and washable) hat! The path is a boardwalk for most of its length, to protect the puffins that nest in burrows dug deep in the soft soil. Around the edges of the island, the shags, guillemots and kittiwakes compete for space among the cliff ledges.

Once the SE-going flood stream has begun, the return to St Aidan's is best started from the northern end of the island. There is little tidal movement along the rocky northern shores of Inner Farne. The tidal streams of Inner Sound are strongest and most turbulent near the southern part of the island. If you wish to avoid the strongest of the tide that runs through the Inner Sound, then you should start by heading west before making your way south through smoother waters close to the mainland beaches. To complete the trip, follow the coast before returning to the beach and St Aidan's Dunes.

Tides and weather

If it seems tough launching though the surf at St Aidan's Beach, then landing here later could be even trickier. Although prevailing south-westerly winds tend to leave the waters close to the shore reasonably calm, such conditions mean that the return crossing can be a bit of a slog through choppy seas.

Additional information

Annstead Farm (www.annstead.co.uk) is beside the road between Beadnell and Seahouses, where you will find a campsite, bunkhouse and cottages for rent.

No trip to this area would be complete without a portion of fish and chips. There are a number of takeaways in Seahouses, and competition keeps the prices reasonable and the quality excellent.

The Ship Inn is an old-fashioned pub that overlooks the harbour. There is always a cosy, friendly atmosphere inside, accentuated by the intriguing, cluttered array of maritime trinkets that hang from the walls and ceilings.

Variations

The above description is best suited for paddling out to the Inner Farnes while crossing the last of the NW-going ebb and returning across the SE-going flood. Another option is to paddle out from The Wynding (NU 179 355) near Bamburgh as described in the following route. With this option, you would cross the SE-going flood stream on the way out and cross the NW-going ebb on the way back.

 # The Outer Farne Islands & Longstone **47**

No. 47 | **Grade C** | **18km** | **OS Sheet 75**

Tidal Port	North Shields
Start	△ Harkness Rocks, The Wynding, Bamburgh (NU 179 355)
Finish	◯ Harkness Rocks, The Wynding, Bamburgh (NU 179 355)
HW/LW	High and low water along this section are around 1 hour before North Shields.
Tidal Times	The SE-going stream begins around 4 hours 30 minutes before HW North Shields and the N-going stream begins around 1 hour 30 minutes after HW North Shields. Off Knivestone, the SE-going stream begins around 3 hours 30 minutes before HW North Shields and the NW-going stream begins around 2 hours 30 minutes after HW North Shields.
Tidal Rates	2 knots in the Inner Sound, 4 knots in Staple Sound and 5 knots off the Knivestone.
Coastguard	Humber, tel. 01262 672 317, VHF weather every 3 hours from 0150

Introduction

The outer part of the Farne Island chain lies beyond Staple Sound, where tides run at 3 knots in open water and 6 knots in some of the narrow channels. There are boils and whirlpools, overfalls with standing waves and reefs awash with swell. Staple Island is prized for the Pinnacles, towers of rock that rise from the sea off the eastern cliffs. Longstone is the outermost island; prepare to feel humbled by the raw power of the North Sea when paddling around here.

Description

The pretty town of Bamburgh is on the B1340 between Seahouses and Belford. Broad village greens and terracotta-roofed cottages stretch out in the shadow of the mighty castle that dominates the coastline here. A narrow street called The Wynding leads north from the village towards the sand dunes and broad beaches between Bamburgh Castle and Harkness Rocks.

There is a small car park that overlooks the beach where a small stream called Mill Burn flows out across the sands. This feature is useful to know about when launching and landing through surf. There is often a rip current here where water from waves running up the beach finds its way back out to sea. Where the rip forms, the surf is usually a little smaller.

This point of departure suits a crossing to Longstone during the last two hours of the SE-going flood; you should therefore reach the outer islands when the tidal streams are weakening. The green Swedman buoy (NU 195 371), lying a little over 2km from the beach and around 1km west of Megstone, shows the starboard hand to boats heading north through the Inner Sound. In order to keep a good course, you should aim to paddle between the Swedman buoy and Megstone. Although you will be able to see the Longstone lighthouse from Megstone, the islands of North and South Wamses will be in the foreground. They lie just to the north of Staple Island and Brownsman. Brownsman Haven is a small sheltered stretch of water between Brownsman Island and South Wamses. The eddies provide a good area to regroup after the crossing from Bamburgh. From here, there is a network of channels with swirling currents between the rocks and skerries that make up the Outer Farne Islands.

North Wamses, South Wamses and Little and Big Harkar are favoured by the grey seals for hauling out and basking in the sun. It is best not to get too close to avoid spooking them, especially between September and November when newly born pups are most vulnerable. Little Harkar and Clove Carr become all but submerged at high water. The channel that separates Clove Carr and Longstone is called Craford's Gut. Tidal streams run strongly through here and the resulting overfalls often have excellent standing waves for surfing. Any paddlesport antics will almost certainly have an audience of local seals; there may even be an element of audience participation.

By the time you reach Longstone, you will be 6–7km offshore. The only places for paddlers to land are two locations immediately below the huge red-and-white-coloured lighthouse. The first is a stony beach among the rocky foreshore on the southwest side, and the second is a narrow seaweed-infested gully on the northeast side. There are usually plenty of seals sprawled out along the beaches and rocks of the Northern Hares just to the north of Longstone.

The final outpost of the Farne Island chain lies 500m northeast of the Northern Hares. In keeping with its name, Knivestone is a long sharp reef that is only exposed at low water. Swell breaks heavily around these rocks and confused breaking seas can develop in the overfalls here.

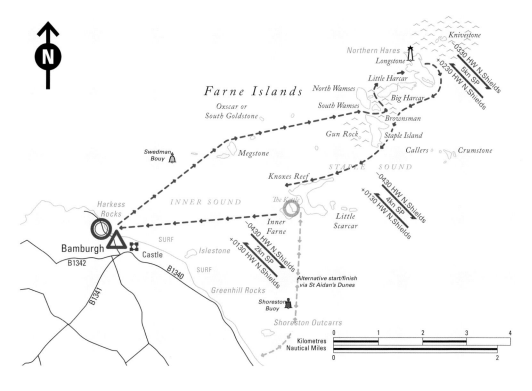

The Whin Sill

It is hard to comprehend the earth-shattering forces that enabled the escape of molten rock from deep below the land that was to become northeast England. Stretched to breaking point, fissures formed and vast quantities of hot, liquid rock rose upwards – multitudes of volcanoes in the making – but it never reached the surface. Instead, it flowed sideways along weaknesses in the layers of rocks, slowed, cooled and solidified into the hard horizontal band we now call the Whin Sill. Over 100m thick in places, it is more resistant to the effects of weathering than the surrounding surface rocks. Well exposed along the coast, it forms many of the Northumberland cliffs, the Farne Islands and the defensive knolls topped by castles such as Bamburgh.

By Royanne Wilding

The return journey will start by crossing Craford's Gut to the shores of Clove Carr and the Harcar group of islands. Beyond Big Harcar and Brownsman Island lie the rocks known as Roddam and Green. Standing waves develop in the exciting chutes of water that rush either side of these rocks. Brownsman Island is over 600m long but only 200m at its widest. The patchy grassland on the top provides perfect nesting for hundreds of terns and eider ducks. Some of the wardens take up residence in the old lighthouse cottages during the summer months; it is difficult to imagine how they put up with the constant piercing calls made by the swarming flocks of terns.

As you round the eastern tip of Brownsman, you will cross Pinnacles Haven before approaching the eastern cliffs of Staple Island and the Pinnacles. Swell from the south and east breaks at the base of the cliffs and stacks, causing spouts of water to shoot high into the air. There can be clapotis away from the cliffs, giving rise to challenging choppy waters. In these conditions, this can easily be one of the wilder parts of the Farnes. On calm days, it is possible to cruise among the towering stacks where guillemots and kittiwakes squabble incessantly over space on precarious nesting ledges.

The Callers and Crumstone lie out on their own just over 1km southeast of Brownsman and the Staple Island. The Callers barely break the surface at low water, whereas Crumstone barely shows at high water. Either way, their presence is almost always known as swell breaks noisily all around them.

Staple Sound separates the outer islands from the inner archipelago. The tide runs quickly through this open stretch of water, with overfalls forming readily either side of Gun Rock and off the southwest tip of Staple Island. The distance across Staple Sound is around 1.5km. After hopping from one island to the next, it will seem appropriate to pay a visit to the Inner Farnes before making the final crossing to the beach at Harkness Rocks. Landing through the surf in the shadow of Bamburgh Castle is a grand finale to an exciting and challenging trip.

Tides and weather

This area is exposed to winds from any direction. It is easy to gauge the conditions when there are winds from the north and east; winds from the south and west often leave the nearshore waters

The Outer Farne Islands & Longstone

The Ship Inn, Seahouses

smooth with an inviting sheltered look. On days like this, however, conditions out at Longstone could be harsh and you would be left with a difficult return paddle into the wind.

Additional information

The Farne Islands and surrounding waters are a national nature reserve and SSSI. The only places where landing is permitted on the Outer Farnes are the two locations described on Longstone. Landing is prohibited on all of the other islands (except the location on Inner Farne described in the previous route).

Parts of Bamburgh Castle are open to the public daily from March to October and at weekends during the winter (www.bamburghcastle.com).

Bamburgh village has a souvenir shop, a delicatessen and two pubs, both of which have B&B accommodation. Budle Bay Campsite is 4km west of Bamburgh along the B1342 at Warren Mill (tel. 01668 214 598; www.budlebaycampsite.co.uk).

Variations

If it is suitable to launch during the last of the NW-going flood, then you can start from and finish at St Aidan's Dunes as described in the previous route.

Lindisfarne Castle

Lindisfarne  48

No. 48 | **Grade B** | **16km** | **OS Sheet 75**

Tidal Port	North Shields
Start	△ Holy Island Harbour (NU 131 419)
Finish	○ Holy Island Harbour (NU 131 419)
HW/LW	Around 45 minutes before North Shields.
Tidal Times	To the west and north of Holy Island, the S-going stream begins around 4 hours 30 minutes before HW North Shields and the N-going stream begins around 1 hour 50 minutes after HW North Shields.
	Between the causeway and Castle Point, the in-going (W) stream begins around 5 hours before HW North Shields and the out-going (E) stream begins around 45 minutes before HW North Shields.
	In the channel to the north of the causeway, the in-going (S) stream begins around 4 hours before HW North Shields and the out-going (N) stream begins around 45 minutes before HW North Shields.
Max Rate Sp	Between the causeway and Castle Point, the streams can reach 2–3 knots. Elsewhere, the streams rarely reach 1 knot.
Coastguard	Humber, tel. 01262 672 317, VHF weather every 3 hours from 0150.

Lindisfarne

Lindisfarne

Introduction

A hilltop Tudor castle, 12th-century priory and shores designated as Sites of Special Scientific Interest await all those who wish to explore this historic island. A circumnavigation by kayak involves tidal streams, remote rocky shores and surf. Tidal planning must begin before you arrive, as the road to the island runs along a causeway that becomes submerged at high tide.

Description

The Holy Island of Lindisfarne is a small low-lying island signposted off the A1 between Belford and Berwick-upon-Tweed. A minor road leads east through the village of Beal and across the Lindisfarne Causeway. Traffic restrictions normally prohibit vehicles from being driven to Holy Island harbour. However, a well-established agreement permits paddlers to drive through the village to the grassy harbour beach area where there are fishermen's sheds made of old upturned fishing boats. Unload your kayaks and kit here, then park your car at one of the nearby pay-and-display car parks.

The shores of Holy Island form a small part of the Lindisfarne National Nature Reserve. The reserve stretches from Cheswick Black Rocks in the north to Budle Point in the south, and was primarily designated to protect the rich and varied birdlife of these shores. It is worth making a telephone call to the reserve office (01289 381470) before setting off. This lets reserve staff know what your plans are and enables them pass on any important up-to-date information.

Once you are on the water, head east out of the bay towards the steep rocky shores beneath the castle. The castle's entrance kiosk and some introductory displays are located on the high ground beside the castle, housed in modern replica boat sheds modelled on those at the harbour beach. Down by the water, there are six lime kilns built on the sheltered pebbly shores that lead to Castle Point. There are usually a few breaking waves here (even on calm days) as you push against some incoming tide in the shallow waters around the headland.

The rugged east-facing shores open up to reveal steep beaches and boulder-strewn rock ledges with rolling grassland beyond. Plough Rock and its cardinal buoy lie around 800m offshore and mark the end of a reef associated with one of the bigger ledges named Broad Stones. These rocky shores are shrouded in pebbles piled into high beaches by the action of the sea. In rougher weather, surf dumps heavily upon these storm beaches that lead all the way to Emmanuel Head. Emmanuel Head is the northeast tip of Holy Island and is marked by a large white-painted pyramid-shaped beacon.

Around the headland, the north-facing shores have low rocky reefs and sheltered sandy coves. There are often grey seals hauled out on Castlehead Rocks and beaches such as Coves Haven will be bustling with wading birds feeding on the last of the exposed sand. To the west, there is another reef called Snipe Point. The rocks here rise gently from the sea, leading to Black Skerrs and a short stretch of sandstone cliffs engulfed by tall dunes at their western end.

As you leave the cliffs behind, you will find yourself paddling alongside a long surf-washed sand bank; this is the eastern extremity of Goswick Sands. After around 4km, you will find a narrow but distinct channel though the sands. You may not be able to spot the gap until you are really close to it. You should resist any temptation to turn in too early, as there is at least one false

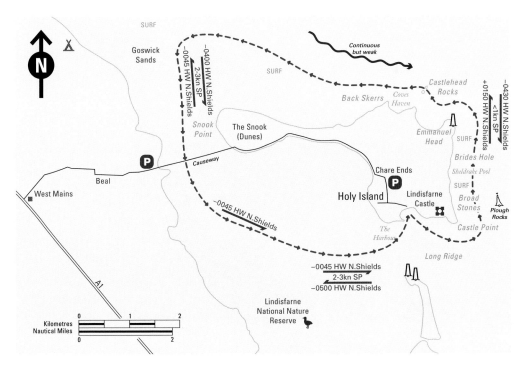

© Lindisfarne causeway

channel. As a double check, you should be around 2km due north of the causeway refuge and 2km due east of the distinctive white buildings of Beachcomber House on the mainland.

The key to making a successful circumnavigation is passing the causeway at local high water. Once past the causeway, follow the flow paddling southeast and keep well away from the shore to avoid sandbanks and shallow water.

This area is particularly rich in birdlife, especially migrating wildfowl and wading birds. There is also a large colony of common seals. Once you can see the castle appear out from beyond the Lindisfarne Priory and the adjacent headland, you can begin to aim for the castle and harbour entrance. At this point, the E-going ebb tide will begin to gather speed. Your approach to the harbour should be as close as possible to Steel End, which shelters the harbour from the south.

Tides and weather

A Holy Island circumnavigation is usually paddled anticlockwise and needs a spring tide so that the causeway and nearby sand banks are well submerged at high water. Carefully planning to paddle past the causeway at local high water is the key to a successful trip.

This trip is exposed to winds from any direction. Swell from the east breaks heavily around Castle Point and along the eastern shores including Emmanuel Head. There is normally some swell from the northeast, which means that there will almost always be surf at Goswick Sands and around the entrance to the channel north of the causeway.

St Cuthbert

There is something reminiscent of Monty Python's Life of Brian in St Cuthbert's story. He came to the Monastery on Lindisfarne in 665, desperate to live a quiet, humble life. His teaching was greatly revered, however, and people flocked to hear him preach. The church thought he would be an excellent figurehead at the strategically important holy site of Lindisfarne, and he was put in charge as the Bishop. After several years, Cuthbert managed to shirk his responsibilities and fled to Farne Island where at last he was able to achieve his ambition to be a hermit. He died there nine years later and was buried, as requested, in a plain grave. He did not lie in peace for long however, as the monks on Lindisfarne felt a grand shrine in their church would be a much more appropriate commemoration for their saint. They dug up and reburied his miraculously intact body.

The monks' dedication to St Cuthbert's holy remains is very impressive: when Lindisfarne was ravaged by Viking raids in 875 they dug him up again. This time they couldn't think of anywhere safe enough to bury him, so they carried his body about with them for 100 years as they roamed Northern England. When eventually the atmosphere settled down, St Cuthbert was interred in Durham Cathedral were he remains today. St Cuthbert's legend lives on in the Northumberland: eider ducks, common visitors to Lindisfarne, are known to locals as St Cuthbert's ducks or 'cuddy ducks'.

By Kirstine Pearson

Variations

A clockwise circumnavigation is less practical because of various tidal issues. Paddling to and landing on any other parts of the Lindisfarne National Nature Reserve is restricted (contact the reserve office for information). There is a designated watersports zone in the south of the reserve at Budle Bay, however, which is open between Easter and the end of October.

Additional information

When you return to the harbour at the end of your trip, the causeway will still be submerged for at least another hour. This time can be spent exploring the 12th-century priory, the castle or some of the island's other historical attractions. There are a couple of pubs and several tea shops in the village. St Aidan's Winery is famous for Lindisfarne Mead, but also sells a range of beers, whiskies, jams, chutneys and local honey.

The Beachcomber Campsite and Stables is a basic site on the mainland shore to the west of Holy Island, near the villages of Cheswick and Goswick (tel. 01289 381 217; www.beachcomber-campsite.co.uk). South Meadows Caravan and Camping Site is just outside the village of Belford. Being over 4km inland, it is a little more sheltered (tel. 01668 213 326; www.southmeadows.co.uk).

River Tweed Estuary 🔄📷

No. 49 | Grade A | 16km | OS Sheet 75

Tidal Port	North Shields
Start	△ Sandstell Point (NU 005 520)
Finish	◯ Sandstell Point (NU 005 520)
HW/LW	40 minutes before North Shields.
Tidal Times	The in-going stream begins around 5 hours 15 minutes after HW North Shields and the out-going stream begins around 1 hour before HW North Shields.
Max Rate Sp	2–3 knots in the lower reaches of the estuary; 1 knot is more typical in the upper reaches.
Coastguard	Humber, tel. 01262 672 317, VHF weather every 3 hours from 0150

Introduction

This trip is ideal for those bad weather days. Paddling on a rising tide up the River Tweed takes you through the historic town with its Georgian buildings, city walls and three impressive bridges. The countryside beyond is beautifully scenic, leading to a stately home with a welcoming café.

Description

Spittal is a suburb that lies between the south bank of the River Tweed and the windswept North Sea shores. If you turn off the A1167 following the sign for Spittal, Billendean Terrace will lead you along its winding route onto Sandstell Road. At the very end of Sandstell Road there is a car park that overlooks the mouth of the River Tweed to the north and surf beaches to the east. A long sand bar extends from Sandstell point, where the border between river and sea is clearly defined. The usual place to launch is from the gravely beach on the north side. The view to the far shore extends from the end of the breakwater, along to the 16th-century town walls and then upstream to the three famous Tweed bridges.

If you launch around 2 hours before high water, the flood tide will quickly carry you upstream and smooth waters will lead you towards the town and the first of the bridges. Before long, the town with its red-roofed Georgian buildings will close in around you and you will almost certainly be accompanied by mute swans; Berwick is famous for them and in the autumn there can be more than 200 in and around the estuary.

Berwick Bridge is made up of 15 elegant sandstone arches. It is sometimes known as the 'old bridge' and dates back to the early 17th century. This was the only road crossing of the Tweed in the area until the Royal Tweed Bridge was built in the 1920s on a site only 100m upstream. Four concrete arches carried the main A1 over the river until a bypass was constructed to the west of the town in the early 1980s. The tallest and by far the most striking of the Tweed bridges is the Royal Border Bridge. Designed by Robert Stephenson, it was completed in 1850 to carry the east coast railway line across the river. This imposing structure spans over half a kilometre with 28 sandstone block arches, and stands nearly 40m above the water.

Upstream of the bridges, the river winds its way through a rolling landscape with grassy hills and patchy woodland. The only brief interruption to the pleasing rural landscape is the bridge that carries the busy Berwick bypass, which is the modern route for the A1. Just upstream of the bridge is Whiteadder Point. This is where the tributary Whiteadder Water joins the Tweed from the distant Lammermuir Hills. The riverbanks here are thick with vegetation and the shallow, slow-moving waters readily support dense beds of reeds.

Some of the pretty riverside dwellings are old fishing houses. There would often be a wooden lookout tower either attached, or very near, to the house. From these towers, shoals of salmon could be seen making their run upstream through the shallows. Nets would then be deployed and the catch would be stored in cellars or bunkers built into the riverbank, before being taken by boat to the market in Berwick the next day.

After around 7km from Spittal, the river becomes the border between England and Scotland. Soon afterwards, the Scottish shore is lined with mature woodland and it is possible to land upon a gravely beach. These are the elegant grounds of Paxton House. A nearby boathouse contains a display telling the story of salmon fishing on this stretch of the Tweed. A short walk through the woods brings you to Paxton House itself, where there is a café in the old stable block.

Around 1km upstream, the tidal limit is marked by Union Bridge. Sometimes referred to as the Chainbridge, this is the oldest surviving suspension bridge in Britain. If you are quiet and patient, there is a good chance of seeing otters playing among the driftwood along the steep wooded banks.

River Tweed Estuary

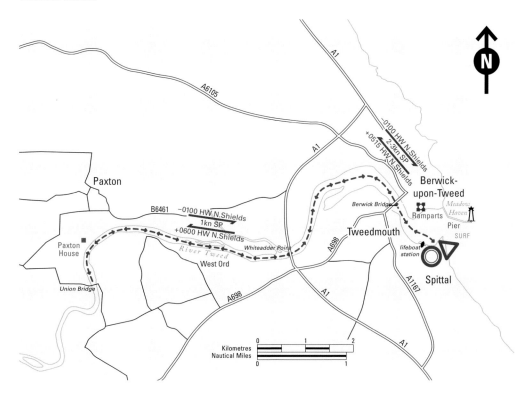

The return to Spittal should be started soon after the tide begins to turn. There is no immediate hurry, however, as there is almost always a channel deep enough to float a kayak in the river.

Tides and weather

Tides run strongly through the town area. Eddies that form behind bridge pillars can be swirling and unpredictable. Strong winds can produce gusts that cause downdraughts along the section through Berwick, especially around the bridges.

Strong winds from the east or west funnel along the stretch between Whiteadder Point and Paxton House. This can make progress laborious and slow if you are paddling into the wind.

Additional information

The village of Scremerston is 2km south of Spittal. To the east of the village at Borewell Farm is a craft centre called Pot-a-Doodle Do, where there are a number of wooden wigwams and canvas yurts for hire (www.potadoodledo.com). This is ideal for small group bookings and family holidays.

Variations

There is a good beach for surfing at the southern side of Sandstell Point. The shore beside the lifeboat station is another popular place to launch and is more sheltered from strong easterly winds.

© Burnmouth

Berwick-upon-Tweed to Eyemouth

No. 50 | Grade B | 12km | OS Sheet 67 & 75

Tidal Port	North Shields
Start	△ Meadow Haven Beach (NU 007 526)
Finish	◎ Eyemouth Beach (NT 944 645)
HW/LW	1 hour 10 minutes before North Shields.
Tidal Times	The SE-going stream begins around 3 hours 35 minutes before HW North Shields and the NW-going stream begins around 2 hours 25 minutes after HW North Shields.
Max Rate Sp	The tidal streams along this section are barely noticeable and rarely reach 1 knot.
Coastguard	Humber, tel. 01262 672 317, VHF weather every 3 hours from 0150

Introduction

This is a wild journey from England to Scotland that is packed with interest. The last of the smooth red sandstone cliffs give way to a more sinister coast north of the border. Once you leave

253

the beaches of Berwick behind, there are few places to land and the only escape route is the tiny fishing harbour of Burnmouth.

Description

Meadow Haven Beach to the north of the Tweed breakwater is a bright and breezy place to set out from, but navigating Berwick's narrow streets can make finding it a mission in itself. On the east side of town, Silver Street runs east from Hide Hill through an arch in the town wall and onto Pier Road. Pier Road then runs alongside the Tweed estuary before making a sharp left turn just before the pier, past a couple of houses and onto a grassy parking area that overlooks the soft sandy beach.

Meadow Haven Rocks lie a short way offshore and are only completely covered at high water. As the water recedes, a lagoon is revealed that forms a shallow natural harbour. Paddling away from the beach will often begin with a rock-hopping session among the reefs of Bucket Rocks and Ladies Skerrs that lead into Fisherman's Haven. This is the first of two bays that are dominated by the Berwick Holiday Park. Each of the bays has a sandy beach that dries to rocks lower down. The coastline then becomes rockier with red sandstone cliffs. Caves and arches at the foot of the cliffs are especially entertaining close to high water. Keep a good look out, however, as rogue waves can break heavily upon reefs that extend from the base of the cliffs out to sea.

As you paddle on, the cliffs grow in stature as you approach the huge sea arch of Needles Eye. Soon afterwards, you will find yourself beneath the towering cliffs of Marshall Meadows Bay. Either side of high water, it is possible to land upon a sandy beach for a short break in the depths of this huge sandstone amphitheatre. A rickety ladder leads up a steep slope to the entrance of a Victorian subway. This dark, slippery, inclined tunnel leads to the cliff-top caravan site that overlooks the area, giving panoramic views along the coast. The Scottish border is only 500m beyond the northern entrance of the bay.

Continuing north, the steep grassy slopes are interspersed with crags and rocky outcrops that cascade down to beaches of pebbles and boulders. Offshore, seals play among the reefs, gullies and stacks. Maiden's Stone stands a little under 10m high and is surrounded by water at high tide. It is left standing high and dry as the tide goes out, surrounded by flat seaweed-strewn slabs. Ross Point and the southern entrance to Burnmouth Bay lie just a little further north.

Burnmouth village consists of little more than a couple of rows of colour-washed houses and a small fishing harbour nestled in a gap between the cliffs. It is possible to land on the steep shingle beach beside the southern part of the village at high water. At low water, the bay dries to a complex series of reefs and the only place to land is on the beach within the harbour walls. The harbour is small, providing shelter for only a handful of traditional crab and lobster fishing boats.

Paddling north from Burnmouth, the coastal scenery takes on a darker and more striking appearance. Towering twisted igneous rock structures and deep caves lead the way as the cliffs rise to over 100m at Fancove Head. The rock hopping here is excellent, with crooked gullies to explore and rock stacks to weave your way around.

The cliffs begin to relent 1km further north as you paddle past Scout Point. There are still a few more jagged reefs and surf-washed gullies to navigate and explore at Nestends, and it is best

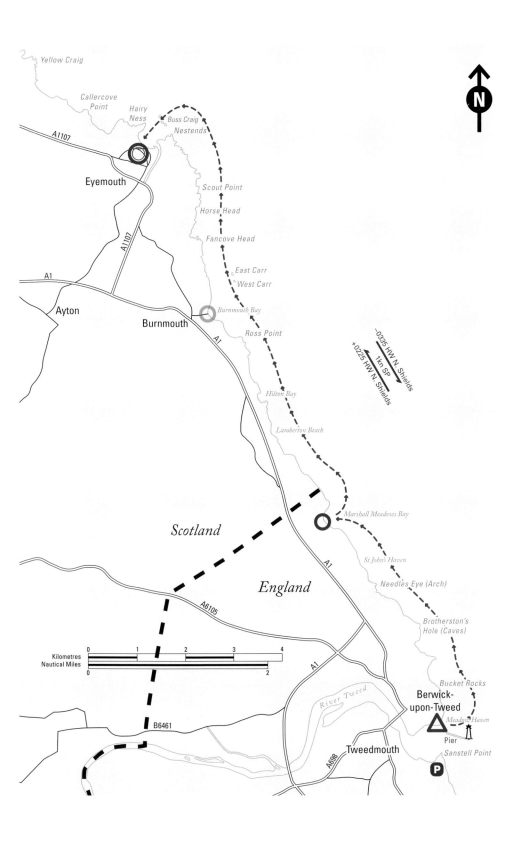

Yellow Craig

Callercove Point

Hairy Ness

Buss Craig

Nestends

A1107

Eyemouth

Scout Point

Horse Head

Fancove Head

East Carr

West Carr

A1107

A1

Ayton

Burnmouth

A1

Burnmouth Bay

Ross Point

-0335 HW N. Shields

1kn SP

+0225 HW N. Shields

Hilton Bay

Lamberton Beach

Scotland

Marshall Meadows Bay

St John's Haven

England

Needles Eye (Arch)

A6105

A1

Brotherston's Hole (Caves)

Kilometres
Nautical Miles

0 1 2 3 4

0 1 2

Bucket Rocks

Berwick-upon-Tweed

A1

B6461

River Tweed

Meadow Haven

Pier

A698

Tweedmouth

Sanstell Point

P

50

Berwick-upon-Tweed to Eyemouth

to make the most of this final headland before entering Eyemouth Bay. The narrow harbour entrance is on the southern side of the bay and is often busy with large, fast-moving fishing vessels. A public car park overlooks the middle part of the beach and promenade.

Tides and weather

The cliffs and high ground offer a great deal of protection from westerly winds but beware of downdraughts. Swell from the north and east breaks heavily upon the reefs and at the base of the cliffs. The beach at Eyemouth is almost completely submerged at high water; the only exception is a small sandy area at the western end of the promenade beside the leisure centre.

Additional information

There is a Co-op supermarket beside the Eyemouth promenade car park. Mackay's fish and chip shop, restaurant and B&B is located on High Street, less than 50m away. Local paddlers favour Giacopazi's take-away and ice-cream parlour at the junction of Harbour Road and Chapel Street. With the Ship Inn on the opposite corner and the Eyemouth Maritime Centre (www.worldof-boats.org) across the road, this part of town is well worth a visit.

Variations

This trip can be paddled just as easily in either direction. Burnmouth can be used as an alternative place to start or finish shorter excursions.

Appendix A – HM Coastguard and Emergency Services

In UK waters, HM Coastguard co-ordinates rescues and emergency services. They also broadcast weather forecasts and inform water users about potential hazards in their area. They monitor VHF channel 16 and you should use this channel to make initial contact; you will then be directed to a working channel. Note the times here are for UTC. During the UK summer months remember to add 1 hour.

There are two HM Coastguard stations that fall within the scope of this book.

HMCG	Telephone	Weather announced on CH16 (UTC)
Liverpool	02392 552100	0130, 0430, 0730, 1030, 1330, 1630, 1930, 2230
Humber	01262 672 317	0150, 0450, 0750, 1050, 1350, 1650, 1950, 2250

IMPORTANT NOTICE

The coastguard information here and throughout this book is correct at the time of writing. However, changes have been proposed that will reduce the number of coastguard stations around the country and alter the way in which they provide services.

Appendix B The Royal National Lifeboat Institution (RNLI)

The RNLI (www.rnli.org.uk) is the charity that saves lives at sea. Its lifeboats cover all UK coastal waters up to 50 miles offshore and are manned almost entirely by volunteer crews. There are 35 stations along the shores of northern England and the Isle of Man. Many of these stations are open to the public, and it is well worth a visit to find out more the RNLI's history, equipment and operations. Furthermore, it might be a nice idea to consider materially supporting the RNLI in their work.

Appendix C – Pilots

WEST COAST

Admiralty Sailing Directions West Coast of England and Wales Pilot, UKHO 2005, ISBN 0707718805

Irish Sea Pilot, David Rainsbury, Imray 2008, ISBN: 085288916X

Sailing Directions, Tidal Streams and Anchorages of the Isle of Man, Iain Fraser Simpson, Andrew Dean and Jerry Colman, Manx Sailing & Cruising Club 2006, ISBN 0955366208

EAST COAST

Admiralty Sailing Directions North Sea (West) Pilot, UKHO 2009, ISBN 0707742145

Forth, Tyne, Dogger, Humber: Blakeney to St.Abbs, Henry Irving, Imray 2002, ISBN 0852885784

Appendix D – Weather Information

The weather is the most discussed topic within the communities that make up the UK coastline. Mariners have always put trust in those who try to predict its fickle nature. The Met Office (www.metoffice.gov.uk) was founded in 1854 to provide information about the weather to marine communities. It was not until 1922 that forecasts were first broadcast by BBC radio, a tradition that still remains today.

The Met Office website provides detailed predictions for the weather all over the UK but if you are away from a computer or phone with web access then there are several other ways of obtaining a reliable weather forecast.

RADIO

BBC RADIO 4 (92.5 – 94.6 FM AND 198 KHZ LW)

0048 – Shipping and inshore waters forecast, coastal station reports

0520 – Shipping and inshore waters forecast, coastal station reports

MANX RADIO (89, 97.2, 103.7 FM AND 1368 MW)

Monday to Friday – 0700, 0800 (FM only), 0900, 1700, 2300

WEB

Met Office - www.metoffice.gov.uk

BBC Weather – www.bbc.co.uk/weather

XC Weather – www.xcweather.co.uk

Appendix E – Mean Tidal Ranges in metres

Tidal Port	Mean Spring Range (m)	Mean Neap Range (m)
Douglas	6.1	3.0
Maryport	7.7	4.1
Barrow-in-Furness	8.2	4.1
Fleetwood	8.0	4.3
Liverpool	8.4	4.5
Immingham	6.4	3.2
Scarborough	4.6	2.3
Hartlepool	4.3	2.2
North Shields	4.3	2.1
Berwick-upon-Tweed	4.1	2.5

Appendix F - Trip Planning Route Card - User's Guide

The trip planning route card is designed to be used in conjunction with the information supplied in each route chapter in the book. In addition to this you will also require a set of relevant tide timetables. If the blank route card is photocopied, all the information for your route to be paddled can be worked out on it. This way it will help you plan your paddle as effectively as possible, and then allow you to have all the information you need on a handy piece of paper. This can be displayed in your map case on your kayak for easy reference. To help you use the card please refer to the following example and guidelines:

Trip Name & Number	*Douglas to Debyhaven (No. 1)*
Page Number *15*	VHF Weather *0730, 1030, 1330*
Date *3rd April, 2011*	Weather Forecast
Coastguard Contact *Liverpool, 0157 931 3341*	*Fair, visibility good, wind NE F2-3*

- Fill in the name, number and page of your chosen trip for easy future reference.
- When choosing the date of the trip, check in the chapter's 'Tide & Weather' section as to whether it will need specific tides that will dictate the date.
- Obtain a weather forecast using information supplied in Appendix B.
- Coastguard contacts can be found in the introductory info for each trip and in Appendix A.

Tidal Port			Mean Sp Range *8.4*		Local Port			
Liverpool			Mean Np Range *4.5*		*Douglas*			
Tidal Port Tide Times (UT)	Height in Metres	Tidal Range in Metres	HW/LW	+1 Hr for BST?	Local Port HW/LW Time Difference	Local Port HW/LW	Sp or Np Tides	
0454	*1.7*		*LW*	*0534*	*0000*	*0534*	*Sp*	
1105	*8.95*	*7.25*	*HW*	*1205*	*0000*	*1205*	*Sp*	
1744	*1.3*	*7.65*	*LW*	*1844*	*0000*	*1844*	*Sp*	

- Identify Tidal Port from the chapter introductory information.
- Identify Mean Spring and Neap Ranges from tide timetable or see Appendix D. These will help identify Spring or Neap Tides and Estimated Maximum Speed.
- Local Port is also found in the chapter introductory information.
- Obtain the Tidal Port Times and Height in Metres from your tide timetables. Usually four times and heights, but occasionally three.
- To work out the Tidal Range in Metres subtract the LW heights from the HW heights.
- Add 1 Hr for BST? Add an hour to your Tidal Port Times if you are in British Summer Time.

- The Local Port HW/LW Time Difference can be found in the chapter introduction.
- To work out Sp or Np Tides compare your Tidal Range to the Mean Sp and Np Ranges.

Location	Direction of Tidal Stream	Tidal Stream Time Diff.	Tidal Port HW (BST?)	Tidal Stream Start Time	Tidal Rate	Est. Max Speed
Douglas Head	S W	- 0300	1205	0905	2 Kn	5 Kn
	N E	+ 0600	1205	1805	2 Kn	1 Kn

Location	Direction of Tidal Stream	Tidal Stream Time Diff.	Tidal Port HW (BST?)	Tidal Stream Start Time	Tidal Rate	Est. Max Speed
Santon Head	S W	- 0400	1205	0805	2 Kn	5 Kn
	N E	+ 0515	1205	1720	2 Kn	1 Kn

Location	Direction of Tidal Stream	Tidal Stream Time Diff.	Tidal Port HW (BST?)	Tidal Stream Start Time	Tidal Rate	Est. Max Speed

- Use the Location as indicated in the chapter introductory and tidal information.
- For the Direction of Tidal Stream there are generally four periods of tidal movement every 24 hours. Direction for the Tidal Stream Start Time soonest after 0000 hours in the first box.
- The Tidal Stream Time Difference is found in the chapter introductory and tidal information.
- Tidal Port HW can be transposed from above converting to BST if appropriate.
- The Tidal Stream Start Time is worked out by subtracting/adding the Tidal Stream Difference from/to the Tidal Port HW time.
- Tidal Rate is the average spring speed for the tidal stream, found in the chapter introduction.
- Estimate Maximum Speed based on whether it is Spring, Neap or in between tides.
- If it is Springs use the speed given in the chapter's introductory and tidal information.

- On Neap Tides halve this spring rate.
- When in between springs and neaps use the average of the spring and neap speeds.
- Note that speeds given are average spring rates. If paddling on a spring tide look to see if your Tidal Range in Metres is bigger or smaller than the Mean Sp Range. If it is bigger the speeds will be faster than average spring rates given.

	Location	Notes	ETA	ETD
Start	Douglas harbour public slipway	Call harbour authorities on VHF ch 12 before launching		0930
1st	Douglas Head	Paddling under cliffs	0950	0950
2nd	Little Ness	Rockhopping	1030	1045
3rd	Port Soderick	Lunch	1100	1215
4th	Santon hd / Port Greanaugh	Possible leg stretch	1300	1330
5th	Santon Burn	Explore the inlet	1345	1400
Finish	Castletown	land on beach near slipway	1430	

- When choosing Locations for the Route Plan use places that have tidal importance and where you may want to stop.
- When working out ETD (Estimated Time of Departure) or ETA (Estimated Time of Arrival) enter key times which need to be met for the best use of tidal stream first, as recommended in Tide & Weather. Work out other times around these.
- To work out the times an average paddling speed of 6km/h or 3 knots can be used. This can be adjusted to suit your needs, or time added for coastal exploration if desired.

Please feel free to photocopy the blank Trip Planning Route Card on the page overleaf.
An A4 downloadable version is available on our website.
For this and other resources go to www.pesdapress.com, follow the links to the Welsh Sea Kayaking page and look for the download symbol in the right-hand column.

www.pesdapress.com

Trip Name & Number	
Page Number	VHF Weather
Date	Weather Forecast
Coastguard Contact	

Tidal Port			Mean Sp Range			Local Port		
			Mean Np Range					

Tidal Port Tide Times (UT)	Height in Metres	Tidal Range in Metres	HW/LW	+1 Hr for BST?	Local Port HW/LW Time Difference	Local Port HW/LW	Sp or Np Tides

Location	Direction of Tidal Stream	Tidal Stream Time Diff.	Tidal Port HW (BST?)	Tidal Stream Start Time	Tidal Rate	Est. Max Speed

Location	Direction of Tidal Stream	Tidal Stream Time Diff.	Tidal Port HW (BST?)	Tidal Stream Start Time	Tidal Rate	Est. Max Speed

Location	Direction of Tidal Stream	Tidal Stream Time Diff.	Tidal Port HW (BST?)	Tidal Stream Start Time	Tidal Rate	Est. Max Speed

	Location	Notes	ETA	ETD
Start				
1st				
2nd				
3rd				
4th				
5th				
Finish				

Trip Planning Route Card

Index

Index of Place Names

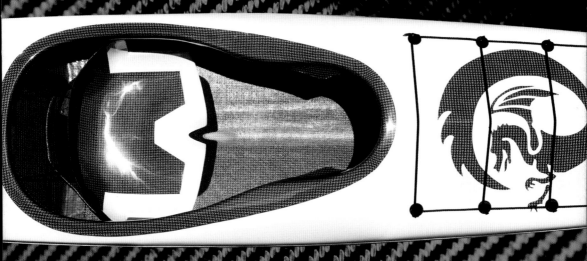

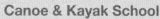